AQA GCSE
English Language
and English Literature

Core Student Book

Series Editors: Sarah Darragh and Jo Heathcote

Sarah Darragh
Phil Darragh
Mike Gould
Jo Heathcote

William Collins' dream of knowledge for all began with the publication of his first book in 1819. A self-educated mill worker, he not only enriched millions of lives, but also founded a flourishing publishing house. Today, staying true to this spirit, Collins books are packed with inspiration, innovation and practical expertise. They place you at the centre of a world of possibility and give you exactly what you need to explore it.

Collins. Freedom to teach

HarperCollins Publishers
1 London Bridge Street
London SE1 9GF

> **Browse the complete Collins catalogue at**
> **www.collins.co.uk**

First edition 2015

10 9 8 7 6 5

© HarperCollins Publishers 2015

ISBN 978-0-00-759679-9

Collins® is a registered trademark of HarperCollins Publishers Limited

www.collins.co.uk

A catalogue record for this book is available from the British Library

Commissioned by Catherine Martin
Project managed by Hamish Baxter
Project management and editing by Judith Walters
Edited by Catherine Dakin
Proofread by Claire Throp
Designed and typeset by Ken Vail Graphic Design
Cover design by We are Laura
Printed by Grafica Veneta S.p.A. in Italy

MIX
Paper from
responsible sources
FSC™ C007454
FSC
www.fsc.org

Approval message from AQA

This textbook has been approved by AQA for use with our qualification. This means that we have checked that it broadly covers the specification and we are satisfied with the overall quality. Full details for our approval process can be found on our website.

We approve textbooks because we know how important it is for teachers and students to have the right resources to support their teaching and learning. However, the publisher is ultimately responsible for the editorial control and quality of this book.

Please note that when teaching the GCSE English Language and English Literature course, you must refer to AQA's specification as your definitive source of information. While this book has been written to match the specification, it cannot provide complete coverage of every aspect of the course.

A wide range of other useful resources can be found on the relevant subject pages of our website: www.aqa.org.uk

Contents

Chapter 6 • Forming a critical response

English Language AO4 • English Literature AO1

6.1 Critical evaluation: form an interpretation

6.2 Critical evaluation: gather and present evidence about language

6.3 Critical evaluation: gather and present evidence about structure

6.4 Critical evaluation: gather and present evidence about mood

6.5 Critical evaluation: construct a convincing response to literary texts

6.6 Critical evaluation: construct a convincing response to non-fiction texts

6.7 Apply your skills to English Language and English Literature tasks

Chapter 7 • Comparing texts

English Language AO3 • English Literature AO2

7.1 Compare views and perspectives in non-literary non-fiction from the twentieth century

7.2 Compare non-fiction prose texts

7.3 Compare the ways viewpoints are presented to the reader in texts from the early twentieth century

7.4 Structure a comparative response to poetry

7.5 Apply your skills to English Language and English Literature tasks

Chapter 8 • Writing creatively

English Language AO5, AO6

8.1 Describe setting and atmosphere

8.2 Describe people and events

8.3 Structure a description

8.4 Build ideas for a descriptive task

8.5 Structure narratives effectively

8.6 Create convincing characterisation and voice

8.7 Generate ideas for your narrative response

8.8 Apply your skills to an English Language task

Chapter 9 • Point of view writing

English Language AO5, AO6

9.1 What is point of view writing?

9.2 Match tone and register to task and audience

9.3 Match features to text types and conventions

9.4 Select appropriate vocabulary to make an impact

9.5 Key techniques: varying sentences and verbs for effect

9.6 Key techniques: using punctuation for effect and impact

9.7 Shape whole texts cohesively

9.8 Shape sentences into paragraphs effectively

9.9 Apply your skills to an English Language task

Introduction

The *Collins AQA GCSE English Language and GCSE English Literature Core Student Book* is designed to develop the skills required for GCSE English Language and GCSE English Literature.

The book is structured on the principle that very similar skills underpin success in both English Language and English Literature. The chapters address the GCSE Assessment Objectives in turn, introducing you to these skills and showing you how to make progress as you apply them to a range of reading and writing tasks. You will notice that each chapter focuses on a maximum of two Assessment Objectives – often one from GCSE English Language and one from GCSE English Literature. This is because, although the two qualifications are separate, the skills are usually exactly the same. Within individual lessons, where relevant to the ideas being explored, additional AOs are sometimes referenced to show the relationships between the skills being taught.

You will be encouraged to read a wide range of literary and non-literary fiction and non-fiction texts, as you strengthen the ways in which you read for meaning, and explain and evaluate writers' choices. You will also develop your ability to write well for a range of different purposes, learning to communicate your ideas accurately and effectively under examination conditions.

This approach should give you the confidence to tackle unseen texts in your GCSE English Language and GCSE English Literature exams, and will support you as you explore and write in depth about the novels, plays and poems you are studying for GCSE.

How the book is structured

The first two chapters of the book introduce you to some fundamental skills and concepts which you will build upon as you progress through your GCSE course.

Chapter 1 is called 'Key technical skills' because these skills are indeed 'key' to being able to communicate effectively, and also to developing a better understanding of the ways in which other writers convey their own ideas. Accuracy is a very important part of the new GCSEs and we have put this chapter first to remind you that whenever you are using the written word, it is really important to do so with precision and technical accuracy.

Chapter 2 then introduces some of the 'Key concepts' you need to understand for GCSE study. This chapter also introduces you to different styles of writing and reminds you of some important principles to think about as you progress further through the book.

Chapters 3–7 focus more closely on how to read and how to write about what you have read. As simple as this may sound, the chapters are designed to ensure that you become a discerning, critical reader of a range of written genres and styles. The chapters build from simpler skills such as comprehension and inference to more sophisticated skills such as explaining and evaluating the effect of writers' choices. Finally, you will learn how to apply these skills in combination to more complex tasks such as producing an extended critical response or a comparison of two texts.

Chapters 8 and 9 focus on helping you become an effective writer, whether you are writing creatively or presenting a point of view. You will look at how to communicate shades of meaning through your choice of words, your choice of structure and form, and how to manipulate what you write to achieve a specific purpose or effect.

How to use the book

Each chapter is divided into a sequence of 'topics' or lessons. The lessons introduce, build and extend the skills identified at the start of the chapter.

a big question to think about at the start of the lesson and to try to answer at the end of the lesson

clear learning objectives

at a glance match to the specification

explains unfamiliar concepts

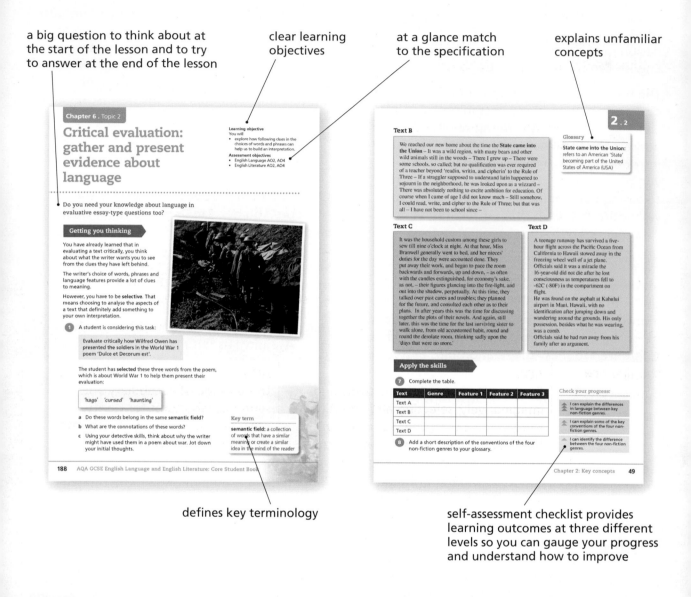

defines key terminology

self-assessment checklist provides learning outcomes at three different levels so you can gauge your progress and understand how to improve

This skills-building sequence leads up to a substantial, synoptic 'Apply your skills' task or series of tasks at the end of each chapter. You can use this section to assess your progress, as sample responses at two levels are provided for you to judge your own work against.

We hope that you enjoy using this book, and that it helps you to make the progress you need to successfully complete your GCSE English Language and GCSE English Literature course.

Sarah Darragh and Jo Heathcote
Series editors

Chapter 1

Key technical skills

What's it all about?

In this chapter, you will learn about words, where they come from and the different jobs they do in sentences. You will also look at how sentences are formed and structured to create effects, as well as considering paragraphing. You will learn some of the correct technical terms to help you in your studies. The understanding of grammatical concepts and terms developed here will inform your work in later chapters, particularly Chapters 4, 6, 8 and 9.

In this chapter, you will learn about

- words and how we spell them
- vocabulary and meaning: nouns and adjectives
- words and meaning: verbs and agreement
- sentences and their functions
- adding meaning and clarity with punctuation
- sentences used for effect
- structure: using different sentence structures
- structure: paragraphing.

	English Language GCSE	English Literature GCSE
Which AOs are covered?	**AO5** Communicate clearly, effectively and imaginatively, selecting and adapting tone, style and register for different forms, purposes and audiences. Organise information and ideas, using structural and grammatical features to support coherence and cohesion of texts **AO6** Candidates must use a range of vocabulary and sentence structures for clarity, purpose and effect, with accurate spelling and punctuation	**AO4** Use a range of vocabulary and sentence structures for clarity, purpose and effect, with accurate spelling and punctuation
How will this be tested?	You will be asked to complete writing tasks under timed conditions. You will need to show accurate spelling and organisation and be able to punctuate varied sentences to create effects as well as paragraph your work accurately and effectively. Some reading questions will ask you to focus in detail on particular words and phrases. Others will identify an area of a text and ask you to look closely at the meanings and techniques being used.	Reading questions will ask you to analyse and comment on the overall text, paying attention to the language, the structure or the literary techniques being used by the writer to communicate meanings and create effects. In writing your responses you will need to show you can do so in a clear and organised way, using accurate spelling and punctuation to help make your meaning clear.

Words and how we spell them

Learning objective
You will learn to
• explore how English spelling has evolved and how we can use this to help us recognise spelling patterns.
Assessment objectives
• English Language AO6
• English Literature AO4

How do you improve your spelling of more complex words?

Getting you thinking

English is made up of a whole host of different words from different languages. These words have become part of our language at different times through our very varied history.

1. Consider the following questions and jot down your ideas.

   a Do you know who the Vikings were and when they invaded our country?

   b What do you know about the Romans and Anglo-Saxons in Britain?

   c Have you heard of the Norman Conquest?

  d Can you name any places that England has ruled in
    the past?

  e Can you think of any ways these different peoples,
    events and places have affected our language?

If English is a patchwork quilt of different languages, each one
brings with it different patterns and ways of spelling.

2 Look up these words in a dictionary to find out which
   language they originally came from:

pyjamas	cake	parliament	tragedy	expensive	umbrella
adventure	history	coffee	jeans	guitar	icon	shampoo

Explore the skills

Many of our everyday words come from Anglo-Saxon and Old
Norse (brought by waves of invaders who settled in Britain,
including the Saxons and later the Vikings). These words are short,
monosyllabic and logical to spell. They 'sound out' easily when we
come to write them down and include many of the nouns, basic
verbs and pronouns we use every day.

3 Look at the words in the box which follows. Using **only** the
   words in the box, write a short poem or description of a
   natural scene.

house	love	you	she	he	I	this	that	can	eat
sleep	live	water	leaf	moon	food	as	and	so	on
in	down	to	when	where	day	night	shall	sun	
day	winter	spring	friend	evil	cold	then	we	us	
under	up	to	heart	grass	water	have	do	be	
	sky	weak	die	get	give	take			

Your poem or description is made up of very familiar words – all
of which are Anglo-Saxon or Norse in origin.

Some of our more complex words, however, tend to come from
Latin: the language brought to England by the Romans (when they
were invaded) in 43 AD. The Romans stayed for nearly 370 years and
brought order and organisation. Their words are very organised too.

Our Latinate vocabulary is often made up of a root word or word
stem. For example:

norm

The root word changes in meaning very slightly when we add
prefixes or **suffixes** to the beginning or ends of the stem.

e+norm+ous

ab+norm+al

Key terms

prefixes: added at the
beginning of words in
order to turn them into
other words

suffixes: 'endings' – used
at the end of words to turn
them into other words

4 The following table lists some common suffixes which often cause confusion when spelling words. Read the golden rule in the table, then add the correct endings to the root word.

Confusing suffixes	Golden rule	Stem words	New words
–cious and –tious	If your stem ends in –ce, then lose the –ce and add –cious. If the stem ends in any other letters just add –tious.	grace space caution ambition	
–ation and –able	If your stem ends in –ce or –ge, keep the –e before adding –able. Words which end in –ation can usually also use –able.	adore notice enjoy consider	

5 Look at these words ending in the prefix –ible.

horrible   forcible   visible   terrible

a Work out the stem word and write some golden rules to help you remember these suffixes.

b Think of some more –ible words to try out your rule.

Develop the skills

By thinking carefully about the word stem, we are often able to find the key to spelling other words in the same family.

For example, take the word **finish**, meaning the end or the limit of something.

finish → add a new ending → finite

If you can spell **finish**, you can also spell **finite** by changing the ending and you can then spell **infinite** by adding a prefix. You can also spell **definite** by adding a different prefix. Then, by adding a further prefix, you can create **indefinite**.

6 How does the meaning of the word shift slightly in each of these examples? Check in a dictionary for any words you are not familiar with.

What does not change, however, is the spelling of the stem 'fini'.

7 Using the prefixes and suffixes in the following table, try to build ten more words from these Latinate stems.

equal – meaning: even or level
cure – meaning: to care
form – meaning: to shape

Examples might be:

> **equal**: un + equal = unequal, equal + ity = equality

Common prefixes						Common suffixes				
ad	ac	as	bi	con	de	–able	–ible	–ant	–ance	–ent
dis	in	per	pre	re	trans	–ence	–acy	–ate	–ity	–ite
un						–sion	–tion			

Apply the skills

8 Read the extract from Charles Dickens's *Nicholas Nickleby*, and work out the missing words by adding prefixes and suffixes to each stem. Then check with a dictionary.

Pale and haggard faces, lank and bony figures, children with the countenances of old men, (form) with irons upon their limbs, boys of (stunt) growth, and others whose long, meagre legs would hardly bear their (stoop) bodies, all (crowd) on the view together; there were the bleared eye, the hare-lip, the (crook) foot, and every (ugly) or (distort) that told of (nature) aversion conceived by parents for their offspring, or of young lives which, from the (early) dawn of (infant), had been one horrible (endure) of (cruel) and neglect.

Charles Dickens, from *Nicholas Nickleby*

Check your progress:

▲▲ I can form and use complex words which do not always follow regular patterns.

▲ I can recognise, use and spell more complex words.

▲ I can recognise, use and spell basic words accurately.

Vocabulary and meaning: nouns and adjectives

Learning objective

You will learn to
- explore some key word classes (nouns and adjectives) and how they create meaning.

Assessment objectives
- English Language AO2, AO5
- English Literature AO2, AO4

What jobs do words do?

Getting you thinking

Nouns

Some of your first words were the names of things around you – teddy, ball, cup. This is how you learn to make sense of the world, by labelling and naming the things you see.

The words that do the job of labelling and naming are called **nouns**. To test whether a word is a noun, see if you can put a **determiner** in front of it. The most common determiners are **a**, **an** and **the**.

Adjectives

As you developed your skills with language, you probably needed to be able to recognise more specific things and to describe specific things – you may have needed to ask for your brown teddy rather than a pink one, a football rather than a tennis ball, and a clean cup rather than a dirty one.

The words that do the job of describing nouns are called **adjectives**.

Key terms

nouns: labelling and naming words – teddy, ball, cup

determiner: a word that goes in front of a noun such as *a*, *an* and *the*

adjectives: words that describe nouns – a *tennis* ball, a *pink* teddy

1 Organise the following words into two columns headed **Nouns** and **Adjectives**.

black	house	web	silvery	chilly	door	torrential
wispy	cat	moon	haunted	breeze	rain	creaking

2 Now look at your lists. Pair up each noun with the most appropriate adjective from the list. An example has been done for you below.

haunted house

If we add a determiner to this pairing, we create a **noun phrase**.

the haunted house – a haunted house

Key term

noun phrase: a noun phrase is a phrase (a group of connected words) with a **noun** as its main word; a **noun phrase** can normally be used in place of a **noun** within a sentence

3 Create noun phrases from all of your pairings by adding 'a' or 'the'.

4 Look again at the noun phrases you have created. What type of story might you be reading if you found these noun phrases in it?

Can you explain why?

Explore the skills

Now look at what happens if you change the adjective in a noun phrase.

> a lonely house
> ↓
> a summer house

This is known as **modification.**

When you change the adjective, you change the picture. When writers use **modification**, they are trying to give you a precise picture.

5 Look at these noun phrases. How does each one change the mental picture you have of a house? Jot down what you see in your mind's eye for each one.

- a newly built house
- an imposing house
- a dilapidated house
- a seaside house
- the family house

6 Look at this extract from a poem called 'Space Poem 3: Off Course' in which the writer uses noun phrases to describe a space mission.

> the turning continents   the space debris
> the golden lifeline   the space walk
> the crawling deltas   the camera moon
> the pitch velvet   the rough sleep
> the crackling headphone   the space silence
>
>   Edwin Morgan, from 'Space Poem 3: Off Course'

Choose four of the noun phrases and write down what you see in your mind's eye.

7 Imagine you are on the space mission in the poem.

   a Replace all of the adjectives in your four chosen noun phrases with ideas of your own.

   b How does this modification change what you might see in your mind's eye?

   For example:

   the turning continents ⟶ the distant continents

Develop the skills

You are now going to read the whole of the poem.

Space Poem 3: Off Course

the golden flood   the weightless seat
the cabin song   the pitch black
the growing beard   the floating crumb
the shining rendezvous   the orbit wisecrack
the hot spacesuit   the smuggled mouth-organ
     the imaginary somersault   the visionary sunrise
     the turning continents   the space debris
     the golden lifeline   the space walk
     the crawling deltas   the camera moon
     the pitch velvet   the rough sleep
     the crackling headphone   the space silence
     the turning earth   the lifeline continents
     the cabin sunrise   the hot flood
     the shining spacesuit   the growing moon
       the crackling somersault   the smuggled orbit
       the rough moon   the visionary rendezvous
       the weightless headphone   the cabin debris
       the floating lifeline   the pitch sleep
       the crawling camera   the turning silence
       the space crumb   the crackling beard
       the orbit mouth-organ   the floating song

Edwin Morgan

In some cases in the poem, the same noun appears two or three times with a different adjective each time. For example:

'the golden flood' becomes 'the hot flood'.

This change of adjective suggests something that was beautiful and 'golden' – perhaps the light of the sun – has become dangerous and a threat, 'the hot flood'.

8 Can you find an example in the poem where the same noun has been used more than once? What does the different adjective suggest about what is happening in the poem?

9 a In other places, the same adjective has been used more than once. What does it suggest in each case about the noun it is describing? For example:

'the crackling headphone' becomes 'the crackling somersault'.

b Find one more example of your own and explain what you think might be happening.

Words can do more than one job. The place that words appear in a sentence is the factor that gives them their technical term.

10 Look at these three noun phrases from the poem.

the orbit wisecrack   the smuggled orbit   the orbit mouth-organ

a What do you notice in each case about the use of the word 'orbit'?

b What job is the writer making the word do in each phrase?

11 Write two noun phrases for each word in the following list: one where the word is used as the adjective, one where the word becomes a noun. An example has been done for you.

village: the village green/the country village

flower   star   thunder
house   dress   television

Apply the skills

12 Now read the following task.

Think about a place or a person you know well.

Construct a poem in the style of 'Off Course' in which you describe that person or place in noun phrases only.

Be as precise as you can in putting your noun phrases together. Experiment with using words in different places and repeating words to create different pictures for your reader.

An example has been given here of a student describing their house to help you get started.

The glittery path

The glassy expanse

The greeting warmth

Check your progress:

- I can recognise that the place a word is used gives it its word class and that, by modifying nouns, we create different meanings.

- I can recognise nouns, adjectives and noun phrases and have learned what modification is.

- I can understand what the terms noun, adjective and noun phrase mean.

Words and meaning: verbs and agreement

Learning objective
You will learn to
- explore the function of verbs within the sentence and understand basic patterns of agreement.

Assessment objectives
- English Language AO5, AO6
- English Literature AO2, AO4

How do you know what verbs do and which ones to use where?

Getting you thinking

You are probably familiar with the idea that a verb is an action or doing word.

A verb is far more than that, however. It is the driving force in any sentence you read, write or say. It represents not only movements and actions, but states of being and communicates *when* these things are happening.

Verbs are also not necessarily single words.

1 Look at the highlighted words and phrases in the extract below. All of them are verbs.

    a Which things seem to be happening now, in the present?

    b What happens when verbs are made up of more than one word?

> Snuggling in my bed, I drift back into consciousness. Then, the numbers on the clock leap out at me. I have slept in, yet again. Stumbling down the stairs, I grab a quick coffee before heading for the bus. Then I realise. Outside the rain is torrential. It is going to be one of those days, yet again.

Explore the skills

Verbs help us to understand the time in which things happen. This is called the **tense** of the verb.

Verbs can tell us about things happening in the present. Texts which contain the **present tense** often have an immediate 'here and now' feel about them – as though you are witnessing what is happening.

2 Read this extract from *The Generation Game* by Sophie Duffy where she describes a memory of school.

School is more bearable now I have Lucas for a friend. He might only be small and thin but he has a voice that even Miss Pitchfork must envy. A voice like a crow having a bad day. A voice he uses sparingly, for greater effect.

Lucas and I soon settle into a shared routine that gets us through the six hour long haul. We play together at break in our corner. We pick each other for teams in gym. I save a place for him on the carpet. He saves a place for me in the hall at lunchtime where I give him my greens in exchange for potatoes. (He is a boy of mystery.)

Sophie Duffy,
from *The Generation Game*

3 Make a list of the present tense verbs in the passage.

4 Thinking about the topic of the passage, why do you think the writer chose to use the present tense? Why did she use such simple verbs to convey the actions of the school day?

5 Complete the table below by placing the verbs from the passage in the past and the future tenses.

Present tense: to play	Simple past tense	Future tense
I play You S/he plays We They	S/he played	You will play

Develop the skills

Other tenses, however, are not so simple.

6   These are the verbs 'to have' and 'to be'. Complete the table with the verb **be** and then with the verb **have**.

Present tense: to be	Simple past tense	Future tense
I am You are S/he is We are They are	You were	I will be

Both 'to be' and 'to have' help us to form special past tenses, acting as **auxiliaries**.

The verb 'to have' modifies (or changes) the main verb when we want to indicate something has ended, but only recently:

Phew! I **have found** my keys.

It also modifies the main verb when something in the past has been going on for a long period of time.

She **has taken** flowers to the grave every week since he died.

7   Write five sentences using the verb 'to have' as an auxiliary.

- I have
- S/he has
- They have
- You have
- We have

The verb 'to be' can indicate that something was continuing to happen in the past.

I **was travelling** on the stretch of lonely road when…

We **were marching** onwards into the night, with no idea of where we were heading.

8   Write five sentences using the verb **to be** as an auxilliary.

- I was
- S/he was
- They were
- You were
- We were

The key thing to remember is always to match the correct form of the verb to your subject or pronoun (I, you, he/she…).

'We ~~was~~ marching …'

Explain why this is incorrect.

> ### Key term
>
> **auxiliaries:** the verbs *to have* and *to be* can be used to assist other words to make verb phrases and communicate actions, states of being and time much more specifically

It can be tricky to choose the correct form of the verb when you are writing in **Standard English** because you may be used to speaking in a less formal way, using local **dialect**.

9 **a** Read the transcript below and then rewrite it in Standard English.

b Make some notes about the changes you have made. Explain why confusion might occur here between the spoken forms and the Standard English written forms.

Key terms

Standard English: the most widely used form of English, which is not specific to a particular place or region

dialect: the form of English used in a particular place

Jack: We was much better off in the old days.

Bill: No doubt about it. I were much happier without computers and mobile phones and all that technology.

Jack: My grandson, he were here the other day and he was never off his phone.

Bill: I were on the bus the other day and there was a young lad just the same. Tap, tapping away.

Jack: In our day, we just talked to each other. We was proper sociable.

Bill: Mind you, Jack, you was always a chatterbox...never shutting up. I might have preferred hearing from you by text message!

Apply the skills

10 Rewrite this extract, also from *The Generation Game,* but this time change the present tense to past.

Sometimes Lucas and I are given complete and utter freedom, freedom that would never be contemplated these days for six-year-olds without serious concerns for their health and safety. We like to wander the local streets. We like to go down the road to Toy Town with our pocket money to add to our growing collection of Dinky TV tie-ins. We like to call in to see Mr Bob Sugar who stocks us up with goodies…. we like to spend hours playing Hide-and-Seek amongst the crosses and angels or Guess-the-Animal-Poo amongst the shrubs and undergrowth. But the time I am happiest in the Bone Yard is when Lucas helps me with my reading. I have mastered several Biblical verses and all the old family names of Torquay. He is a good teacher.

Start like this:

Sometimes Lucas and I *were given* complete and utter freedom, freedom that would never be contemplated these days…

Check your progress:

 I can change tenses and ensure the verb always matches the pronoun correctly.

 I can understand what 'tense' means and how to change the tense of verbs.

 I can understand what a verb is and its job in a sentence.

Sentences and their functions

Learning objective
You will learn to
- explore how different messages can be created from different sentence functions.

Assessment objectives
- English Language AO2, AO6

What are sentences for?

Getting you thinking

When you write, you are probably conscious of the need to write in clear sentences, but it isn't very often that we worry about whether or not we are speaking in them. We also create other perfectly clear forms of communication without sentences in them, for example, lists or revision notes.

1 Can you think of any other forms of clear communication – spoken, written or multi-modal – that do not use sentences?

Believe it or not, sentences are a pretty recent invention! In medieval times, the word 'sentence' meant a judgement or decision and came from a Latin word 'sentential'.

2 What other meaning of the word 'sentence' is still used today which links with this?

In the 1600s, Ben Jonson used the line 'Thou speakest sentences' in one of his plays. Back then 'sentences' seemed to mean speaking wisely, with judgement, or with good common sense.

Only later did 'sentences' come to be associated with the content of writing and with communicating ideas using specific groupings of words that make clear sense to all of us.

Explore the skills

3 Look at these sentences and decide what is different about each one.

> Have we got any homework tonight?
>
> Tuesday is homework night.
>
> Homework is a total nightmare!
>
> Get that homework done now.

Each sentence here has a different job to do. We call these jobs **sentence functions**. The different functions are as follows:

- making a **statement**
- asking a question or making a request
- giving a **command**
- making an **exclamation**.

Match the sentences in Activity 3 above to their correct function.

4 Read the extract below from the novel *Junk* by Melvin Burgess. The character Gemma has been in a disagreement with her parents.

> **1** I didn't go back that day. **2** In fact, I stayed away all weekend as a protest.
>
> **3** Response: banned from going out of the house at weekends.
>
> **4** My next plot was to stay out until ten each night during the week. **5** They couldn't keep me off school in the name of discipline, surely? **6** They got round that by my dad picking me up from school. **7** My God! **8** Everyone knew what was going on. **9** He actually came into the class to get me! **10** I thought I was going to die of humiliation.
>
> Melvin Burgess, from *Junk*

Key terms

statement: a sentence that declares something and presents it as a fact or opinion

command: a sentence that tells us to do something by putting the verb first to emphasise the action

exclamation: a sentence that expresses an emotion such as shock, anger, joy, surprise

5 **a** What function does each sentence in the extract have?

b What do the statements provide for us?

c Who is the question addressed to?

d What tone do the exclamations suggest? What mood is Gemma in?

e What is the benefit for the writer in being able to use different sentence functions?

Develop the skills

6 Which sentence functions are used to introduce this charity campaign? Can you identify two possible purposes this text might have? What clues do the sentence functions give us?

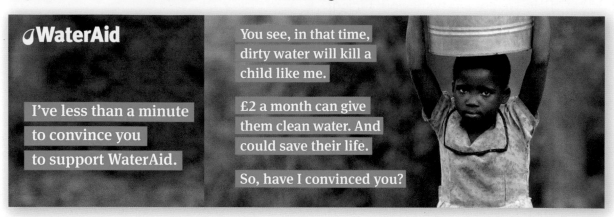

7 Now read the rest of the text and use the questions in the annotations to help you explore its use of different sentences.

⟨WaterAid

One child is dying with every minute that passes. That's 2,000 children every single day. Not because of war or disaster. But simply because of dirty water and poor sanitation.

Hard to stomach, isn't it?

What's even more sickening is that all these deaths could be so easily prevented.

WaterAid works across the globe with some of the world's poorest people. Every hour we build a new water point. And every hour we help over 100 people to get safe, clean water.

But it's still not enough. Which is why we need your help.

Your donations will be used to buy things like cement and bricks for wells. To help communities build pumps. And to make sure children get safe, clean water and sanitation – for life.

Have we convinced you?

Complete the form below and send it back to us please. Before another child dies.

These sentences are stark statements presented to us as facts. Why do you think the writer chose this type of sentence to be the first thing you read when you look inside the leaflet?

Why choose a question here? Who is it addressed to? What answer is the writer expecting?

By using more statements here, how is the charity able to communicate more about its work?

These sentences are still statements but they have a different tone. Can you work out what they are trying to do here? Are these statements like the more formal ones we had earlier?

How does changing the topic of the statements here help the charity remind you of its key message?

Why was it important for the writer to use another question at this point?

The leaflet finishes with a command followed by a statement. Why put them in this order?

Apply the skills

8 Complete the following task.

Imagine you are heading up an event at your school to raise funds for a local children's charity. Compile a one-page informative poster using the key facts below. Use all four different sentence functions to help your poster meet its purpose and target its audience.

- There are a number of children living in poverty in the local area.
- Many children have no adequate winter coats or shoes and will not have gifts at Christmas.
- Your school is going to organise a collection of outgrown clothes, shoes and toys.
- You need volunteers to help wash, package and label the items.
- The local children's charity is called The Rainbow Group.
- You need to get items to them in the next three weeks.

Check your progress:

- I can understand that different sentence functions can add to the impact of a text and help to fulfil its purpose and engage its reader.
- I can name the different sentence functions and understand how they can add to the meaning of a text.
- I can understand that sentences have different functions.

Add meaning and clarity with punctuation

Learning objective
You will learn to
- recap and revise the importance of accurate basic punctuation.

Assessment objectives
- English Language AO6
- English Literature AO4

Why is punctuation important in making things clear?

Getting you thinking

Long ago, early forms of writing had no punctuation at all. Not everyone could write and those who could did not even use spaces between their words. It must have made reading very difficult indeed.

1   Try reading the following passage from Lewis Carroll's *Alice in Wonderland*. Is it as straightforward to read and understand as the kinds of punctuated writing you are used to?

CuriouserandcuriousercriedAliceshewassomuchsurprisedthatfor
themomentshequiteforgothowtospeakgoodEnglishnowImopening
outlikethelargesttelescopethateverwasgoodbyefeetforwhenshelooked
downatherfeettheyseemedtobealmostoutofsighttheyweregettingsofar
offohmypoorlittlefeetIwonderwhowillputonyourshoesandstockingsfor
younowdearsImsureIshantbeableIshallbeagreatdealtoofarofftotrouble
myselfaboutyouyoumustmanagethebestwayyoucanbutImustbekindto
themthoughtAliceorperhapstheywontwalkthewayIwanttogoletmesee
IllgivethemanewpairofbootseveryChristmasandshewentonplanningto
herselfhowshewouldmanageithowfunnyitllseemsendingpresents
toonesownfeetohdearwhatnonsenseImtalking

Explore the skills

2   Make a copy of the passage on a large sheet of paper, inserting the spaces between the words.

3   Now think about the four sentence functions you have learned about:

- statements
- questions
- commands
- exclamations.

Which sentence function ends with:

- **?** a question mark
- **!** an exclamation mark?

The remaining two sentence functions end with full stops.

4 Work out where Lewis Carroll is using statements, questions or exclamations. Add them in to your copy using a coloured pen.

Already, you should start to see the passage beginning to make more sense, but other types of punctuation also help make writing clearer.

Apostrophes help us to create clear meaning in two ways.

Apostrophes of omission

The first is by pinpointing where you have joined two words together to make a more informal version. If someone sends you an email asking for the arrangements for a party, you are unlikely to reply with:

I do not know. It has not been decided yet.

Much more likely would be:

I don't know. We haven't sorted it out yet.

Apostrophes help you to create that friendly, informal tone. They are known as **apostrophes of omission** as the apostrophe replaces the letters you have missed out. The general rule is that you need to identify which letters are removed and join the words back together with the apostrophe.

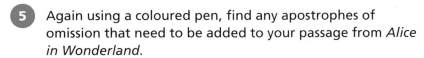

5 Again using a coloured pen, find any apostrophes of omission that need to be added to your passage from *Alice in Wonderland*.

Apostrophes of possession

The second way apostrophes add clarity to your writing is by showing belonging.

These are known as **apostrophes of possession.** These apostrophes change their place depending on whether you are showing belonging to one person or thing, or many.

For example: | The boy's books

This places the apostrophe straight after the word 'boy' and before the 's'.

This tells you there is only one boy and all the books belong to him.

However: | The boys' books

This places the apostrophe after the 's' of 'boys'. This tells us there is a group of boys with books belonging to all of them.

6 Look at the sentences below which all use apostrophes incorrectly. Identify the problem and write out the sentence correctly.

 a Whos seen Lydia's shoes?

 b The student's revision notes were in their books.

 c The builder was late putting in all my window's and door's.

 d The two girl's bicycles were left in the driveway.

 e There is'nt any point in reading the newspaper's today.

Develop the skills

Commas

Commas have a variety of uses but are often overused or misplaced.

Commas form a mini break or boundary in a sentence where you want to separate different aspects of an idea or description.

7 The table below gives some of the most common uses of the comma that you will need in your writing. Look at the examples provided and then write an example of your own for each usage.

Use of comma	Example
Commas are used to separate out the items in a list.	In the cake shop I couldn't decide between the chocolate eclairs, the strawberry tarts, the vanilla slices – they all looked delicious.
Commas are used to link adjectives when more than one is used to describe something.	The black, stormy night filled me with dread. The thrashing, pounding waves made a dramatic sight on the beach.
At the beginning of a sentence they create a pause after names, discourse markers or answers like 'yes' and 'no'.	Alex, can you stop playing on the computer now. However, the story ends happily. Yes, it's going to be a good day.
They can be used in pairs to drop extra pieces of information into a sentence.	The day, which began gloomily, ended on a high note. The river, which was polluted, burst its banks and flooded the nearby village.

Speech punctuation

When characters are in conversation with each other in a novel or short story, this is called **dialogue**.

We present the words they speak in speech marks. However, other punctuation marks are also used alongside the speech marks.

> "Are you absolutely serious?" Phil said.
>
> "Of course," Sheila replied, "I'm deadly serious."

What do you notice about what the dialogue begins with?

Where does the sentence punctuation go?

What happens when a new speaker begins to speak?

What is needed when the speaker hasn't finished speaking?

What is needed before the speaker begins again?

8 Now look back at *Alice in Wonderland* and add in any commas you feel would help to clarify the meaning. Add any speech punctuation to show where Alice is using dialogue.

Apply the skills

9 Complete the following task.

There are eighteen punctuation marks missing from the following passage from the novel *A Kestrel for a Knave* by Barry Hines. The sentence punctuation is in place, but the following have been left out:

- apostrophes • commas • speech marks.

Identify where all the missing punctuation marks go, using the rules you have just learned to help you.

Im sick of you boys youll be the death of me. Not a day goes by without me having to deal with a line of boys. I cant remember a day not one day in all the years Ive been in school and how longs that? … ten years and the schools no better now than it was on the day that it opened. I cant understand it. I cant understand it at all.

The boys couldnt understand it either and they dropped their eyes as he searched for an answer in their faces. Failing to find one there he stared past them out of the window.

The lawn stretching down to the front railings was studded with worm casts and badly in need of its Spring growth. The border separating the lawn from the drive was turned earth and in the centre of the lawn stood a silver birch tree in a little round bed.

Adapted from Barry Hines, *A Kestrel for a Knave*

Check your progress:

▲▲ I can demarcate sentences and use both forms of the apostrophe, the comma and speech punctuation accurately nearly all the time.

▲ I can demarcate sentences and use both forms of apostrophe in the right place, as well as use the comma correctly most of the time.

▲ I can use full stops, question marks and exclamation marks to mark the end of my sentences. I sometimes remember apostrophes.

Sentences used for effect

Learning objective
You will learn to
- explore how different sentence functions can be used to create special effects in writing.

Assessment objectives
- English Language AO2, AO6
- English Literature AO2

Does using different types of sentences make any difference?

Getting you thinking

You've discovered already that sentences can do different jobs in writing and help to make clear the purpose of a text. They can also be used, though, to add to the impact of a text and to create special effects within it.

 1 Look at these sentences.

I love you.

I... love you?

How does the use of a different sentence function dramatically alter the meaning? You could experiment by saying both versions in different tones of voice to help you identify the differences.

Explore the skills

Look at the following extract. It is from a speech by Barack Obama as he unveiled a statue of Rosa Parks, an important figure in the American **Civil Rights Movement**.

Glossary

Civil Rights Movement: a political movement for equal rights; Rosa Parks, a black protester, refused to give up her seat on the bus for a white man

> Rosa Parks tells us there's always something we can do. She tells us that we all have responsibilities, to ourselves and to one another. She reminds us that this is how change happens – not mainly through the exploits of the famous and the powerful, but through the countless acts of often anonymous courage and kindness and fellow feeling and responsibility that continually, stubbornly, expand our conception of justice – our conception of what is possible.
>
> Rosa Parks's singular act of disobedience launched a movement. The tired feet of those who walked the dusty roads of Montgomery helped a nation see that to which it had once been blind. It is because of these men and women that I stand here today. It is because of them that our children grow up in a land more free and more fair; a land truer to its founding creed.
>
> http://www.whitehouse.gov/the-press-office/2013/02/27/remarks-president-dedication-statue-honoring-rosa-parks-us-capitol

Statement sentences – also known as **declaratives** – are used here.

Key term

Declaritive: a sentence that declares something and presents it as a fact or opinion

2 Why is that same statement sentence function used repeatedly? How does this enhance the serious tone?

3 Does the sentence function make the piece feel formal or informal? Why would this register be most appropriate here?

4 By using declarative statements, how does Obama emphasise the importance of Rosa Parks and what she did?

5 Do you notice anything about the choice of verbs in the sentences and the tenses that are used? How do these help present Obama's opinions of Rosa Parks as facts?

6 Can you suggest any reason why Obama did not choose to use any of the following in his speech?

- questions/interrogatives
- commands/imperatives
- exclamations

By contrast, now look at the following poem.

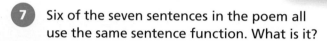

How Not to be a Woodlouse

Avoid damp, dark places. Try not to hide. Your shell is for protection only.

Seek sunshine, dry weather, fresh flowers. Develop a taste for clean, clear water, and the smooth, pungent skin of just-picked fruit.

Celebrate the lightness of your touch, the way your feathery caress holds people still.

Remember, that, like you, the world is not black and white, but made up of delicate shades of grey.

Patricia Debney

7 Six of the seven sentences in the poem all use the same sentence function. What is it?

8 We often think of this sentence function as giving us instructions, but is that what Debney is doing here?

9 What is surprising about the tone Debney has managed to create?

10 Debney is perhaps using the idea of the woodlouse to suggest we should not hide ourselves away or be shy. What do you think is the meaning and impact of the one declarative sentence in the poem?

Develop the skills

Now you are going to consider how different sentence forms in the same text can add to subtle meanings and create startling effects. The following extract is from Shakespeare's play *Othello*. Iago, a lower ranking officer, is plotting against his superior by suggesting his wife is having an affair with Othello's trusted officer, Cassio.

11 Consider the questions in the annotations and make a note of your responses.

IAGO
My noble lord!
OTHELLO
       What dost thou say, Iago?
IAGO
Did Michael Cassio, when you woo'd my lady,
Know of your love?

OTHELLO

He did, from first to last: why dost thou ask?

IAGO

But for a satisfaction of my thought –
No further harm.

OTHELLO

        Why of thy thought, Iago?

IAGO

I did not think he had been acquainted with her.

OTHELLO

O, yes; and went between us very oft.

IAGO

Indeed!

OTHELLO

Indeed! Ay, indeed. Discern'st thou aught in that?
Is he not honest?

IAGO

        Honest, my lord?

OTHELLO

Honest? Ay, honest.

IAGO

        My lord, for aught I know.

OTHELLO

What dost thou think?

IAGO

        Think, my lord?

OTHELLO

Think, my lord! By heaven, he echoes me,
As if there were some monster in his thought
Too hideous to be shown.

William Shakespeare, from *Othello* (Act 3, Scene 3)

> Iago has been asking devious questions but now switches to the declarative. What response does he know he is going to get here?

> Usually the person asking the questions in a situation is the one in authority but what do you notice about the questions Othello is asking so far? Do they put him in charge here or Iago? Why?

> What kind of tone does Iago's exclamation suggest here? How might that add to Othello's concern?

> What does the repetition of the exclamation and the series of questions now tell you about Othello's thoughts and feelings?

> How does the use of the declarative here add to Iago's success in disturbing Othello?

> How does Othello's declarative here suggest Iago has been successful?

Apply the skills

12 Choose one of the texts you have studied in this section and write up your notes and ideas in 200–300 words, exploring the following task.

How does the choice of sentence function in the text add to the meaning and impact of the text?

Checklist for success

- Identify the different sentence functions.
- Give clear examples.
- Explain in detail how they might add to the purpose, the meaning and the impact of the text on its audience or reader.

Check your progress:

⬆⬆ I can understand that when writers use different sentence functions they are able to add to the meaning and impact of a text for the reader or audience.

⬆ I can see that using different sentence functions creates different moods or feelings within a text.

⬆ I can identify the different sentence functions in a text.

Structure: using different sentence structures

Learning objective
You will learn to
- explore how sentences can be built.

Assessment objectives
- English Language AO6
- English Literature AO4

What's the difference between a simple, compound and complex sentence?

Getting you thinking

Look at the sentences below. They are all on the same topic.

a I like reading.

b I hate reading, so I listen to texts on my MP3.

c I liked reading until I had to read that awful book in school.

d I hate reading usually, but that book which we read in class, was totally brilliant.

1 Look at sentences **a** and **c**. What is the main idea in each?

2 Look at sentence **b**. If you took out the word 'so' and changed the comma to a full stop would the ideas still make sense?

3 Look at sentence **c**. If you took out the word 'until' and added a full stop, would the two ideas make sense together?

4 What are the two key ideas in sentence **d**? Which part of the sentence provides additional information to us?

The four sentences above are the four main ways we can build or structure sentences in English. Their names are:

Simple   Complex   Compound-complex   Compound

5 Which label belongs with which sentence? Decide how each one got their name.

Explore the skills

Simple sentences

A simple sentence:

- contains one idea
- has one verb or verb phrase
- has one action, event, or state within it
- contains at least one noun or pronoun that is linked or attached to the verb.

> We **1** bought **2** a house.

1 **Pronoun** / subject
2 Verb

> The house **1** was painted **2** red.

1 Noun / subject
2 Verb phrase

Simple sentences tend to be short and punchy. They can create a clipped effect in a text. They can often indicate a kind of tension. Simple sentences are not necessarily easy to read or understand. The simplicity is linked to their structure, not their ideas.

Read this extract from the short story 'Everything Stuck to Him' by Raymond Carver.

They stared at each other. **1** Then the boy took up his hunting gear and went outside. **2** He started the car. **3** He went around to the car windows and, making a job of it, scraped away the ice. **4**

He turned off the motor and sat awhile. **5** And then he got out and went back inside. **6**

The living-room light was on. **7** The girl was asleep on the bed. **8** The baby was asleep beside her. **9**

The boy took off his boots. **10**

Raymond Carver, from 'Everything Stuck to Him'

6 a Identify all of the verbs and verb phrases.

b Identify the six **simple sentences**.

c Look carefully at sentence 1 and then sentence 10. What tension do you detect in the story? What has changed from the beginning of the extract to the end?

d Now look closely at the remaining sentences and make notes on why they are not **simple**.

e Look at sentences 2, 5 and 6. How does the writer link the two ideas in each sentence?

Compound sentences

A compound sentence happens when two simple sentences are joined together. They are joined with coordinating conjunctions.

> We **1** bought **2** a house and **3** painted **4** it red.

1 Pronoun **2** Verb

3 Conjunction to join the ideas. No second noun or pronoun is needed as we know what is being referred to.

4 A second verb is needed though to show the second action and idea.

A common mistake is to join two simple sentences together without using a conjunction:

> We bought a house, it was painted red.

This is called a comma splice and is not an accurate way to build or punctuate a sentence.

Key term

coordinating conjunctions: joining words such as *and*, *nor*, *but*, *or*, *yet*, *so*

7 Look back at the extract from the Raymond Carver story. The writer has used compound sentences for sentences 2, 3 and 5.

   a Why do you think he did this?

   b What do you think is the impact of using simple sentences for sentences 1 and 10?

   c Why did the writer also choose simple sentences for sentences 7, 8 and 9? Do they create a particular feeling for you when you read the extract? Do they affect the pace at which you read? What do all the full stops force you to do as a reader?

Complex sentences

A **complex sentence** still has, at its core, a simple sentence. However, it develops the idea contained in the simple sentence and adds more detail and information in little subsections.

> It was way back in '56 that **2** **we bought the house** **1**, painted it up in a pillar box red and planted out the garden. **3**

In a **complex sentence**, the simple sentence is known as the **main clause**.

The subsections are known as the **subordinate clauses** as they can't make sense alone, without the main one.

Complex sentences can take us on a journey of thoughts, to create a vivid picture in our minds. They are not necessarily difficult to understand!

1 The simple sentence is still at the core of the sentence and makes sense in its own right.

2 The subsections *depend* on the simple sentence, as they don't make sense on their own.

3 The subsections add to the idea and provide more detail, and more information about time, place or manner.

Key terms

main clause: a simple sentence with a subject and a verb

subordinate clauses: clauses attached to the main clause to add extra detail and information; they don't make sense alone without the main clause

8 **a** Rewrite the passage from 'Everything Stuck to Him' changing the six simple sentences into complex sentences by adding subordinate clauses, telling us something about time, place or manner.

> *For a good while,* they stared at each other, *anger and resentment behind their eyes.*

b Explore the differences your changes in sentence structure have made to the text. What is added? What is taken away? How has the tension changed?

Apply the skills

A student wrote in an analysis:

> Simple sentences are short and easier to understand, so texts with simple sentences must be for younger readers. Complex sentences are for an older audience.

9 Read the analysis above, then complete the following task.

Using the following extract, from a storybook for very young children, *The Princess and the Pea* by Lauren Child, as evidence, write 200–250 words explaining whether you agree or disagree with the student.

The prince came back very downcast.

He refused to eat anything for supper, not even the very delicious rook pie the royal cook had prepared as a welcome home. He lit a candle in his window and just stood and gazed into the night sky.

Not so very far away, in a treetop house just over the mountain, there was a girl, with the most beautiful black, black hair you have ever seen, or possibly never seen. **4**

She woke up that night to see the moon dancing on her ceiling, and she popped on her favourite pea-green dress and glided down the stairs into the garden. **5**

Lauren Child, from *The Princess and the Pea*

Check your progress:

▲▲ I can understand how each sentence type is constructed and how they can create different effects within a text.

▲ I can understand the difference between simple, compound and complex sentences.

▲ I can understand that sentences can be structured in different ways.

Before you begin, think about:

- the different types of sentences the writer has used
- the different impact and effects of sentences 1 and 4.

Structure: paragraphing

Learning objective
You will learn to
• explore how ideas can be organised in a piece of writing.

Assessment objectives
• English Language AO6
• English Literature AO4

Does it really matter when you start a new paragraph?

Getting you thinking

Stop and think for one minute about your journey into school today.

Chances are that most days this involves a clear routine, a set route of places where you are likely to be by a certain time. The bus stop perhaps, the newsagents to pick up a snack, a specific spot to meet a friend.

Your journey has a structure and a sequence that allows you to get where you want to be, logically and without confusion.

1 Picture your journey to school in five clear stages. Make a bullet-pointed list of the five stages.

2 Can you remember a time when you were in a strange place – perhaps on holiday? What does it feel like to try and set out to find somewhere in a strange place?

A piece of writing without a clear structure makes the reader feel as you did in your strange place. That is why, in most types of writing, structure is important.

Explore the skills

When you write in prose, the most logical way of showing order is to use paragraphs. Paragraphs show a logical change in a text, rather like the different stages in a journey.

3 Look at the statements below. Are they are true or false?

• Paragraphs should have a single focus.
• Paragraphs can go in any order.
• Paragraphs are there to make the page look neater.
• Paragraphs should begin with an introductory sentence.
• Paragraphs should be no more than ten lines long.
• Paragraphs change to show a different time, place, person or subject.

4 Imagine you are going to write a description of the scene in the photograph below, or another one of your choice. Pay close attention to the order your eye takes in the details in the photograph.

Make a list of the different details you feel should be in your description. Ensure your list reflects the order in which you recorded each detail in your mind.

Following the picture is a list that a student compiled into a grid. They have put the details in a **logical order**. Each detail is going to be **the single focus** of a different paragraph of their description. They have gone on to start to write a clear introductory sentence – known as **a topic sentence** – for each paragraph.

5 Help the student to finish the grid by compiling some more possible topic sentences.

Detail from the picture	Topic sentence
Para 1: The large red house with blue shutters	Mandula's house dominated the bay of the small Greek fishing village.
Para 2: The sweep of soft sand	Like a continuing blanket of comfort, the sweep of soft sand always dried swiftly in the sun at low tide.
Para 3: The blueness of the sea and the sky	
Para 4: The figure in blue	
Para 5: The boats on the shore	Dotted along the shore, the tiny boats with their bright paint were a reminder of the struggling livelihood of the locals.

6 By placing the details here in **a logical order** from the most obvious to the more subtle, how do you think this will add interest to the description?

7 Does each paragraph deal with **one place, person or subject**? How will this allow the writer to develop more depth to their ideas?

Develop the skills

Imagine now that the photograph is to accompany an article in a broadsheet newspaper on the subject of the Greek economy.

8 Look at the **topic sentences** the journalist has prepared below. Reorder the sentences so that their paragraphs will be more coherent for the readers of the article.

a) The tourism industry has benefited from a wide range of visitors – those who have taken longer trips and those who have spent more money on luxury holidays.

b) The local Minister for Tourism concluded: 'Tourism remains an important driving force in our recovery from recession.'

c) In the past year, more money came into the country than went out, which is good news at last for locals.

d) Record spending by tourists has helped the Greek economy out of a big recession.

e) A spokesperson for a major bank warned there is a long way to go.

f) This news is little help though to the 28% of Greeks who are still unemployed.

9 Read the following extract which was inspired by the photograph you studied earlier. Make notes on your responses to the questions in the annotations.

It was just as I'd remembered. The village shimmered in the bright, luminous light of the morning.

Returning now, through the sun-baked streets, I looked for familiar faces that weren't there. The old women, sitting outside shops, occupied in their lace making, their black dresses stark against the white-painted walls, paid me no heed. The fishermen on the quay-side, bronzed and weather-beaten – their skin burnished through years of struggle on these waters, continued mending their nets.

Eyes that did not recognise me.

Past the harbour and across the soft, sweep of sand, the bar still dominated the view. Red walls amongst the white dots of houses, blue shutters open like a smile to the morning. It was impossible to believe she would still be here, after all these years: that she'd brought out those cold beers and dark-treacle coffees the locals sipped. A handful of tourists were seated outside, taking in the depth of the blue from shoreline to the edge of the heavens, shading their eyes with Ray Bans.

Eyes that did not recognise me.

> Why is the first paragraph so short and what does its change indicate a change in?

> The writer has used a paragraph which is only one sentence long. How does that make you feel as a reader? Does it tell you anything about the narrator? Does it add to the ideas connected with time?

> How does repeating the one-sentence paragraph add interest for the reader and communicate even more fully the feelings of the narrator?

Apply the skills

10 Now look at this practice task and think about how you would approach it.

Continue writing the story above, adding three more paragraphs that:

- are varied in length
- have a single focus
- mark a change in time, person, place or subject
- have a strong introductory sentence.

If you prefer, you could write your own story based on the picture and the table you made in Activity 5.

Check your progress:

⬆⬆ I can understand that paragraphs shift to show changes in writing – changes about time, place, person and subject and can use these in my own writing.

⬆ I can understand that paragraphs should come in a logical sequence with a topic sentence to open them and can use these in my own writing.

⬆ I can understand that writing needs paragraphs to be clear and can use these in my own writing.

Check your progress

- I can form and use complex words which do not always follow regular patterns.
- I can recognise that the place a word is used in a sentence gives it its word class and that by modifying nouns I can create different meanings.
- I can change tenses and ensure the verb always matches the pronoun correctly.
- I can understand that different sentence functions can add to the impact of a text and help it to fulfil its purpose and engage its reader.
- I can demarcate sentences and use both forms of the apostrophe, the comma and speech punctuation accurately nearly all the time.
- I can understand that when writers use different sentence functions they are able to add to the meaning and impact of a text for the reader or audience.
- I can understand how each sentence type is constructed and how they can create different effects within a text.
- I can understand that paragraphs shift to show changes in writing – changes about time, place, person and subject.

- I can recognise, use and spell more complex words.
- I can recognise nouns, adjectives and noun phrases and have understood what modification is.
- I can understand what 'tense' means and how to change the tense of verbs.
- I can name the different sentence functions and can understand how they can add to the meaning of a text.
- I can demarcate sentences and use both forms of apostrophe in the right place as well as use the comma correctly most of the time.
- I can see that using different sentence functions creates different moods or feelings within a text.
- I can understand the difference between simple, compound and complex sentences.
- I can understand that paragraphs should come in a logical sequence with a topic sentence to open them.

- I can recognise, use and spell basic words accurately.
- I can understand what the terms noun, adjective and noun phrase mean.
- I can understand what a verb is and its job in a sentence.
- I can understand that sentences have different functions.
- I can use full stops, question marks and exclamation marks to mark the end of my sentences. I sometimes remember apostrophes.
- I can identify the different sentence functions in a text.
- I can understand that sentences can be structured in different ways.
- I can understand that writing needs paragraphs to be clear.

Chapter 2

Key concepts

What's it all about?

In this chapter, you will learn some of the key concepts and ideas that will help your study of texts for both English Language and English Literature. The concepts you learn in this chapter will underpin your study in other chapters of the book. You will not be focusing on one particular skill or Assessment Focus in this chapter.

In this chapter, you will learn to

- understand literary forms
- understand non-fiction genres
- understand narrative perspective
- understand theme
- understand structure
- understand literal and metaphorical reading
- understand the effect of writers' choices
- understand attitude and viewpoint.

	English Language GCSE	English Literature GCSE
Where will this be useful?	In your exams, you will be expected to read and understand some previously unseen sources. You will be expected to explain the ideas in them. You will also be asked to think about the ways in which they have been written, including the words that have been used and the ways in which the sources have been structured and organised.	In your exams, you will be writing about the ways in which writers communicate their ideas and viewpoints to the reader. You will write about a range of different genres. You will be expected to consider the range of ways a writer has communicated their ideas, including the language they use, the literary techniques they employ, and the ways in which the text is structured and organised.

Understand literary forms

Learning objectives
You will learn how to
- identify the four main literary forms
- understand some of the main features and conventions of these forms.

Assessment objectives
- English Language AO1, AO2
- English Literature AO1, AO2

Why do we tell stories and how do we tell them?

Getting you thinking

Cave paintings are the earliest examples of humans telling stories.

1 Look at the cave painting on the right. What's the story here? What is this painting about?

Stories are one of the ways we make sense of the world around us.

2 Why do humans love to tell and hear stories?

  a Rank the following statements. Which is the most important? Place them onto a diamond nine when you have decided.

Stories give information about events.	Stories provide entertainment.
Stories allow people to share an important idea or concept or feeling.	Stories have to have an event; it's not a story if nothing happens.
Stories send messages or warnings about an aspect of human behaviour.	Stories allow us to enter another world or another person's experiences.
Stories pass ideas down through history.	Humans tell each other stories in a variety of different ways, or forms.
Stories teach us about other people and about ourselves.	

most important

least important

  b Look at the top three ranked statements. Can you think of an example from a story you know well to support each one?

3 Look at the following three descriptions. Which one is describing 'fiction', which one is describing 'poetry' and which one is describing 'drama'?

a Narrating an event or experience, using lots of descriptive detail, several characters, and taking the reader on a journey towards a conclusion.

b Condensing ideas, using the ideas behind the words, the sounds of the words, and the ways they are organised, to tell a story or describe a feeling or idea.

c Presenting a story, using dialogue and movement to present the events and characters to the reader / audience.

Explore the skills

Prose fiction, poems and plays are the three main **forms** of creative literary writing. Each one has its own set of conventions, which are rules or things we expect to see.

What is a short story?

A short story usually focuses on one main event or idea. There tend to be few characters and we don't find out much about them. Short stories often concentrate on one 'slice of life' such as an event, a decision or a particular incident.

What is a novel?

A novel is a long narrative organised into chapters. Novels are longer than short stories so they have the space to develop characters and they often contain many more events. Novels became very popular during the eighteenth century.

4 What are the main differences between a short story and a novel?

5 Think about a novel you have read recently. See if you can summarise the plot into fifty words or fewer. Aim to explain:

• who tells the story (the writer / a character)

• what the reader learns from the story (the ideas / characters / themes)

• what the time span of the story is (years / months / days).

> **Key term**
>
> **Prose:** spoken or written language, distinguished from poetry by its lack of formal metrical structure

> **Key term**
>
> **forms:** a set of agreed conventions, or rules, that give an identifiable shape to a piece of literary writing; these rules might relate to structure and organisation, layout, content or language

What is poetry?

Poetry communicates in a more condensed way than prose, using sounds, imagery and word association to express ideas or emotions. Before most people could read, poetry was the most familiar literary form because the use of patterns (of rhythm and rhyme) meant that the poems were easier to remember and could therefore be passed on by word of mouth. As printing became more popular, the look of the poem on the page became more important.

6 Read the following ten definitions of poetry. Choose the three that you think best describe poetry.

a Poetry is when an emotion has found its thought and the thought has found words.

b Poetry says more in fewer words than prose.

c Poetry is thoughts that breathe, and words that burn.

d The language beneath the language; that is poetry.

e Poetry is the best words in the best order.

f Poetry gives you permission to feel.

g Poetry is the rhythmical creation of beauty in words.

h Poetry is the art of uniting pleasure with truth.

i Poetry is painting that speaks.

j Poetry is an echo, asking a shadow to dance.

What is a play?

7 Think of three main differences between a play and a novel. What would you expect a play to look like on the page? What are some of the key conventions of a play?

8 Think of three ways in which a play can be brought to life by a director and a group of actors. How might they turn a play from something written down into something live for an audience?

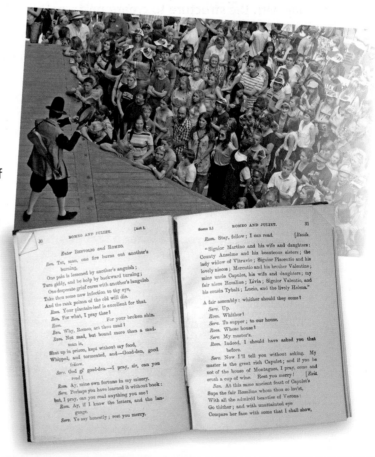

Develop the skills

Read the following extract from *Great Expectations*.
In this extract, Dickens is describing the appearance
of Magwitch, an escaped convict.

> A fearful man, all in coarse grey, with a great iron on his leg. A man
> with no hat, and with broken shoes, and with an old rag tied round
> his head. A man who had been soaked in water, and smothered in
> mud, and lamed by stones, and cut by flints, and stung by nettles, and
> torn by briars; who limped and shivered, and glared and growled;
> and whose teeth chattered in his head as he seized me by the chin.
>
> Charles Dickens, from *Great Expectations*

9 Which literary form does this passage
belong to? What conventions does it use?

10 Because this passage is from a novel, it is written in prose.
Without adding any new words, rewrite this passage into a
poem. Think about how you could:

- turn sentences into lines
- use repetition
- play with the structure to create patterns
- emphasise particular words.

11 What different conventions do you use when you turn a
passage from a novel into a poem?

Apply the skills

You can use the information you learn in this chapter as a
reference guide to help you as you go through your GCSE course.
This is the beginning of a 'glossary' you will work on over the rest
of this chapter.

12 Complete the following task.

List the features and main conventions of the four main literary
forms:

- short story
- novel
- poetry
- play.

Think about:

- structure / organisation / layout
- content / themes
- language.

Check your progress:

- I can understand why different literary forms have different conventions.
- I can explain the conventions of different literary forms.
- I can recognise the main differences between literary forms.

Understand non-fiction genres

Learning objectives

You will learn how to
- identify some of the main non-fiction genres
- understand some of the features and conventions of these genres.

Assessment objectives
- English Language AO1, AO2
- English Literature AO1, AO2

What is the difference between different types of non-fiction?

Getting you thinking

1. Look at the book covers on the right. Which of these texts are fiction and which are non-fiction?

2. How many non-fiction text types can you think of?

   A   Advert

   B   Blog

   C   Chatroom entry

3. Which of the following extracts is fiction and which one is non-fiction?

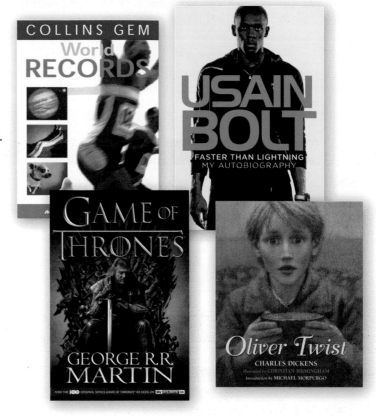

Text 1

Children's behaviour has worsened over the past five years, according to a survey of teachers which found that a fifth thought girls were more likely to cause trouble than boys.

The survey, published after teachers at a Lancashire school went on strike over discipline, found low-level disruption, including chatting and 'horsing around', was the biggest problem. Boys were more likely to be physically aggressive while girls tended to ostracise other pupils.

The behaviour of boys was more of a challenge than that of girls but the actions of each sex had deteriorated, according to 56.5% of staff surveyed by the Association of Teachers and Lecturers (ATL).

Among male pupils the most challenging behaviour for teachers was physical aggression, such as pushing, spitting, kicking and hitting. A secondary teacher quoted in the survey said boys were usually aggressive with other pupils, while girls tended to call one another names.

Text 2

'Fight! Fight!'

The news was relayed round to the yard, and within seconds the swirling pattern of activity changed to a linear form as boys abandoned their games and raced round to the back of the school. Billy and MacDowall had rolled the peak of the coalheap into a plateau, and gradually, as more and more spectators arrived, the first arrivals were forced up the heap, and the coke was trampled backwards and levelled out across the asphalt.

4 **a** How did you tell the difference between the fiction and the non-fiction extract?

b Complete the table of features below.

Feature	Text 1	Text 2
factual statements		
use of descriptive language		
past / present tense		
use of statistics / data		
complex punctuation		
a narrative sequence		
quotations		
objective / subjective		

Explore the skills

The main purpose of a fiction text is to entertain, whereas the main purpose of a non-fiction text is to relay information.

Here are four of the main **genres** of non-fiction that you are likely to encounter during your GCSE English Language course.

> **Key term**
>
> **genres:** particular types or categories of writing with their own purpose, features and conventions

5 Match each of these genres of non-fiction to the list of features below.

a Broadsheet article   c Biography

b Travel writing   d Autobiography

> * describes a journey or visit to a new place
> * contains information about the place
> * includes personal commentary, anecdote and opinion
> * uses descriptive language
> * usually written in first-person perspective (uses 'I')

> * an objective report on a current event or topic
> * reports facts about the event or topic
> * can often present the writer's viewpoint on the issue
> * focuses on serious national and international political / financial / ethical or social issues

> * a written account of someone's life, written by another person
> * tends to be organised chronologically and tells the story of the subject's life
> * written in third person (uses *he / she / they*)
> * usually objective, informative and descriptive

> * a written account of someone's life written by that person
> * sometimes written by a 'ghost-writer'
> * more subjective than a biography

Develop the skills

6 a What genre is each text A, B, C and D?

b Which features help you to identify this?

Text A

The next morning I caught a taxi north of Yulin, where the Great Wall ran through the desert. Tourists rarely came to see the wall here, because it was unrestored and the northern Shaanxi roads were so bad. There was no mention of the wall in my guidebook, but I had a Chinese map of the province that marked the ruins clearly.

The cabbie took me to a big Ming Dynasty fort that stood five miles outside of town, where Yulin's irrigated fields ended and the desert began. From the fort's highest tower the view stretched northward for miles. Occasionally, the barrenness was punctuated by a slice of green where water had found its way – a stand of trees, a lonely field – but mostly it was just sand and low brown hills and a vast thoughtless sky.

Text B

We reached our new home about the time the **State came into the Union** – It was a wild region, with many bears and other wild animals still in the woods – There I grew up – There were some schools, so called; but no qualification was ever required of a teacher beyond 'readin, writin, and cipherin' to the Rule of Three – If a straggler supposed to understand Latin happened to sojourn in the neighborhood, he was looked upon as a wizard – There was absolutely nothing to excite ambition for education. Of course when I came of age I did not know much – Still somehow, I could read, write, and cipher to the Rule of Three; but that was all – I have not been to school since –

Glossary

State came into the Union: refers to an American 'State' becoming part of the United States of America (USA)

Text C

It was the household custom among these girls to sew till nine o'clock at night. At that hour, Miss Branwell generally went to bed, and her nieces' duties for the day were accounted done. They put away their work, and began to pace the room backwards and forwards, up and down, – as often with the candles extinguished, for economy's sake, as not, – their figures glancing into the fire-light, and out into the shadow, perpetually. At this time, they talked over past cares and troubles; they planned for the future, and consulted each other as to their plans. In after years this was the time for discussing together the plots of their novels. And again, still later, this was the time for the last surviving sister to walk alone, from old accustomed habit, round and round the desolate room, thinking sadly upon the 'days that were no more.'

Text D

A teenage runaway has survived a five-hour flight across the Pacific Ocean from California to Hawaii stowed away in the freezing wheel well of a jet plane. Officials said it was a miracle the 16-year-old did not die after he lost consciousness as temperatures fell to -62C (-80F) in the compartment on flight.

He was found on the asphalt at Kahului airport in Maui, Hawaii, with no identification after jumping down and wandering around the grounds. His only possession, besides what he was wearing, was a comb.

Officials said he had run away from his family after an argument.

Apply the skills

7 Complete the table.

Text	Genre	Feature 1	Feature 2	Feature 3
Text A				
Text B				
Text C				
Text D				

8 Add a short description of the conventions of the four non-fiction genres to your glossary.

Check your progress:

- I can explain the differences in language between key non-fiction genres.
- I can explain some of the key conventions of the four non-fiction genres.
- I can identify the difference between the four non-fiction genres.

Understand narrative perspective

Learning objectives
You will learn how to
- identify the difference between 'the writer' and 'the speaker' in a text
- understand perspective and point of view.

Assessment objectives
- English Language AO1, AO2
- English Literature AO1, AO2

What is narrative point of view and why is it important that you understand it?

Getting you thinking

1　Read the following three texts. What is the difference in **perspective** between them?

Key term

perspective: point of view

Text 1

All of a sudden, I found myself on the ground. Shots whistled past my head. Scrambling forward, I slithered on my belly towards the doorway I could still just about make out through the mist and the looming terror that threatened to envelop me.

Text 2

Emma Woodhouse, handsome, clever, and rich, with a comfortable home and happy disposition, seemed to unite some of the best blessings of existence; and had lived nearly twenty-one years in the world with very little to distress or vex her.

Text 3

An old woman grabs
hold of your sleeve
and tags along.

She wants a fifty paise coin.
She says she will take you
to the horseshoe shrine.

You've seen it already.
She hobbles along anyway
and tightens her grip on your shirt

She won't let you go.
You know how old women are.
They stick to you like a burr.

2　a　Which text is written using first person?

　b　Which text is written using a mixture of third and second person?

　c　Which text is written using third person?

3　Make a list of the **pronouns** from each text.

4　Through whose eyes are we seeing each text? Is it a character or the writer?

Key term

pronouns: words that we use in place of a name: *I, you, they,* for example

Explore the skills

Writers make deliberate choices about viewpoint in order to create particular effects on the reader:

- close to the action
- part of the action
- distant from the action.

First-person perspective tells the story from the point of view of one of the characters:

'All of a sudden I stopped. Someone was behind me. I could hear nothing; I could see nothing. But I knew.'

Second-person perspective addresses the reader directly. It is an unusual perspective to take in literary fiction:

'You know how it is… one minute you're walking along minding your own business, admiring your reflection in the shop window, and the next thing you know, you've walked into a lamppost.'

Third-person perspective tells the story from the point of view of a narrator. Sometimes the narrator seems to look over the shoulder of one particular character and can see into their mind:

'Never had she felt so agitated, mortified, grieved, at any circumstance in her life. She was most forcibly struck. The truth of this representation there was no denying. She felt it at her heart. '

Sometimes the person who tells the story can't be trusted.

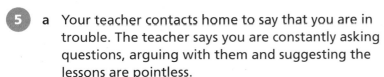

5 **a** Your teacher contacts home to say that you are in trouble. The teacher says you are constantly asking questions, arguing with them and suggesting the lessons are pointless.

Tell the story of what happened, making yourself look good and avoiding trouble.

Begin: It really wasn't like that…

b Is your story true and reliable?

Develop the skills

Although writers create speakers or narrators, they are not the same thing.

Writers make deliberate choices of narrative perspective to shape the reader's view of the events and characters being described.

In *The Curious Incident of the Dog in the Night-Time*, Christopher narrates the story. Christopher often looks at the world from a different perspective, which means his views of the world are sometimes surprising.

6 Look at the following extract. What is interesting or surprising about Christopher's viewpoint?

> The policeman looked at me for a while without speaking. Then he said, 'I am arresting you for assaulting a police officer'.
>
> This made me feel a lot calmer because it is what policemen say on television and in films.
>
> Mark Haddon, from The Curious Incident of the Dog in the Night-time

Christopher's reactions to events are often very unusual. Look at this next extract:

> Mother died two weeks later.... Father said that she died of a heart attack and it wasn't expected.
>
> I said, 'What kind of heart attack?' because I was surprised.
>
> Mother was only 38 years old and heart attacks usually happen to older people, and Mother was very active and rode a bicycle and ate food which was healthy and high in fibre and low in saturated fat like chicken and vegetables and muesli.
>
> Father said that he didn't know what kind of heart attack she had and now wasn't the moment to be asking questions like that.
>
> I said that it was probably an aneurysm.

7 What is surprising about Christopher's reactions to the news of his mother's 'death'? How is it different from what you might expect?

Later in the novel, Christopher finds some letters from his mother and realises that she has not died. Look at this next passage:

> I felt giddy. It was like the room was swinging from side to side, as if it was at the top of a really tall building and the building was swinging backwards and forwards in a strong wind (this is a simile, too). But I knew that the room couldn't be swinging backwards and forwards, so it must have been something which was happening inside my head.
>
> I rolled onto the bed and curled up in a ball.

In the play version of *The Curious Incident of the Dog in the Night-Time*, this sequence is presented differently.

8 Compare the two extracts. What is the difference between reading the story from Christopher's viewpoint and watching Christopher's reactions in the play?

> Christopher moves to the middle of the track. He crouches down. He rolls himself into a ball. He starts hitting his hands and his feet and his head against the floor as the letter continues. His thrashing has exhausted him. He has been sick. He lies still for a while, wrapped in a ball.
>
> Mark Haddon and Simon Stephens, from *The Curious Incident of the Dog in the Night-Time: The Play*

Apply the skills

Because Christopher is an unreliable narrator, the reader has to think carefully about what is really happening outside the world of Christopher's head.

Read this next extract from the novel and complete the task below.

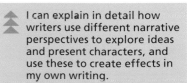

> And then I heard Father come up the stairs and walk into the room.
>
> He said, 'Christopher, what the hell are you doing?'
>
> And I could tell that he was in the room, but his voice sounded tiny and far away, like people's voices sometimes do when I am groaning and I don't want them to be near me.
>
> Mark Haddon, from *The Curious Incident of the Dog in the Night-time*

Imagine you are Christopher's father. You have hidden the truth about Christopher's mother from him, and have just discovered that Christopher has found the letters that you were hiding. He knows that his mother is alive, and knows that you have lied.

Describe the same scene from Christopher's father's point of view. Imagine:

- you walk upstairs, shouting for Christopher
- he is not in his bedroom
- you go to your bedroom and find Christopher there
- he is curled in a ball, surrounded by the letters from his mother that you had hidden.

9 Add the following terms to your glossary:
- first-person perspective
- second-person perspective
- third-person perspective.

Check your progress:

🔺🔺 I can explain in detail how writers use different narrative perspectives to explore ideas and present characters, and use these to create effects in my own writing.

🔺 I can explain how and why writers use different narrative perspectives, and try these out in my own writing.

🔺 I can explain the difference between first-, second-, and third-person narrative perspective, and try these in my own writing.

Understand theme

Learning objective
You will learn how to
* understand the difference between content and theme in literary texts.

Assessment objectives
* English Language AO1, AO2
* English Litereature AO1, AO2

How can a text be 'about' more than one thing at the same time?

Getting you thinking

What is the difference between content and theme? Look at this conversation.

> **A:** Have you heard the theme tune of the latest Bond movie? I love it! Are you going to see the film?
>
> **B:** I don't know. There's some violent content in it, so I bet my mum won't want me to watch it.
>
> **A:** They're all pretty much the same, though, aren't they? Same old content – another evil genius wants to take over the world, James single-handedly saves the day. Same themes – the 'one man against the world', what it's like being a spy who can't live like normal people…

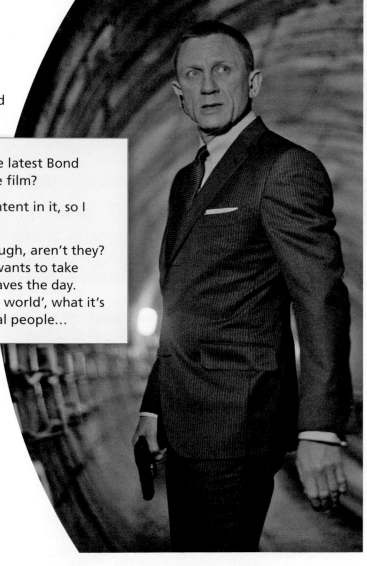

1. Look at these two definitions. Which one defines 'theme' and which one defines 'content'?

   * The overall, recurring 'big' ideas in a text.
   * The story, literal events and characters in a text.

Explore the skills

Read the following poem.

2. Which one of these statements is true?

   a The poem is about a man who plants a tree.

   b The poem is about what happens to your anger when you bottle it up.

A Poison Tree

I was angry with my friend:
I told my wrath, my wrath did end.
I was angry with my foe:
I told it not, my wrath did grow.

And I water'd it in fears,
Night and morning with my tears:
And I sunned it with smiles,
And with soft deceitful wiles.

And it grew both day and night,
Till it bore an apple bright.
And my foe beheld it shine,
And he knew that it was mine.

And into my garden stole,
When the night had **veil'd the pole**;
In the morning glad I see,
My foe outstretched beneath the tree.

William Blake

3 **a** What is the content of the poem?

b What is the theme of the poem?

Do you remember the story of Adam and Eve in the Garden of Eden? They were cast out from the 'garden' of heaven because they ate an apple that was growing on the Tree of Knowledge of Good and Evil.

4 In the poem, the tree has an 'apple bright' which his enemy steals, and presumably eats. What do you think this apple represents?

5 Why do you think Blake chose to focus the content of the poem on planting a tree? Think about how this links to the theme.

Develop the skills

The following painting is called *Landscape with the Fall of Icarus*. In Greek mythology, Icarus and his father escaped from a cliff-top prison by flying with wings invented from wax and feathers. In spite of his father's warning to not fly too close to the sun, Icarus ignored his advice and plunged to his death in the ocean.

Glossary

veil'd the pole: clouds covered up the stars

6 Look carefully at the painting. Can you find Icarus?

What is interesting about this painting is the way the painter has used structure, organisation, colour and light to suggest meaning.

Notice how:

- our eyes are drawn to the ploughman by his position, his size and his red sleeves
- our eyes are drawn to the ship, the sea, the sunset and the cliffs of Athens in the distance
- everyone in the painting is facing towards the left
- Icarus is in the darkest corner of the painting, away from all the 'action'.

7 Why do you think the painter has put Icarus in the darkest corner of the painting?

One student said:

Another student said:

> The painter seems to be suggesting that enormous, mythological events can take place but because of the pressure of daily life, people just don't see them – or even worse, ignore them. Everyone in the painting has something to do and somewhere to go, so even when Icarus crashes into the sea, nobody notices. It's like a comment on society.

> Icarus was known for being arrogant and not listening to the advice of his father. He doesn't listen and he is kind of punished for it – he crashes to his death. The painting seems to suggest the idea of pride coming before a fall; he thinks he's better than his father and the result is he just gets plunged into obscurity and nobody even notices. It's like a comment on the results of arrogance.

8 Discuss these two views. Which one do you think is 'correct'? Could they both be?

9 **a** What is the story or content of the painting?

  b What do you think are the themes it explores?

Apply the skills

10 Read the following poem. As you read, make a note of the 'plot' or 'content' of the poem. What is the sequence of events?

Cold

It felt so cold, the snowball which wept in my hands,
and when I rolled it along in the snow, it grew
till I could sit on it, looking back at the house,
where it was cold when I woke in my room, the windows
blind with ice, my breath undressing itself on the air.
Cold, too, embracing the torso of snow which I lifted up
in my arms to build a snowman, my toes, burning, cold
in my winter boots; my mother's voice calling me in
from the cold. And her hands were cold from peeling
then dipping potatoes into a bowl, stopping to cup
her daughter's face, a kiss for both cold cheeks, my cold nose.
But nothing so cold as the February night I opened the door
in the Chapel of Rest where my mother lay, neither young, nor old,
where my lips, returning the kiss to her brow, knew the meaning of cold.

Carol Ann Duffy

---

11 Is 'Cold' about a child playing in the snow or is it about something else? Using some of the words below, write a paragraph explaining what the *theme* of the poem is.

Childhood	Protection	Powerlessness
Parenthood	Vulnerability	Fear
Death	Love	Grief

12 Write a summary of the difference between **theme** and **content** in your glossary.

Check your progress:

- I can explain in detail how writers use content to explore themes and ideas.

- I can explain the difference between content and theme and how writers use content to present themes.

- I can understand that there is a difference between content and theme.

Understand structure

Learning objective
You will learn how to:
• understand what is meant by 'structure' in English Language and in English Literature.

Assessment objectives
• English Language AO1, AO2
• English Literature AO1, AO2

Why does structure matter?

Getting you thinking

A mini-saga is a story written in exactly 50 words. The form is designed to distil a story down to its essential elements.

> She buried John in the woods, wrapped in his coat. After what he tried to do, she didn't owe him more.
>
> What if the police had decided it wasn't self-defence?
>
> The next morning, after her third shower, her phone rang. A smiling picture and a name on the screen:
>
> 'John'.

 a After reading this mini-saga, what else do you want to know? How could you turn this 50-word story into a longer narrative? What else would you add?

b Can you identify the beginning, the middle and the end of this mini-saga?

Explore the skills

The term 'structure' refers to the ways in which a text is organised. It can refer to:

• the shape or organisation of the whole text and how the writer starts and ends it
• what is revealed to the reader in what order
• how paragraphs are organised and sequenced
• the order and positioning of particular words
• the use and effect of particular sentences: simple / complex / compound
• patterns created by techniques such as repetition.

You will be familiar with the basic narrative structure of beginning, middle and end.

Look at the diagram below.

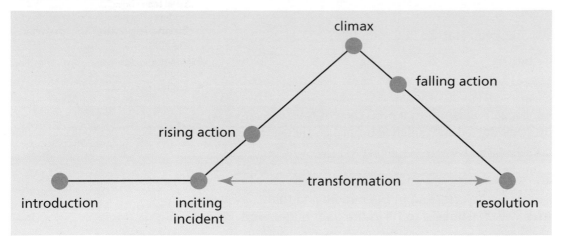

A Freytag pyramid describes the way most narratives are structured.

Take a story that you might know:

- rebellious and disobedient young male
- warned by caring mother to stay away from a dangerous local man who attacked and killed the boy's father
- young male ignores warning because of greed and arrogance
- is chased and almost killed by local man
- finally escapes unharmed
- learns his lesson and is changed by his experience.

Do you recognise this story? It is *The Tale of Peter Rabbit* by Beatrix Potter. Look at how the story has been structured:

Rebellious and disobedient young male	Introduction
Warned by caring mother to stay away from a dangerous local neighbour who attacked and killed the boy's father	Inciting incident
Young male ignores warning because of greed and arrogance	Rising action
Is attacked and almost killed by neighbour	Climax
Escapes unharmed but learns his lesson	Transformation and resolution

2 Choose another children's story that you know and apply this structure to it.

The Tale of Peter Rabbit is a story that is organised **chronologically**.

Would this story work if you started in the middle?

Imagine the story began:

> All of a sudden, he realised he was trapped. There was no way out. Frantically, Peter tugged and pulled at his jacket. He felt the footsteps before he heard them. Closer and closer they came…

In a more sophisticated story, starting in the middle and then working backwards with **flashbacks** to fill in the gaps might work very well.

3 Why might a writer decide to start their story in the middle – at the moment of crisis?

Develop the skills

In the opening chapter of *The Year of the Flood*, Margaret Atwood starts her story in the middle of the action. Her opening asks the reader to work out who the characters are and what their situation is.

4 **a** What can you work out about the story from its title?

   b What do we learn about Toby and her situation in the first two paragraphs of the passage?

   As you read, look at the annotations that point out structural features.

> In the early morning Toby climbs up to the rooftop to watch the sunrise. She uses a mop handle for balance: the elevator stopped working some time ago and the back stairs are slick with damp, and if she slips and topples there won't be anyone to pick her up.
>
> As the first heat hits, mist rises from among the swath of trees between her and the derelict city. The air smells faintly of burning, a smell of caramel and tar and rancid barbecues, and the ashy but greasy smell of a garbage-dump fire after it's been raining. The abandoned towers in the distance are like the coral of an ancient reef – bleached and colourless, devoid of life.

Key term

chronologically: in the order in which it happens

Key term

flashbacks: past events inserted into a narrative

first sentence of the novel explains the first thing Toby does in the morning

this seems strange; there is something wrong. What has happened?

by the end of the first paragraph we know that she is alone and in a strange place. We want to know why she is there and what has happened.

start of the second paragraph tells the reader that the city is 'derelict'

'abandoned' is linked to 'derelict'

'devoid of life' is linking with 'abandoned' and 'derelict' and emphasising the fact that Toby is alone

There still is life, however. Birds chirp; sparrows, they must be. Their small voices are clear and sharp, nails on glass: there's no longer any sound of traffic to drown them out. Do they notice the quietness, the absence of motors? If so, are they happier? Toby has no idea. Unlike some of the other Gardeners – the more wild-eyed or possibly overdosed ones – she has never been under the illusion that she can converse with birds.

The sun brightens in the east, reddening the blue-grey haze that marks the distant ocean. The vultures roosting on hydro poles fan out their wings to dry them, opening themselves like black umbrellas. One and then another lifts off on the thermals and spirals upwards. If they plummet suddenly, it means they've spotted carrion.

Vultures are our friends, the Gardeners used to teach. *They purify the earth. They are God's necessary dark Angels of bodily dissolution. Imagine how terrible it would be if there were no death!*

Do I still believe this? Toby wonders.

Everything is different up close.

Margaret Atwood, from *The Year of the Flood*

5 What is revealed about Toby in the rest of the passage? Re-read the passage and make notes on the structural features used. How do these features tell us more about Toby and her situation? Think about:

- what is revealed in each paragraph
- the length of each paragraph
- the types of sentences (questions, statements) and length of sentences used
- any repetitions or patterns – similar words or ideas.

Check your progress:

Apply the skills

6 Read the opening of *The Year of the Flood*, your own notes and the annotations carefully and answer this task.

How does the writer use structure in this passage to engage the interest of the reader at the start of the novel?

 I can examine the ways structural features have been used to engage the reader.

 I can explain the effect of some structural features on the reader.

 I can identify some structural features in a text.

Understand literal and metaphorical reading

Learning objectives
You will learn how to
• understand the difference between literal and implicit meaning
• understand what is meant by 'metaphor' and how to comment on it.

Assessment objectives
• English Language AO1, AO2
• English Literature AO1, AO2

Why do writers use metaphors when they could just say what they mean?

Getting you thinking

Human beings tell stories as a way of communicating ideas about the world and our place in it. We know that non-fiction texts can have these purposes:

inform	explain	entertain	warn
instruct	advise	persuade	argue
describe	guide	recount	

But what about literary texts?

Read the following section from *Little Red Riding Hood*.

Once upon a time there lived in a certain village a little country girl, the prettiest creature who was ever seen. Her mother was excessively fond of her; and her grandmother doted on her still more. This good woman had a little red riding hood made for her. It suited the girl so extremely well that everybody called her Little Red Riding Hood.

One day her mother, having made some cakes, said to her, 'Go, my dear, and see how your grandmother is doing, for I hear she has been very ill. Take her a cake, and this little pot of butter.'

Little Red Riding Hood set out immediately to go to her grandmother, who lived in another village.

As she was going through the wood, she met with a wolf, who had a very great mind to eat her up, but he dared not, because of some woodcutters working nearby in the forest. He asked her where she was going. The poor child, who did not know that it was dangerous to stay and talk to a wolf, said to him, 'I am going to see my grandmother and carry her a cake and a little pot of butter from my mother.' …

Charles Perrault, from *Little Red Riding Hood*

1. What are the possible purposes, of this text? Look back at the list of purposes.

2. Who is the audience for this text?

The fairy story, although entertaining, has a moral purpose – to warn young girls about the dangers of the world.

Little Red Riding Hood is an allegory, which is a metaphorical story designed to illustrate a point. It has an **implicit** meaning.

Key term

implicit: below the surface, implied rather than stated directly

Explore the skills

Literal meaning is different from implicit meaning. When we are looking at language, we are often more interested in the implicit meaning behind the literal. In *Little Red Riding Hood*, the literal meaning is that a young girl is nearly killed by a wolf. The implicit meaning, however, is a warning to young girls about the dangers in the world.

Implicit meaning can work at a word level as well as a whole-text level. Different words, depending on their context, can have different **connotations** – they can create different ideas in the mind of the reader.

Look at the following three sentences, which all communicate the same information, but suggest a slightly different meaning.

> The girl was very thin.
> The girl was very slender.
> The girl was very scrawny.

The first sentence presents a fact.

The second sentence implies that the girl's 'thinness' is a good thing.

The third sentence implies that the girl's 'thinness' is a bad thing.

Key term

Literal: surface, basic, obvious meaning

Key term

connotations: associations

3 Look at the following lists of words. Which words have positive connotations and which have negative connotations?

careful / frugal / miserly
interested / inquisitive / nosy
slight / delicate / flimsy

4 Think of some triplets of your own that provide neutral, positive and negative connotations of words with similar implicit meanings.

Develop the skills

Imagery takes the idea of implicit meaning even further.

When you want to describe something to someone else so they can really picture what you mean, a **figure of speech** is a very useful language tool. There are three main forms of figures of speech that are used to create imagery:

* simile   * metaphor   * personification.

5 Read the three definitions below and identify which one matches each figure of speech listed above.

* A figure of speech that states that one thing 'is' another thing
* A figure of speech that describes an inanimate object as if it has human qualities, characteristics or abilities
* A figure of speech which compares one thing to another using 'like' or 'as'

Key terms

Imagery: language used in a particular way to create a picture (image) in the mind of the reader

figure of speech: a word or phrase that means something additional, or different, to its literal meaning

6 Look at this famous example of imagery in action. There are several examples of imagery in the poem. Look at the highlighted sections as you read.

Daffodils

I wandered lonely as a cloud
That floats on high o'er vales and hills,
When all at once I saw a crowd,
A host, of golden daffodils;
Beside the lake, beneath the trees,
Fluttering and dancing in the breeze.

Continuous as the stars that shine
And twinkle on the Milky Way,
They stretched in never-ending line
Along the margin of a bay:
Ten thousand saw I at a glance,
Tossing their heads in sprightly dance.

The waves beside them danced, but they
Out-did the sparkling waves in glee:
A poet could not but be gay,
In such a jocund company:
I gazed—and gazed—but little thought
What wealth the show to me had brought:

For oft, when on my couch I lie
In vacant or in pensive mood,
They flash upon that inward eye
Which is the bliss of solitude;
And then my heart with pleasure fills,
And dances with the daffodils.

William Wordsworth

7 **a** Which of the highlighted sections are similes?

b Which are metaphors?

c Which are personification?

8 Wordsworth uses imagery in this poem to create an image of how the sight of the daffodils has affected him. Choose one of the figures of speech and write a short paragraph explaining its effect.

We use metaphors in order to open up meanings or to make our meaning clearer. When we compare one thing to another, it helps explain what we mean. Learning to 'read the picture' of the words is one of the most important skills of studying English Language and English Literature.

Apply the skills

9 Think about this famous adage, or saying:

'The pen is mightier than the sword.'

What does this actually mean?
• Is the pen literally stronger or 'mightier' than the sword?

Could you use it in a fight?
• How can a pen be 'mighty'?
• What are the properties of a pen and a sword?
• Why are they being compared here?

In other words, what is the effect of this metaphor?

Check your progress:

I can explain in detail how a writer uses imagery to create a range of meanings.

I can identify and explain the effect of an image on the reader.

I can identify examples of imagery and give examples.

Understand the effect of writers' choices

Learning objective
You will learn how to
- understand how to comment on 'effect'.

Assessment objectives
- English Language AO1, AO2
- English Literature AO1, AO2

What are effects and how do you write about them?

Getting you thinking

In everyday life, an effect is what happens after a related event.

You shake up a canned drink → it sprays everywhere.
                                                    ⁄
                                                  effect

In texts, the process is similar. A writer has something they want to write about. They convey this to their reader through text and the reader gets 'the effect'.

When you read a text, ask yourself questions such as:

- What does this make me see / imagine?
- What does this make me think?
- How does this make me feel?
- How might this change the way I behave / respond?

Look at the example of a charity advert on the right.

Such a lovely little boy, but always getting shouted at. Maybe his mum's just stressed.

He has some nasty bruises though. Perhaps he fell over.

It's really none of my business. Whose is it though?

Should I ignore it? Should I do something?

Don't talk yourself out of it. Talk to us.
When you're worried about a child, call the NSPCC Helpline. We're here to offer help, advice and support. You could help us to protect a child. You don't have to say who you are.
Call 0808 800 5000 or email help@nspcc.org.uk

NSPCC
HELPLINE
0808 800 5000
help@nspcc.org.uk

1. What is the **purpose** of this advert? What is it designed to encourage you to *do*?

2. What is this advert designed to make you *feel*? In other words, what *effect* is this advert designed to have on the reader? What is it designed to make the reader do?

Key term

purpose: the reason a text is written

3. What techniques are used to have this desired *effect* on the reader? Think about:

   - words and phrases such as 'lovely little boy', 'stressed', 'nasty bruises'
   - organisation on the page (structure)
   - who is asking the questions
   - who is giving the answers.

4. Choose one of the techniques and write a sentence explaining how it creates a particular effect on the reader.

5. How does the picture add to the overall effect?

Explore the skills

In a novel, poem or play or a non-fiction text writers make choices to create an effect on the reader.

However, a text can be read and interpreted in a variety of different ways. It is the effect on you, the reader, that is important.

Here is a checklist of questions for when you read a literary text.

- What is the overall **purpose** of this text?
- How is this making me feel – what emotions is this text / line / word provoking?
- How might other readers respond to this text / line / word?
- Do I think the text / line / word communicates its meaning successfully?

6 Look at this line from the poem 'Havisham' by Carol Ann Duffy:

'I've got dark green pebbles for eyes'

What is the effect of this metaphor? What does it suggest to you about the speaker?

7 Now look at the two sample responses below.

Student A

Carol Ann Duffy is very clever the way she has used language for effect in this line. She uses 'dark green pebbles' to create an effect and to make the line stand out for the reader. The word 'green' makes you notice the way she describes her eyes. The word 'pebbles' is a metaphor and the line makes the reader want to read on to see what else she is going to say.

Student B

Duffy's use of a metaphor to describe her eyes gives the effect of harshness and bitterness. 'Pebbles' are hard and cold and lifeless, which creates the effect that this is how she sees her eyes — as hard cold windows to her soul. The use of 'green' has connotations of envy, which creates the effect that her soul is consumed by jealousy.

What are the differences between the two responses? Which is better?

8   Read this extract and think about the purpose of the text and what effects the writer wants to achieve.

> Everything is as it always is! Ice-white gulls scream joyously and sticky toddlers wrestle over plastic spades, giggling carelessly. Their melodic voices and the sweet smell of candyfloss waft along the pebbled beach towards me. Striped deckchair canvases billow in the breeze and the beckoning flags advertise ice-cream companies, arching like stretching beauties as the warm wind catches them.
>
> The frothy waves race towards us and their white crest curves up and over, scooping sand and stray flip-flops in its grasp. I lurch as the water sucks at my feet, pulling me towards its glistening jade depths, and I shriek happily as the salt spray lingers on my stinging lips and tongue.

9   Pick out some details to suggest that the memory is a happy one.

A word can have different **connotations** depending on how it is used:

> 'giggling carelessly' suggests carefree and happy = positive **connotation**
>
> He attached the bolts to the wheel carelessly: nobody would ever notice and he was in a hurry. = negative **connotation**

Key term

connotations: ideas or feelings invoked by a word because of its associations

What is the effect of changing word choices? Look at how the tone of the second paragraph changes.

> The frothy waves race towards us and their white crest looms up and over, scooping sand and stray flip-flops in its grasp. I lurch as the water sucks at my feet, pulling me towards its gloomy jade depths, and I shriek as the salt spray lingers on my stinging lips and tongue.

10 Rewrite the first paragraph. Change the words, phrases and details that suggest 'happy' so that you create the effect that the memory is an unhappy one. Start with:

giggling   joyously   sweet   waft

Develop the skills

11 Read the first verse of 'The Chimney Sweeper' by William Blake and think about what effect Blake wants to create.

> When my mother died I was very young,
> And my father sold me while yet my tongue
> Could scarcely cry 'Weep! weep! weep! weep!'
> So your chimneys I sweep, and in soot I sleep.
>
> William Blake, 'The Chimney Sweeper'

What is the effect of starting with this phrase?

Why does Blake tell us this?

What effect does this have on the reader?

Why does Blake repeat this word?

Why does he tell us that the little boy sleeps in 'soot'?

Overall, what effect is Blake creating with these details? How does he want the reader to feel about the chimney sweep?

You might say:

Blake starts the poem with 'my mother died when I was very young'. This creates the effect of sympathy in the reader straight away, as it makes the child seem young and very vulnerable as if he is in need of protection. This elicits an emotional response from the reader right from the first line of the poem.

12 Choose another detail from this verse and write a short paragraph about the effect it creates.

Apply the skills

13 Complete the following task.

Add definitions of the following terms to your glossary:
- effect • affect • purpose

Check your progress:

▲▲ I can explain precisely why a particular technique has a specific effect on the reader.

▲ I can explain what the writer is doing to create a particular effect.

▲ I can identify that the writer is doing deliberate things to create a particular effect.

Understand attitude and viewpoint

Learning objectives
You will learn how to
• understand what is meant by attitude and viewpoint
• identify how writers use different methods to present their attitude and viewpoint.

Assessment objectives
• English Language AO1, AO2
• English Literature AO1, AO2

How do you know what a writer feels about what they are writing about?

Getting you thinking

1 Read the following statement:

> We're going on holiday to Portugal again.

Can you tell anything about how the writer feels from this statement?

2 Now look at what happens when the writing is slightly altered:

> We're going on holiday to Portugal. Again.

a What is the difference in feeling between this statement and the first statement?

b Does the writer suggest that they are happy about going to Portugal on holiday again?

c How has the writer changed the sentence to suggest this feeling?

3 Rewrite the statement again, this time to suggest that you are very excited about going to Portugal on holiday again. You could add one or two words and / or change the punctuation.

Explore the skills

Tone is one of the ways a writer expresses their attitude, feelings or viewpoint about a particular topic.

Tone can be:

• objective (expressing no particular attitude towards the topic)

or

• subjective (expressing a clear, strong attitude towards the topic).

4 Look at the list of text types. Which would you expect to be 'objective' and which 'subjective'?

- A news report
- A letter to a friend about a recent holiday
- A review of a rock album
- A science textbook
- A recipe
- An article about child labour in Bangladesh

Read the following text, an article about the amount of time spent watching television in the UK.

Text 1

Britons 'watch four hours of TV a day'

British viewers watched a record of more than four hours of TV a day in the first three months of 2010 – and a record 48 ads a day as a result. TV viewers notched up an average of four hours and 18 minutes a day in front of the box, an increase of close to 8% year on year, in the first quarter of this year according to a report published today by TV marketing body Thinkbox, based on official Broadcasters' Audience Research Board ratings figures.

This is up from an average of three hours and 56 minutes recorded in the first quarter last year. The figures show that the number of ads that people watch on commercial TV were up 4.9% year on year in the first quarter from 45 a day to 48. This is up 22% over the past five years.

In total British viewers watched 30 hours and 4 minutes of TV a week on average in the first quarter, an increase of two hours and 29 minutes year on year.

Mark Sweney, *The Guardian, 4 May 2010*
http://www.theguardian.com/media/2010/may/04/thinkbox-television-viewing

5 Can you tell what the writer's opinion is from this article? How?

Now read the following text.

Text 2

Forget the Fiction: Live Your Own Adventure

When reflecting on life, do you find the moments spent watching sitcoms or action movies are the moments when your life seems most purposeful and fulfilling? While there is something to be said about the intrinsic value of relaxation and release that visual entertainment can provide, I would wager that the average person has probably surpassed healthy limits of entertainment and amusement.

Yes: we can find enjoyment in these things. And yes: they can serve a purpose in our lives when used intentionally. But it seems safe to say that most of us could stand to do without a few hours of entertainment each week for the sake of actually living a life worthy of the adventures that our hearts desire.

http://www.tripleblaze.com/blog/2014/02/13/opinion-forget-the-fiction-live-your-own-adventure/

6 Can you tell what the writer's opinion is from reading this article? How?

7 Which of the following features can you find in Text 1 and which in Text 2?

Feature	Text 1 examples	Text 2 examples
facts		
opinions		
statistics		
personal pronouns (I / you / we)		
descriptive language		
questions		

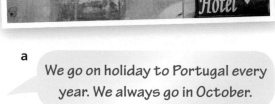

Develop the skills

Writers can express their attitude and viewpoint towards a particular topic in a range of different ways. This might include:

* their choice of language
* their use of sentence forms
* their use of punctuation
* their use of particular language techniques
* the tone of their writing.

Tone can tell the reader a lot about the writer's attitude and viewpoint.

8 Read the speech bubbles on the right. Each one uses a particular tone in order to express an attitude and viewpoint.

9 a Which word would you use to describe the tone of each of the four sentences?

* detached
* sentimental
* irritated
* sarcastic

b How has the writer used tone in sentences **a**, **b**, **c** and **d** to present their viewpoint? What particular detail about each sentence helped you to decide the tone being created?

a

We go on holiday to Portugal every year. We always go in October.

b

We stay in the same hotel every year; it might be a bit run down and old fashioned, but it's where we met and fell in love so it's got a special place in our hearts.

c

Because my parents can't make a decision to save their lives, we have to go to the same miserable, dull and depressing place every year – I can't wait until I'm old enough to make my own holiday plans.

d

According to their website, our hotel is apparently very popular with tourists… tourists who love cockroaches, enjoy the hunt for bed bugs and live for the thrill of a bit of food poisoning, apparently!

Apply the skills

In 1871, some people in Paris rose up to protest against the French government. This was called the 'Paris Commune'. It was suppressed in a week of bitter fighting, during which 20,000 people were killed.

Read the following extract from an article about the suppression of the uprising by Archibald Forbes, then complete the task below.

> As I ride up the broad slope of the avenue between Viroflay and Versailles, I pass a very sorrowful and dejected company. In file after file of six each march the prisoners of the Commune – there are over two thousand of them together – patiently and it seems to me with some consciousness of pride they march, linked closely arm in arm. Among them are many women, some of them the fierce barricade **Hecate**, others mere girls, soft and timid, who are here seemingly because a parent is here too. All are bareheaded and foul with dust, many **powder-stained** too, and the burning sun beats down on bald foreheads.
>
> Archibald Forbes, from *The Suppression of the Paris Commune,*
> *Daily News, 26 May 1871*

Glossary

Hecate: the Greek goddess of witchcraft

powder-stained: covered in traces of gunpowder

10 Now look at this practice task and think about how you would approach it.

What is the writer's attitude towards what he is describing? Aim to write 200–300 words.

Checklist for success

Comment on:

- two or three examples of emotional vocabulary
- two or three examples of descriptive language
- the details the writer chooses to focus on.

Check your progress:

⬆ I can use details and techniques from a text to provide a thoughtful consideration of how a writer is presenting a particular attitude and viewpoint.

⬆ I can explain the tone of a piece of writing and identify some of the ways the writer's attitude is communicated.

⬆ I can identify the tone of a text.

11 Add the following terms to your glossary:

- tone
- attitude
- viewpoint

Check your progress

- I can understand why different literary forms and non-fiction genres have different conventions.
- I can explain in detail how writers use content to explore themes and ideas.
- I can examine the ways structural features have been used to engage the reader.
- I can explain in detail how a writer uses imagery to create a range of meanings.
- I can explain precisely why a particular technique has a particular effect on the reader.

- I can explain the conventions of different literary forms and non-fiction genres.
- I can explain the difference between content and theme and how writers use content to present themes.
- I can explain the effect of some structural features on the reader.
- I can identify and explain the effect of an image on the reader.
- I can explain what the writer is doing to create particular effects on the reader.

- I can recognise the main differences between literary forms and non-fiction genres.
- I can understand that there is a difference between content and theme.
- I can identify some structural features in a text.
- I can identify imagery and give examples.
- I can identify that the writer is doing deliberate things to create a particular effect.

Chapter 3

Reading, understanding and responding to texts

What's it all about?

In this chapter, you will learn some basic and then more developed tools to help show your reading comprehension skills. You will learn how to read unseen texts both on the surface and for deeper meanings. When it comes to writing about them, you will learn a helpful method to ensure you always show your understanding.

In this chapter, you will learn how to

- retrieve basic information from unseen texts
- support ideas with evidence and quotation
- show your understanding of inference and implication
- make and present inferences about people
- make and present inferences about places

- make and present inferences about ideas and attitudes
- summarise and synthesise: selecting and collating information from more than one text
- apply your skills to English Language and English Literature tasks.

	English Language GCSE	**English Literature GCSE**
Which AOs are covered?	AO1 Identify and interpret explicit and implicit information and ideas Select and synthesise evidence from different texts	AO1 Read, understand and respond to texts. Students should be able to: • maintain a critical style and develop an informed personal response • use textual references, including quotations, to support and illustrate interpretations
How will this be tested?	All the texts you will be responding to will be previously unseen. Shorter tasks will expect you to be able to locate key information in texts. Longer tasks will expect you to show that you understand key ideas in a text and can use the text to support your thoughts. You need to be able to demonstrate your understanding by writing about what the text suggests to you.	Sometimes you will be responding to a whole play, novel or poetry that you have studied in class and sometimes you will be writing about two previously unseen poems. Tasks will expect you to show that you understand key ideas in a text and can use the text to support your thoughts as well as write about what is suggested to you in terms of possible meanings.

Retrieve basic information from unseen texts

Learning objective
You will learn how to
• establish basic skills in selecting and retrieving explicit information.

Assessment objective
• English Language AO1

What is 'explicit information'?

Getting you thinking

In your day-to-day life, you spend a lot of time **skimming** and **scanning** different texts for information. You will also make hundreds of decisions every day, accepting some of this information and rejecting other aspects of it.

> **Key terms**
>
> **skimming:** reading for gist; a speed read without reading every word
>
> **scanning:** reading to pick out particular information such as the cost of an item or the closing date for an application

1 Think about a typical day. Which of these information sources do you make use of?

- cooking instructions on food packaging
- traffic information
- weather forecast
- homework diary
- content labels on sandwiches, snacks or drinks
- a 'to do' list
- text messages from friends

2 Think about your day today.

   a Make a list of information sources you have come across so far.

   b What are the three most important sources on your list? Why? How did you decide?

Explore the skills

Being able to select the key factual information is the first stepping-stone to understanding any text you read.

3 Now you are going to read through the text to pick out key factual information.

   a **Scan** through the text to pick out references to the man and references to the car.

Read this extract from a newspaper article.

How did Swedish man survive in this frozen car at –30C for TWO MONTHS?

A Swedish man has been pulled barely alive from his snow-covered car having survived on nothing but snow for two months in sub-zero temperatures. Peter Skyllberg, 44, had eaten nothing but handfuls of snow since December 19 when his car became bogged down in snowdrifts in northern Sweden.

Pictures of the vehicle's interior show the dashboard and seats covered in ice after temperatures plunged to –30C.

Experts think he went into a kind of human hibernation which slowed down his metabolism and pulled him through the ordeal in what they have described as the 'case of a lifetime'.

Mr Skyllberg had driven off the main road on to forest tracks where his car became stuck fast.

On Friday a passing man on a snowmobile stopped to scrape snow from the windscreen of the vehicle and saw movement inside.

[…]

Mr Skyllberg survived by taking handfuls of snow from the roof of the car.

[…]

'Absolutely incredible that he is alive, in part considering that he hasn't had any food, but also bearing in mind that it was really cold for a while there after Christmas,' said a member of the emergency services team deployed to rescue him.

[…]

'He was at the end of his tether,' said a police spokesman. 'It was doubtful he could have survived one or two more days.'

He was wrapped up in a sleeping bag in the car but he had no other warmth; the fuel had run out long ago as he kept the heater running to try to survive as the thermometer plunged on some nights to –30C.

[…]

Policeman Nyberg added: 'He was in a very poor state when we found him.

He could not speak, just a few broken sentences and the words snow … eat. And he managed to say he hadn't eaten anything since December.'

Allan Hall, *Daily Mail*, 22 February 2012

b Now sort the information you have identified and complete the table below. Present your information clearly in either:

– short crisp sentences   – bullet-pointed lists.

Things we know about the man who was trapped	Things we know about his car
He is Swedish.	

Think about how you could identify and mark up the information in an exam when you don't have much time. You could:

* use different colours to highlight information about the man and the car

* underline the information in different styles

* number each example you find.

Develop the skills

By using this same ability to identify and make selections, you will be able to develop your understanding of texts.

You are now going to select and consider information to find out more from a text. The extract is from 'Snow Story', a short story by George Packer.

The trouble began Sunday night. Just as the storm was blowing at its wildest, I trudged out to buy milk and found two women trying to maneuver a helpless old-model compact off our Brooklyn street, two-thirds of the way down the block. Stuck at an angle near a buried fire hydrant, they were pushing and spinning and getting nowhere, with the smell of burning rubber noxiously sharp in the cold air. 'Do you need some help?' No one ever answers right away, 'Yes, thank you.' They're too caught in the immediate distraction of their trap, too angry or embarrassed or wary. The women, black and in their thirties, considered the offer of a stranger emerging out of the blizzard. I explained that we could move the car fifty or sixty feet up the street, following the tracks of another car that was stuck farther up. 'And how is that going to be helpful?' one of them demanded. My idea was to guide the car into a row of free parking spaces ahead of mine, but she was right: the tracks were disappearing in the snow even as we stood talking, and though we got the car out of its rut, we couldn't advance more than five feet.

George Packer, from 'Snow Story'

4   Find the answers to questions a–f. You will need to locate the relevant information, then consider what it tells you.

    a   TRUE/FALSE The car is stuck in the snow.

The information relevant to question a has been highlighted for you. Now consider what the highlighted sections tell you about whether or not the car is stuck in snow.

    Continue to answer these questions using the same approach.

    b   TRUE/FALSE The narrator is an interfering neighbour.

    c   TRUE/FALSE The women are glad of a helping hand.

    d   TRUE/FALSE The snow is a light covering.

    e   TRUE/FALSE The woman is losing patience.

    f   TRUE/FALSE The situation is getting worse rapidly.

Apply the skills

5   Now read the following task.

Look back at the first article 'How did Swedish man survive in this frozen car at −30C for TWO MONTHS?'.

List four things we learn about the rescue of Peter Skyllberg.

Checklist for success

- Present your work in a numbered list.
- Use clear sentences.
- Use only things that are given to you in the article and that you can identify as being true.

Check your progress:

▲▲ I can read texts, selecting information and presenting it clearly.

▲▲ I can read texts and select the information I need.

▲ I can read texts carefully.

Support ideas with evidence and quotation

Learning objective
You will learn how to
- identify appropriate supporting quotations and how to present them.

Assessment objective
- English Language AO1

Isn't quotation just copying out bits of the text?

Getting you thinking

To develop your comprehension skills beyond the simple identification of key facts, you need to be able to back up your selected points with evidence. This is also a useful life skill.

1 Imagine a lawyer standing up in a courtroom defending an innocent person. What would happen if they simply said, 'He didn't do it!' and then sat down again. Would they win their case? Why not?

When you come to present your facts and ideas, you need to support them with evidence, too. In your case, the evidence will be quotation from the text.

Explore the skills

2 Look at these responses that a student has made to this task:

What do you learn about the rescue of Peter Skyllberg from the article in 3.1?

> I learned that Peter Skyllberg was rescued after 'a passing man on a snowmobile stopped to scrape snow from the windscreen of the vehicle and saw movement inside'. I also learned that when he was found he was in a very poor state 'He was in a very poor state when we found him.'

a   In the first sentence, can you identify the point that the student is making? Have they used the quotation to support their idea?

b   In the second sentence, can you clearly identify what the student has actually understood? What is the difference between their statement and their supporting quotation?

c   What do you notice about the way the student has used punctuation to present their quotations? Is it correct?

3   Now look at a second student's work in response to the same question and identify the key differences in their approach.

From the text we learn that Peter Skyllberg was rescued by chance after a man out on a snowmobile identified his car in the forest. The man apparently 'stopped to scrape snow from the windscreen…'. and saw movement inside'. The rescue seems to have taken place at a critical time for the trapped man, who was in danger of losing his life as 'It was doubtful he could have survived one or two more days.'.

Begins with a strong, clear statement in the student's own words.

This quotation is genuinely 'embedded' in the sentence as it begins with 'The man apparently' and continues to make sense from there.

The student does not waste time copying out a lengthy quotation; they use ellipsis to ensure we have the key point whilst still making sure it makes sense to us.

Punctuation to close the sentence is placed after the quotation mark.

Again, we have a strong clear sentence in the student's own words.

4   Using the annotations to help you, write a set of clear instructions for this stronger method of supporting ideas and using quotations. You could begin as follows:

Remember to

Make a strong clear statement in my own words that is directly linked to the question.

Develop the skills

5   In the following extract, four quotations have been highlighted by a student about to answer this question:

What do you learn about the impact of the snowstorm in this extract?

The trouble began Sunday night. Just as the storm was blowing at its wildest, I trudged out to buy milk and found two women trying to maneuver a helpless old-model compact off our Brooklyn street, two-thirds of the way down the block. Stuck at an angle near a buried fire hydrant, they were pushing and spinning and getting nowhere, with the smell of burning rubber noxiously sharp in the cold air. 'Do you need some help?' No one ever answers right away, 'Yes, thank you.' They're too caught in the immediate distraction of their trap, too angry or embarrassed or wary. The women, black and in their thirties, considered the offer of a stranger emerging out of the blizzard. I explained that we could move the car fifty or sixty feet up the street, following the tracks of another car that was stuck farther up. 'And how is that going to be helpful?' one of them demanded. My idea was to guide the car into a row of free parking spaces ahead of mine, but she was right: the tracks were disappearing in the snow even as we stood talking, and though we got the car out of its rut, we couldn't advance more than five feet.

George Parker, from 'Snow Story'

The student highlights quotations that link directly to the focus of the task: the snowstorm.

The student picks out quotations that show different problems the snowstorm is causing.

The student chooses quotations that show a direct impact on the people in the story by using something that tells us about their mood.

The student uses quotations which range right the way through the extract, showing they are using all the material they are given.

6 Construct four clear statement sentences that respond to this question and that may be supported effectively by the quotations chosen for you.

> What do you learn about the impact of the snowstorm in this extract?

At times, we need to use longer extracts from a text. Rather than embedding the quotation within your own sentence you need to set out the quoted material in a clear way.

7 Read the extract from this student essay and make notes on how the quotation is presented differently to the ones in Activity 3.

Shakespeare is comparing man to nature and is suggesting that, whilst harsh, nature is not so deliberately cruel as man can be. This is exemplified by Amiens in his song: **1**

    2 Amiens: **3** Blow, blow, thou winter wind,
       4 Thou art not so unkind
        As man's ingratitude;

Key term

colon: a colon is a punctuation mark which goes before a list, description or explanation. It must always be preceded by a complete sentence

1 The quotation is not embedded into the text but begins on a new line and is preceded by a **colon**.

2

3

4

Apply the skills

8 This passage is from a short story where a girl becomes lost in a 'palace' of ice, constructed as a winter attraction. Read the following extract, then complete the task below.

> 'Harry!'
>
> No answer. She started to run straight forward, and then turned like lightning and sped back the way she had come, enveloped in a sudden icy terror.
>
> 'Harry!'
>
> Still no answer. The sound she made bounced mockingly down to the end of the passage.
>
> Then on an instant the lights went out, and she was in complete darkness. She gave a small, frightened cry, and sank down into a cold little heap on the ice. She felt her left knee do something as she fell, but she scarcely noticed it as some deep terror far greater than any fear of being lost settled upon her. She was alone with this presence that came out of the North, the dreary loneliness that rose from ice-bound whalers in the Arctic seas, from smokeless, trackless wastes where were strewn the whitened bones of adventure. It was an icy breath of death; it was rolling down low across the land to clutch at her.
>
> With a furious, despairing energy she rose again and started blindly down the darkness. She must get out. She might be lost in here for days, freeze to death and lie embedded in the ice like corpses she had read of, kept perfectly preserved until the melting of a glacier.
>
> F. Scott Fitzgerald, from 'Ice Palace'

What do you understand about the girl's feelings from the extract?

Checklist for success

- Write up two to three clear ideas in statement sentences.
- Support your ideas with appropriately selected quotations, using annotations 1–4 from Activity 5 to guide you.
- Use the correct method of presentation and punctuation.

Check your progress:

▲▲ I can choose my quotations carefully to support my points and show that I understand texts fully.

▲ I can use quotations to support the point I am making.

▲ I can remember to put quotations in my reading responses.

Show your understanding of inference and implication

Learning objective
You will learn how to
• demonstrate understanding of implicit ideas and meanings through the use of inferential statements.

Assessment objectives
• English Language AO1, AO4
• English Literature AO1

What are inferences and why do you need them?

Getting you thinking

To really show that you understand a text, you need to be able to demonstrate that you can move beyond the **explicit meanings**.

This means thinking about the content of the text and showing that you can 'read between the lines'.

This is called making **inferences**.

1 Imagine this conversation taking place between friends:

A: What do you think to my new top? Cool or what?

B: It's certainly got short sleeves, mate.

> **Key terms**
>
> **explicit meanings:** the basic information on the surface – the true or literal; what is stated directly
>
> **inferences:** the explanation of what you have been able to read between the lines
>
> **implicit meanings:** the meaning that you have to work out by reading between the lines; something suggested rather than stated

Is B agreeing or disagreeing with A? Are they being serious or sarcastic?

If this is not said explicitly, how do you know? How could you work out B's meaning?

Once you can make inferences confidently, you are showing the ability to extract **implicit meanings** as well as explicit. This is a higher-level skill.

Explore the skills

When you have identified a key point and used evidence to support it, you can go one step further and question yourself about it in order to work out what is suggested or implied. This is how you make your inference.

Read the following extract from the short story 'Your Shoes' by Michelle Roberts.

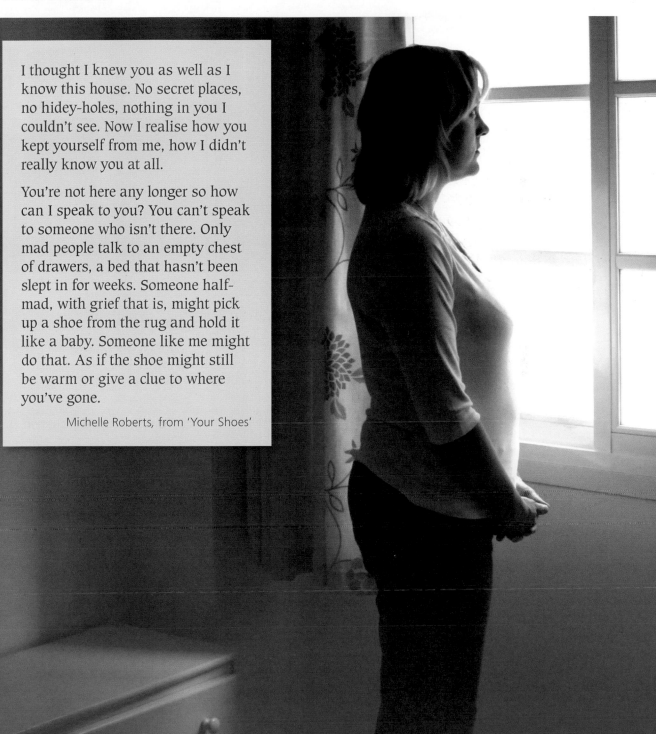

I thought I knew you as well as I know this house. No secret places, no hidey-holes, nothing in you I couldn't see. Now I realise how you kept yourself from me, how I didn't really know you at all.

You're not here any longer so how can I speak to you? You can't speak to someone who isn't there. Only mad people talk to an empty chest of drawers, a bed that hasn't been slept in for weeks. Someone half-mad, with grief that is, might pick up a shoe from the rug and hold it like a baby. Someone like me might do that. As if the shoe might still be warm or give a clue to where you've gone.

Michelle Roberts, from 'Your Shoes'

2 Look at these quotations from the text and make notes as to what is suggested to you by each one. What is implied here that isn't being said explicitly? The first one has been done for you.

a

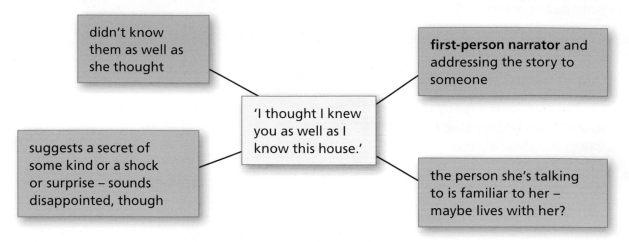

didn't know them as well as she thought

first-person narrator and addressing the story to someone

'I thought I knew you as well as I know this house.'

suggests a secret of some kind or a shock or surprise – sounds disappointed, though

the person she's talking to is familiar to her – maybe lives with her?

b 'You're not here any longer so how can I speak to you?'

c 'a bed that hasn't been slept in for weeks.'

d 'Someone half-mad, with grief that is, might pick up a shoe from the rug and hold it like a baby.'

3 The narrator of the story is a woman. From the inferences you have made, what do you understand about her so far? Who might the person be that she is addressing?

Develop the skills

4 Now go on to read a second extract from the same story and select four quotations of your own that you feel tell us more about the woman in the story.

What did you have for lunch today? I hope you ate something. Did you beg for the money to buy a burger or a sandwich? I'd like to think you had a proper lunch. Something hot. Soup, perhaps, in a Styrofoam cup. You used to love tinned tomato soup. Cream of. I always urged you to eat proper meals, meat and two veg or something salady, when you got home from school. You liked snacks better as you got older, it was the fashion amongst your friends I think, all day long you ate crisps and buns and I don't know what, at teatime when you came in you'd say you weren't hungry then late at night I'd catch you raiding the kitchen cupboards. Fistfuls of currants and sultanas you'd jam into your mouth, one custard cream after another, you'd wolf all my supply of chocolate bars.

5 Write out your four quotations and make notes on what is suggested or implied by them.

    a How does this now add to your understanding of the woman and the situation she may be in?

    b Have you worked out who is missing, just from your inferences?

Now you are going to put together all of the different elements that show your understanding:

- your ability to **retrieve** key information
- your ability to **support** your idea with evidence
- your ability to demonstrate your understanding with an **inference**.

6 Look at the example below and work out what the student has done to cover all three of these areas. Note down for yourself the method they have used.

> The woman in the story is addressing someone with whom she is familiar 'I thought I knew you as well as I know this house'. This suggests that the person maybe lived with her and has done something that has come as a shock or surprise to the woman, something out of character for the person she is addressing.

Apply the skills

7 You are now going to use both extracts from the story, your ideas and quotations and the inferences you have made so far to complete the following task.

What do you understand about the woman in the story and how she is feeling?

Write 250–300 words using the following method to show that you really understand the text.

Checklist for success

- Make clear statements in your own words addressing the question directly.
- Support those statements with your selected quotations.
- Demonstrate your understanding using the inferences you have made.

Check your progress:

▲▲ I can read between the lines of a text and present my inferences with supported statements to demonstrate my clear understanding.

▲ I can read between the lines of a text and present my thoughts as inferences.

▲ I can sometimes read between the lines and show what a text suggests to me.

Make and present inferences about people

Learning objective
You will learn how to
- develop inferential skills with reference to people and characters.

Assessment objectives
- English Language AO1, AO4
- English Literature AO1

How do we know what writers want us to see about characters?

Getting you thinking

Charles Dickens was famous for creating hundreds of interesting characters, all telling us something about the time and the society in which he lived, as well as showing us different sides to human nature.

Sometimes even the names of the characters Dickens created were significant and give us clues from which we could draw inferences about who they were and what they were like.

1 Look at this list of names of characters from Dickens. Choose one to focus on.

Uncle Pumblechook	Vincent Crummles	Paul Sweedlepipe
Lucretia Tox	Luke Honeythunder	Mr M'Choakumchild
Charity Pecksniff	Sissy Jupe	Augustus Snodgrass

2 What kind of a character does your chosen name conjure up in your imagination?

- How old are they?
- What might they be wearing?
- What accent do they have?
- Are they rich or poor, kind or mean?

3 Create a spider diagram around your chosen character name with everything you can imagine about their character, personality and appearance.

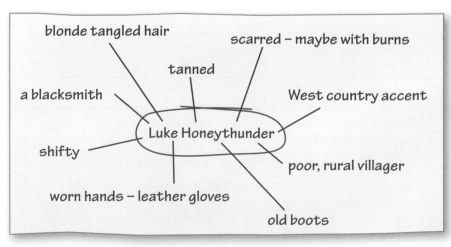

Explore the skills

In order to make inferences about people and characters, we need to be able to make some judgements about them. We need to develop the questions we asked ourselves in Activity 2 to consider the way they are presented to us or described. For example, what do we learn about their:

- appearance
- mannerisms
- any dialogue they may use
- the situation they are in
- the place they are in and how they seem to be responding to it
- the mood or atmosphere surrounding them.

4 Read this extract from Charles Dickens's novel *Great Expectations,* where the narrator, Pip, meets a strange character for the first time.

She was dressed in rich materials – satins, and lace, and silks – all of white. Her shoes were white. And she had a long white veil dependent from her hair, and she had bridal flowers in her hair, but her hair was white. Some bright jewels sparkled on her neck and on her hands, and some other jewels lay sparkling on the table. Dresses, less splendid than the dress she wore, and half-packed trunks, were scattered about. She had not quite finished dressing, for she had but one shoe on – the other was on the table near her hand – her veil was but half arranged, her watch and chain were not put on, and some lace for her bosom lay with those trinkets, and with her handkerchief, and gloves, and some flowers, and a Prayer-book, all confusedly heaped about the looking-glass.

Charles Dickens, from *Great Expectations*

5 Using the categories listed above, make some detailed notes about what we can infer about this character, whose name is Miss Havisham. To get you started, an example has been given below.

Appearance: She's dressed in white with a veil and seems to be about to get married? She seems wealthy – mention of jewels, etc....

Develop the skills

6 Now go on to read some further details about Miss Havisham. What further inferences can you draw from the highlighted quotations?

It was not in the first few moments that I saw all these things, though I saw more of them in the first moments than might be supposed. But, I saw that everything within my view which ought to be white, had been white long ago, and had lost its lustre, and was faded and yellow. I saw that the bride within the bridal dress had withered like the dress, and like the flowers, and had no brightness left but the brightness of her sunken eyes. I saw that the dress had been put upon the rounded figure of a young woman, and that the figure upon which it now hung loose, had shrunk to skin and bone.

7 Collect together all of your notes about Miss Havisham, the quotations that support your ideas and the inferences you have made in Activities 5 and 6. Use them to answer the following task:

> From the way the narrator presents Miss Havisham in this extract, what do you understand about her?
>
> Write up **four** separate ideas using the method:
>
> Statement in response to the task + supporting quotation + inference

Apply the skills

8 The following extract is another passage from a Charles Dickens novel, this time describing the character of the Artful Dodger from *Oliver Twist*.

Read the extract carefully and, using the same method as you have practised, write 200–250 words exploring what you understand about the character of the Artful Dodger from the extract.

Checklist for success

Remember the method:

- statement in response to the task
- + supporting quotation
- + inference.

He was a snub-nosed, flat-browed, common-faced boy enough; and as dirty a juvenile as one would wish to see; but he had about him all the airs and manners of a man. He was short of his age, with rather bow-legs: and little, sharp, ugly eyes. His hat was stuck on the top of his head so lightly, that it threatened to fall off every moment; and would have done so very often, if the wearer had not had a knack of every now and then giving his head a sudden twitch: which brought it back to its old place again. He wore a man's coat, which reached nearly to his heels. He had turned the cuffs back, half-way up his arm, to get his hands out of the sleeves: apparently with the ultimate view of thrusting them into the pockets of his corduroy trousers; for there he kept them. He was, altogether, as roistering and swaggering a young gentleman as ever stood four feet six, or something less, in his bluchers.

'Hullo, my covey, what's the row?' said this strange young gentleman to Oliver.

'I am very hungry and tired,' replied Oliver, the tears standing in his eyes as he spoke. 'I have walked a long way. I have been walking these seven days.'

'Walking for sivin days!' said the young gentleman. 'Oh I see. Beak's order, eh? But,' he added, noticing Oliver's look of surprise, 'I suppose you don't know what a beak is, my flash com-pan-i-on?'

'Going to London?' said the strange boy.

'Yes.'

'Got any lodgings?'

'No.'

'Money?'

'No.'

The strange boy whistled; and put his arms into his pockets as far as the big coat sleeves would let them go.

Charles Dickens, from *Oliver Twist*

Check your progress:

▲▲▲ I can read into character descriptions to make inferences about the character from specific details within the text.

▲▲ I can look at character descriptions and pick out specific quotations to help me work out what they are like.

▲ I can look at character descriptions and imagine what characters look like.

Make and present inferences about places

Learning objective
You will learn how to
• develop inferential skills with reference to place.

Assessment objectives
• English Language AO1, AO4
• English Literature AO1

How do we know what writers want us to see about places?

Getting you thinking

Many different types of text allow us to make inferences about places. Some actively encourage us to make positive inferences for persuasive purposes.

 What is suggested by these phrases in a travel brochure?

> • lush tropical beaches
> • a birdwatcher's paradise
> • the party capital of the Mediterranean

Writers create particular impressions of places for you, the reader. You have to be alert to the precise details the writer has chosen to include. These details will help you to make inferences about the places they describe.

Explore the skills

You need to ask questions and make judgements. A good way to start is to select and 'zoom in' on precise details about how the place is described.

• Where is the place located?

• What kind of weather is associated with it?

• What is the reader allowed to 'see' about the place, for example, if the place is outside what aspects of the landscape are drawn to your attention; if inside what details of the rooms are given to you?

• Are there any people in the place and what are they like?

2 Read the following extract from Emily Brontë's novel *Wuthering Heights,* where two children Cathy and Heathcliff peep through the windows of a house called Thrushcross Grange.

Explore the questions in the annotations and make notes on your responses.

We crept through a broken hedge, groped our way up the path, and planted ourselves on a flower-plot under the drawing-room window. The light came from thence; they had not put up the shutters, and the curtains were only half closed. Both of us were able to look in by standing on the basement, and clinging to the ledge, and we saw – ah! it was beautiful – a splendid place carpeted with crimson, and crimson-covered chairs and tables, and a pure white ceiling bordered by gold, a shower of glass-drops hanging in silver chains from the centre, and shimmering with little soft tapers. Old Mr and Mrs Linton were not there. Edgar and his sister had it entirely to themselves; shouldn't they have been happy? We should have thought ourselves in heaven! And now, guess what your good children were doing? Isabella – I believe she is eleven, a year younger than Cathy – lay screaming at the farther end of the room, shrieking as if witches were running red-hot needles into her. Edgar stood on the hearth weeping silently, and in the middle of the table sat a little dog, shaking its paw and yelping, which, from their mutual accusations, we understood they had nearly pulled in two between them.

Emily Brontë, from *Wuthering Heights*

Does the reference to the drawing room give you any thoughts about wealth or class?

What image does this create for the reader? What are we meant to think about this house? Can you compare it to anything? How does the narrator feel about it?

What does this tell you about how Cathy and Heathcliff see the house?

Is this serious or ironic?

Is this place as beautiful and regal as it first seemed? Why not?

What does the writer seem to be telling you about the people who live in such grand houses as this?

Develop the skills

By contrast, the house that Cathy and Heathcliff grow up in is called Wuthering Heights. Read this second extract describing their home. Some key ideas and quotations have been highlighted to help you with the task which follows.

Wuthering Heights is the name of Mr Heathcliff's dwelling. 'Wuthering' being a significant provincial adjective, descriptive of the atmospheric tumult to which its station is exposed in stormy weather. Pure, bracing ventilation they must have up there at all times, indeed: one may guess the power of the north wind [...] Happily, the architect had foresight to build it strong: the narrow windows are deeply set in the wall, and the corners defended with large jutting stones [...] One step brought us into the family sitting-room, without any introductory lobby or passage: they call it here 'the house' pre-eminently. [...] One end, indeed, reflected splendidly both light and heat, from ranks of immense pewter dishes, interspersed with silver jugs and tankards, towering row after row, in a vast oak dresser, to the very roof. The latter had never been underdrawn, its entire anatomy lay bare to an inquiring eye, except where a frame of wood laden with oatcakes, and clusters of legs of beef, mutton, and ham, concealed it. Above the chimney were sundry villainous old guns, and a couple of horse-pistols, and, by way of ornament, three gaudily painted canisters disposed along its ledge. The floor was of smooth, white stone: the chairs, high-backed, primitive structures, painted green: one or two heavy black ones lurking in the shade. In an arch, under the dresser, reposed a huge, liver-coloured bitch pointer surrounded by a swarm of squealing puppies and other dogs haunted other recesses.

3 Answer the following questions about Wuthering Heights, supporting your ideas with quotations (you could select extracts from the highlighted sections to help you) and making inferences in each response.

a What impression does the name of this house make on you?

b What kind of location is it in, city or country? How does the weather make an impact on it?

c What about its building materials? How is it constructed and what does this suggest?

d Consider the details inside: pewter dishes / oak dresser – is this house ancient or modern? What is implied about how long it has been there? Does it belong there?

e Think about the details of the meats and the guns. Is this a place of work or a place of rest and luxury?

Apply the skills

4 Emily Brontë creates a different impression for her readers of the two important houses in her novel *Wuthering Heights*. Complete the following task:

What different impressions does Emily Brontë give the reader of the two houses in her novel?

- Thrushcross Grange
- Wuthering Heights

Write two to four paragraphs presenting your ideas, supporting them with quotations and incorporating the inferences you have made from your study.

Check your progress:

I can read into descriptions to make inferences about the place from specific details within the text.

I can look at descriptions of places and pick out specific quotations to help me work out what they are like.

I can look at descriptions of places and imagine what they are like.

Make and present inferences about ideas and attitudes

Learning objective
You will learn how to
- develop inferential skills when reading texts presenting viewpoints.

Assessment objectives
- English Language AO1
- English Literature AO1

You can make inferences about creative writing but how can you do it with newspaper articles?

Getting you thinking

Many kinds of journalism do more than just tell us the news – they present ideas about the world and our society, communicating the viewpoint or attitude of the writer. Making inferences from this type of writing can help us to see things from different viewpoints.

Read the opening of this piece of journalism.

> No bell marks the start of our day. Instead, a slow drip-feed of men in grey tracksuits amble their way into classes. Sometimes 10 sit in front of me, aged 21 up to 60 or 70. They are the disaffected and the despicable. They are the proud, the defensive and the downright disagreeable; funnelled into education during their first days inside, where they complete assessments in literacy and numeracy. Their scores determine their placement into a classroom, and their subsequent opportunities for work.
>
> The Secret Teacher, from *The Guardian*, 3 May 2014

1. Using your skills in making inferences about place, can you identify the place that is being described? Make a note of the clues that helped you decide.

2. Using your skills in making inferences about people, what do you understand about the people being described here?

3. Would you say the writer has a positive or negative impression of the people he describes? Select two pieces of evidence that suggest this.

Explore the skills

To build up a picture of the viewpoint in a text, it helps to work through it paragraph by paragraph, using your inference skills as you go, noting down your evidence, key quotations and thoughts as you read between the lines.

Now read the second paragraph of the article.

The most challenging part of working with offenders is the disparity between students in the classroom – the range of ages, their level of literacy and their attitude to learning. Often their only common ground is their criminality. Some learners arrive spoiling for a fight, desperate to avoid the torture of school all over again, determined to prove themselves. Behaviour is an issue, with many refusing to work. Challenging inappropriate language is a constant battle when, for some, the f-word is used in every sentence.

4 Does this paragraph add to or challenge your thoughts in Activity 3? What is your evidence?

5 What impression has been created of the prisoners so far?

6 Now read paragraph three of the article and think about the words and phrases that have been highlighted for you. Consider what is implied by each highlighted word or phrase. Jot down what you can infer from each one.

The biggest rewards working in offender learning come when someone makes you rethink your first impressions of them, when someone proves you wrong. A learner once came to my class, asked what subject it was, reeled off a load of expletives and refused to stay. He was a London lad, a football hooligan. Three weeks later, he returned, calmer, and took his seat. Three months later, I nominated him for an adult learner award because of his success in literacy. I saw him change from this thuggish brute with a bad attitude to one of the most dedicated learners I have had – he even went on to support a young man who was struggling. It's so satisfying as a tutor when, despite initial reluctance, your pupils relax, and begin to trust you and your teaching. They begin to realise that if they attend, and they listen, and they try, they can actually do this.

7 Do you think the writer now has positive or negative feelings about the prisoners?

8 Has the writer made you think differently about the prisoners? Can you work out why?

9 By this point, can you work out what job the writer of this article does?

Develop the skills

10 The writer goes on to use another specific anecdote. Read the extract and consider the questions in the annotations.

Another memorable student was a man in his 50s **1** with very low literacy and numeracy levels. **2** We worked together one-to-one, and his resilience and effort were outstanding. **3** His fear of exams **4** was his big downfall: he would clam up and be unable even to write. He never used a calculator, and instead would perform long multiplications on scraps of paper. **5** After several weeks, I told him we were doing a practice exam. When he passed, I revealed that he had taken his entry level 2 maths and he cried with relief. **6**

What impression are we given here? What is suggested about the man?

1 How do you feel about the age of the man who is in a classroom learning basic maths?

2 What does this tell you about the education he has had previously?

3 What does this tell you about his capacity for learning and his character? Why might this surprise some readers?

4 What might this tell you about his past experiences?

5 What does this tell you about how he learned maths? What does it also tell you about his real mathematical ability?

6 What does this achievement mean to the prisoner and the teacher?

Apply the skills

11 Go on to read the final extract on your own and complete the following task.

How does the writer use a stereotype here to challenge us to see things his way and change our attitude?

You know that difficult, unruly lad in bottom set maths? You know that boy who's been suspended countless times? You know that one they talk about in the staffroom, who throws chairs and spits and swears and tests everyone paid to care for him to the point of tears? Recent figures show he stands a high chance of entering the criminal justice system, and even more so if he gets expelled (with pupils thrown out aged 12 four times more likely to go to jail). If he does, if he's lucky, and brave, and determined, we'll pick him up, dust him down and carry on where he left off. And maybe second, third or 20th time around, he'll succeed.

Checklist for success

- Select some key words and phrases.
- Ask yourself what is suggested by them.
- Consider what the writer is challenging us to do.
- Consider if he has successfully changed our attitude.

Check your progress:

I can explain the main ideas, attitudes and viewpoints in a text, with support and show my understanding through the inferences I can make from it.

I can work out the main viewpoints and attitudes in a text and select evidence or quotations to prove this.

I can read texts and work out the main ideas and points of view.

Summarise and synthesise: selecting and collating information from more than one text

Learning objective
You will learn how to
- expand basic comprehension skills to enable you to deal with more than one text at a time.

Assessment objective
- English Language AO1

How do you work with two texts at once?

Getting you thinking

1 You're in a sports shop. You've got two pairs of trainers in front of you. You like them both.

How do you choose which pair to buy?

Chances are you will start to weigh up the things you know about them:

- the fit
- the colour
- the brand
- the price.

In your mind, you are pulling together or collating information about both pairs in order to make a decision.

This is almost exactly the same process you use when you are asked to collate information or ideas from two or more texts.

Explore the skills

Look at these two short extracts of non-fiction. Text A is from Captain Scott's diary recounting his doomed expedition to the South Pole in 1912. Text B is from *Race to the Pole*, an account of a race between six teams of explorers to conquer the South Pole in 2008.

Text A

We started at 7.30, none of us having slept much after the shock of our discovery. We followed the Norwegian sledge tracks for some way; as far as we make out there are only two men. In about three miles we passed two small cairns. Then the weather overcast, and the tracks being increasingly drifted up and obviously going too far to the west, we decided to make straight for the Pole according to our calculations. At 12.30 Evans had such cold hands we camped for lunch – an excellent 'week-end one.' ... To-night little Bowers is laying himself out to get sights in terrible difficult circumstances; the wind is blowing hard, T. –21 degrees, and there is that curious damp, cold feeling in the air which chills one to the bone in no time.

from Captain Scott's Diary, 1912

Text B

The next day was one of those where the place you wake up in feels totally different from the one you went to bed in. Everything about the start of the next day was grey. The cloud cover and wind totally changed the appearance of the plateau; it was as if we'd been inside the tent for a month rather than a night, or as if we'd gone to bed in summer and woken up on the edges of winter. The sky was dark, the wind was already blowing hard and the temperature had dropped 15 degrees. With wind chill, it was down to minus 41.

James Cracknell and Ben Fogle,
from *Race to the Pole*

In both extracts, we are given key information about:

- the place
- the temperature
- the weather.

2 Collect together this information and remember to select quotations which can be used as evidence.

Organise it in a chart or grid like the one below.

	In Text A I learn ...	Evidence from the text	In Text B I learn ...	Evidence from the text
The place				
The weather				
The temperature				

Checklist for success

To write an effective summary of ideas from two or more texts, it is important to:

- ask yourself what the extracts have in common
- organise that information into logical categories
- select evidence that you can use in support.

A summary, however, does not require a lot of detail. Present your ideas in a crisp, clear, concise way, making only the key points.

Look at this example paragraph from a student, summarising the first key idea about the place and using their evidence concisely and usefully.

> Both sets of explorers are in a harsh, inhospitable place: for example, the tracks in Text A are described as 'drifted up' and it's impossible to see too far ahead, 'to get sights in terrible difficult circumstances,' And in Text B, 'the sky was dark' and the environment has changed drastically overnight.
>
> The weather…

3 Go on to complete a second paragraph, summarising your key ideas about the weather, using your evidence to help you make your point.

Develop the skills

You are going to go on to work on summarising the similarities between the expeditions of 1912 and 2008.

4 Read these further extracts from both texts.

    a What other key information categories are there? Add them to your notes or table.

    b Add in your ideas and evidence.

Text A

After lunch, and Evans still not appearing, we looked out, to see him still afar off. By this time we were alarmed, and all four started back on ski. I was first to reach the poor man and shocked at his appearance; he was on his knees with clothing disarranged, hands uncovered and frostbitten, and a wild look in his eyes. Asked what was the matter, he replied with a slow speech that he didn't know, but thought he must have fainted. We got him on his feet, but after two or three steps he sank down again. He showed every sign of complete collapse. Wilson, Bowers, and I went back for the sledge, whilst Oates remained with him. When we returned he was practically unconscious, and when we got him into the tent quite comatose. He died quietly at 12.30 A.M.

It is a terrible thing to lose a companion in this way, but calm reflection shows that there could not have been a better ending to the terrible anxieties of the past week. Discussion of the situation at lunch yesterday shows us what a desperate pass we were in with a sick man on our hands at such a distance from home.

Text B

Ed came up alongside, then moved ahead and rammed his pole into the ground.

'We're stopping!' he stated defiantly. 'You're recovering from pneumonia, and you need to rest.'

'I'm Ok; I can carry on,' I protested weakly.

'We're not carrying on. For the last three days we've done fewer kilometres each day, and for the last two days we've been all over the shop. We haven't even skied as a group. We need to rest, otherwise we'll be even weaker tomorrow.'

Suddenly all the anger and frustration came pouring out. 'I've let you down, my blisters have slowed us down, I've got pneumonia, frostbite and now I can't pull my weight. I trained so hard for this. I'm so sorry.'

Apply the skills

5 You are now going to put together all of your ideas and evidence to complete the following task.

Write a summary of the similarities between the expeditions of 1912 and 2008.

You could begin with the example paragraph from Activity 2 and continue from there.

Check your progress:

- I can present the ideas from two texts in a crisp summary, supported by quotations and accompanied with inferences to show my understanding.
- I can organise the ideas in a logical way and support them with quotations.
- I can identify the ideas that two texts have in common.

Apply your skills to English Language and English Literature tasks

Learning objectives
You will learn to
- apply the key skills from this chapter to an unseen English Language task
- apply the key skills from this chapter to an English Literature task
- reflect on your progress through looking at different responses to both tasks.

Assessment objectives
- English Language AO1
- English Literature AO1

Responding to English Language tasks

1 There are two texts below. One is from a broadsheet newspaper published recently; the other is an extract from a non-fiction text, *Sketches by Boz* by Charles Dickens. As you read them, think about the following questions:

- What are these extracts about?
- What are we learning about the issues of homelessness both today and in the past?

Text A

Sleeping rough for charity hides the real homelessness crisis

The public needs to understand the true face of what life without a home means, and sleeping rough is only part of it

Organising a sponsored sleep-out is a preferred strategy for many homelessness charities up and down the country.

Jollies under the stars, making a mattress from cardboard and bedding down – these Bear Grylls excursions just perpetuate the myth that homelessness is about rough sleeping, and is therefore a much smaller problem than it really is.

The truth is that rough sleeping is the tip of the iceberg. It doesn't begin to cover the extraordinary scope of homelessness. Each year homelessness affects around 400,000 people.

Imagine if 'experiencing homelessness' was sold to you as it really is. Most homeless people do not sleep in the street. You would most likely be sofa surfing, squatting, staying in hostels or being passed around B&Bs by the local council.

During this period you would also now be three times more likely to go to hospital, 13 times more likely to be a victim of violence and 47 times more likely to be victims of theft. One in five would have been robbed. Your life-span would be reduced from a healthy 81 years to just 47.

Since 2007, running a hostel for homeless people has been completely unregulated. Some landlords are fair and generous, but many force tenants to wallow in unhygienic conditions. 'Worse than prison,' is how one charity key worker I know described conditions in some London hostels.

Long spells in these hostels are common-place. One in 10 will stay for more than two years, most will stay for 12 months. If you don't like the conditions, or feel threatened, a refusal to take the option excludes you from any housing support in the future. Yet 8,000 people each year still take this course of action.

[…]

Every one of the 70,000 people in this hostel system is stuck in a grim and dangerous situation.

[…]

The number of full-time support workers in hostels is dropping dramatically. Cuts have put countless in-house mental health and substance misuse projects at risk. As the state recedes, the proportion of truly dangerous hostels increases.

Tens of thousands more homeless live in filthy squats, far out of reach of help. Charities can only enter to offer aid when accompanied by the police, such is the danger. Interventions are rare. Frustrated landlords turn to private security, who care little for the law and prefer to beat squatters out with garden hoses and cricket bats. Hundreds of thousands more float from sofa to sofa, the legion of 'hidden homeless.'

This problem is widespread. Rough sleeping is not. Society needs to understand how bad a situation we are really in.

Alastair Sloan, *The Guardian*, 29 October 2013

Text B

It is nearly eleven o'clock, and the cold thin rain which has been drizzling so long, is beginning to pour down in good earnest; the baked-potato man has departed – the kidney-pie man has just walked away with his warehouse on his arm – the cheesemonger has drawn in his blind, and the boys have dispersed.

The constant clicking of **pattens** on the slippy and uneven pavement, and the rustling of umbrellas, as the wind blows against the shop-windows, bear testimony to the inclemency of the night; and the policeman, with his oilskin cape buttoned closely round him, seems as he holds his hat on his head, and turns round to avoid the gust of wind and rain which drives against him at the street-corner, to be very far from congratulating himself on the prospect before him.

The little chandler's shop with the cracked bell behind the door, whose melancholy tinkling has been regulated by the demand for quarterns of sugar and half-ounces of coffee, is shutting up. The crowds which have been passing to and fro during the whole day, are rapidly dwindling away; and the noise of shouting and quarrelling which issues from the public-houses, is almost the only sound that breaks the melancholy stillness of the night.

There was another, but it has ceased. That wretched woman with the infant in her arms, round whose meagre form the remnant of her own scanty shawl is carefully wrapped, has been attempting to sing some popular ballad, in the hope of wringing a few pence from the compassionate passer-by. A brutal

laugh at her weak voice is all she has gained. The tears fall thick and fast down her own pale face; the child is cold and hungry, and its low half-stifled wailing adds to the misery of its wretched mother, as she moans aloud, and sinks despairingly down, on a cold damp door-step.

Charles Dickens, from *Sketches by Boz*

Your task

Using details from both sources, write a summary of the issues that the homeless poor seem to face today compared to the past.

Glossary

pattens: clogs

Checklist for success

Before you begin, remember to:

- ask yourself which key ideas the extracts have in common
- organise that information into logical categories
- select evidence that you can use in support.

A successful response should include:

- clear statements in your own words addressing the question directly
- support for those statements with selected quotations
- inferences to show your understanding.

Reflecting on your progress

2 Read the following response to this task. As you read, think about what the student has done well and what advice they might need in order to make more progress.

Response 1

The article shows that today we have homeless charities 'Organising a sponsored sleep-out is a preferred strategy for many homelessness charities up and down the country' which shows that there are people trying to help the homeless. However, in the Dickens text no-one seems to be helping the poor mother and her baby, which tells us that even in the cold and rain she is still not being helped.

makes a clear statement and uses quotation to support

has made an inference on both texts

Today some homeless people are able to use hostels '8000 people each year still take this course of action.' Which shows there is sometimes a place for people to go, even though it is often not very nice 'Worse than prison'. In the Dickens text though, the mother does not seem to have anywhere to go with her baby.

is usefully summarising key points in an organised way

Homelessness must have been a very serious problem in Victorian times as you would not expect to see a young baby out on the streets today. A similarity though, is that homelessness is still a very big problem today as the article tells us 'Each year homelessness affects around 400,000 people.'. This is a very shocking figure and implies that we still have to do more to help the homeless.

is thinking about similarities as well as differences

Comments on Response 1

This response focuses on the task and uses three separate ideas to build the summary. They find two clearly different ideas but also a useful similarity to help show more ideas. Most ideas are supported with a useful and sensible quotation. There are inferences here – some on a rather simple level.

3 How could this sample response be improved? Using the middle rung of the Check your progress ladder at the end of this chapter, think about what advice you might give to this student in order to improve their work.

4. Now read Response 2. As you read, think about what the student has done that is an improvement on Response 1.

Response 2

The broadsheet article tells us about the charity work that is being done to help the homeless, describing sleep-outs as 'Jollies under the stars' which implies these events don't always take the problem seriously enough. In the past however, it seems the problem is not taken seriously either, as people openly laughed at the homeless woman, 'A brutal laugh at her weak voice …'

presents a very clear idea with embedded support and inference from both texts

The woman in Victorian England is left on the streets at night as everywhere was closing and the rain poured down, but in the present the article suggests homelessness is not necessarily living on the streets, 'sofa-surfing, squatting, staying in a hostel' are all classed as being homeless now.

uses close textual reference and quotation effectively to make a second clear point

In the present however, the hostels seem not to be always safe places to stay 'Worse than prison' is how they are described, but this still seems a better option than in the past where a woman and a young baby are left out 'on a cold damp doorstep'.

continues to use the key words from the question to stay on task and help organisation of ideas

Homelessness seems to have been a desperately serious problem in the past, but the article suggests it is also a desperately serious problem now 'homelessness affects around 400,000 people'.

makes a concise summarising link between the texts, showing a good overview of both

Comments on Response 2

This is a crisp, clear and organised response, which selects and organises four sensible ideas. It takes into account similarities and differences. This response uses quotation and support effectively and sensibly and draws a number of interesting inferences whilst summarising the key ideas well.

5 How might this response be improved even further? Using the top rung of the Check your progress ladder at the end of this chapter, decide what feedback and advice you might give to this student.

Responding to English Literature tasks

The following extract is from a short story 'The Veldt' by Ray Bradbury, about a family who live in a technology filled house with gadgets that do everything for them. The children's room is a virtual reality room that is able to connect with the children telepathically to reproduce any place they imagine.

As you read, think about the following questions:

- What ideas and feelings about the impact of technology do you think the writer is communicating?

- What do you notice about the ways language and structure have been used to communicate these ideas and feelings to the reader?

'George, I wish you'd look at the nursery.'

'What's wrong with it?'

'I don't know.'

'Well, then.'

'I just want you to look at it, is all, or call a psychologist in to look at it.'

'What would a psychologist want with a nursery?'

'You know very well what he'd want.' His wife paused in the middle of the kitchen and watched the stove busy humming to itself, making supper for four.

'It's just that the nursery is different now than it was.'

'All right, let's have a look.'

They walked down the hall of their soundproofed Happylife Home, which had cost them thirty thousand dollars installed, this house which clothed and fed and rocked them to sleep and played and sang and was good to them. Their approach sensitized a switch somewhere and the nursery light flicked on when they came within ten feet of it. Similarly, behind them, in the halls, lights went on and off as they left them behind, with a soft automaticity.

'Well,' said George Hadley.

They stood on the thatched floor of the nursery. It was forty feet across by forty feet long and thirty feet high; it had cost half again as much as the rest of the house. 'But nothing's too good for our children,' George had said.

The nursery was silent. It was empty as a jungle glade at hot high noon. The walls were blank and two dimensional. Now, as George and Lydia Hadley stood in the center of the room, the walls began to purr and recede into crystalline distance, it seemed, and presently an African veldt appeared, in three dimensions, on all sides, in color reproduced to the final pebble and bit of straw. The ceiling above them became a deep sky with a hot yellow sun.

George Hadley felt the perspiration start on his brow.

'Let's get out of this sun,' he said. 'This is a little too real. But I don't see anything wrong.'

'Wait a moment, you'll see,' said his wife.

Now the hidden odorophonics were beginning to blow a wind of odor at the two people in the middle of the baked veldtland. The hot straw smell of lion grass, the cool green smell of the hidden water hole, the great rusty smell of animals, the smell of dust like a red paprika in the hot air. And now the sounds: the thump of distant antelope feet on grassy sod, the papery rustling of vultures. A shadow passed through the sky. The shadow flickered on George Hadley's upturned, sweating face.

'Filthy creatures,' he heard his wife say.

'The vultures.'

'You see, there are the lions, far over, that way. Now they're on their way to the water hole. They've just been eating,' said Lydia. 'I don't know what.'

'Some animal.' George Hadley put his hand up to shield off the burning light from his squinted eyes. 'A zebra or a baby giraffe, maybe.'

'Are you sure?' His wife sounded peculiarly tense.

'No, it's a little late to be sure,' he said, amused. 'Nothing over there I can see but cleaned bone, and the vultures dropping for what's left.'

'Did you hear that scream?' she asked.

'No.'

'About a minute ago?'

'Sorry, no.'

The lions were coming. And again George Hadley was filled with admiration for the mechanical genius who had conceived this room. A miracle of efficiency selling for an absurdly low price. Every home should have one. Oh, occasionally they frightened you with their clinical accuracy, they startled you, gave you a twinge, but most of the time what fun for everyone, not only your own son and daughter, but for yourself when you felt like a quick jaunt to a foreign land, a quick change of scenery. Well, here it was!

And here were the lions now, fifteen feet away, so real, so feverishly and startlingly real that you could feel the prickling fur on your hand, and your mouth was stuffed with the dusty upholstery smell of their heated pelts, and the yellow of them was in your eyes like the yellow of an exquisite French tapestry, the yellows of lions and summer grass, and the sound of the matted lion lungs exhaling on the silent noontide, and the smell of meat from the panting, dripping mouths.

The lions stood looking at George and Lydia Hadley with terrible green-yellow eyes.

'Watch out!' screamed Lydia.

The lions came running at them.

Lydia bolted and ran. Instinctively, George sprang after her. Outside, in the hall, with the door slammed he was laughing and she was crying, and they both stood appalled at the other's reaction.

'George!'

'Lydia! Oh, my dear poor sweet Lydia!'

'They almost got us!'

'Walls, Lydia, remember; crystal walls, that's all they are. Oh, they look real, I must admit - Africa in your parlor - but it's all dimensional, superreactionary, supersensitive color film and mental tape film behind glass screens. It's all odorophonics and sonics, Lydia. Here's my handkerchief.'

Ray Bradbury, from 'The Veldt'

6 Now look at this practice task and think about how you would approach it.

Your task

'"The Veldt" is a story warning us about the use of too much technology in our lives.' How far do you agree with this statement?

Write about:

- what some of the ideas about the impact of technology are
- how Bradbury presents these ideas in the way he writes.

You would use the skills you have learned in this chapter to answer the **first bullet point** of this type of task. (You will learn the skills to answer the second bullet point in Chapter 4.)

Checklist for success

A successful response should:

- demonstrate your understanding of ideas in the story
- include some well-selected evidence
- make some inferences to demonstrate your understanding.

Reflecting on your progress

7 Read the following response to this task. As you read, think about what the student has done well and what advice they might need in order to make more progress.

Response 1

Technology seems to have a very positive impact in the story at first as it tells us 'this house which clothed and fed and rocked them to sleep and played and sang and was good to them'. It seems like the technology does everything and makes life a lot easier.

presents a useful idea and uses a key word from the question. The quotation is a little lengthy. Makes an inference

But the story goes on to say it is also negative. George says at one point 'This is a little too real' implying things are getting a bit much especially in the nursery where the technology makes it seem like Africa.

sees another possibility and makes an inference, though not developed

This scene is so real it seems to be very scary, especially for children. The mum is very scared of the lions even though they are not real but they are very frightening.

'The lions stood looking at George and Lydia Hadley with terrible green-yellow eyes'. I agree this is warning us about — the dangers of technology as it makes me think of how we are warned about video games and the dangers of the internet today. How it can be risky.

links the point usefully to the question

The parents also seem to have different attitudes which is also like people today. The mum is frightened and warning her husband about what they have let the children play — with but he is not listening to the warning saying 'crystal walls, that's all they are'. He is not thinking about the impact on his children.

is thinking carefully about the message of the text or the 'warning' and presents a strong idea here

Comments on Response 1

This response has a good focus on the ideas connected to technology and selects some key points sensibly. The student chooses some useful quotations to support their ideas. There is a nice approach to making inferences and the candidate is working hard to think about Bradbury's message in the text and the idea of the warning.

8 How could this sample response be improved? Using the middle rung of the Check your progress ladder at the end of this chapter, think about what advice you might give to this student in order to improve their work.

9 Now read Response 2. As you read, think about what the student has done that is an improvement on Response 1, and what advice this student might need in order to make even more progress.

Response 2

On the surface, the writer suggests that all of the technology in the house is a useful and positive thing and 'was good to them'. The implication is that it makes life a — lot easier for the family and is efficient, saving time and energy.

a crisp, clear start with embedded quotation and an inference

The house is called the 'Happylife Home' which seems somewhat ironic as the wife is clearly not so happy with the situation in the virtual reality nursery. The impact of technology here seems overwhelming with the walls, ceiling and 'hidden odorophonics' almost transporting them to another land. Bradley seems to be warning us that technology can help to remove us from reality and from real life issues, like some people become so absorbed in computer games they don't know what's real anymore.

This seems extra creepy as this is a nursery, filled with vultures and lions with 'panting, dripping mouths' not like the childlike images of animals you usually see in a nursery. This seems to warn us that technology can make things too frightening or as George says, 'too real'.

George though seems to think the technology is a good thing, 'Nothing's too good for our children', and seems not to care about the risks. He thinks it's all 'a miracle' but his wife does not. She is 'tense' and at the end 'crying' when the dangers become almost larger than life and the lions seem to be coming to attack them. This seems to be a clear warning about how technology can take over your life and even though useful, can have hidden dangers.

another clear explanation of the ideas in the story with well-chosen evidence

good strong inference linked to the task and the writer's message

this is a lovely thoughtful inference, showing the candidate is reading between the lines

uses the text concisely to support these points

clear summary linking back to the task

Comments on Response 2

This is a very confident response with a clear focus on the task and shows a range of ideas, all usefully supported with appropriate textual references and quotations. The inferences are thoughtful and detailed in places and show understanding and some original thinking.

10 How might this response be improved even further? Using the top rung of the Check your progress ladder at the end of this chapter, decide what feedback and advice you might give to this student.

Check your progress

- I can read texts, selecting information and presenting it clearly.
- I can choose my quotations carefully to support my points and show that I understand texts fully.
- I can read between the lines of a text and present my inferences with supported statements to demonstrate my clear understanding.
- I can read into character descriptions to make inferences about the character from specific details within the text.
- I can read into descriptions to make inferences about the place from specific details within the text.
- I can explain the main ideas, attitudes and viewpoints in a text, with support and show my understanding through the inferences I can make from it.
- I can present the ideas from two texts in a crisp summary, supported by quotations and accompanied with inferences to show my understanding.

- I can read texts and select the information I need.
- I can use quotations to support the point I am making.
- I can read between the lines of a text and present my thoughts as inferences.
- I can look at character descriptions and pick out specific quotations to help me work out what they are like.
- I can look at descriptions of places and pick out specific quotations to help me work out what they are like.
- I can work out the main viewpoints and attitudes in a text and select evidence or quotations to prove this.
- I can organise the ideas in a logical way and support them with quotations.

- I can read texts carefully.
- I can remember to put quotations in my reading responses.
- I can sometimes read between the lines and show what a text suggests to me.
- I can look at character descriptions and imagine what characters look like.
- I can look at descriptions of places and imagine what they are like.
- I can read texts and work out the main ideas and points of view.
- I can identify the ideas that two texts have in common.

Chapter 4

Explaining and commenting on writers' methods and effects

What's it all about?

In this chapter, you will learn about how writers make conscious decisions about the words they choose, the techniques they use, and the way they structure and shape their texts in order to create meanings and communicate their ideas to their readers.

In this chapter, you will learn how to

- explain and comment on writers' use of language
- explain and comment on writers' use of language techniques
- explain the way writers use language to create character
- explain and comment on writers' use of structural features
- explain and comment on writers' use of openings
- explain and comment on the ways writers create meanings and effects with language, structure and form
- apply your skills to English Language and English Literature tasks.

	English Language GCSE	English Literature GCSE
Which AOs are covered?	AO2 Explain, comment on and analyse how writers use language and structure to achieve effects and influence readers, using relevant subject terminology to support their views	AO2 Analyse the language, form and structure used by a writer to create meanings and effects, using relevant subject terminology where appropriate
How will this be tested?	Some questions will ask you to focus in detail on particular words and phrases. Others will identify a particular area of a text and ask you to look closely at the meanings and techniques being used in that particular part. All the texts you will be responding to will be previously unseen.	Wider questions will ask you to analyse and comment on the overall text, paying attention to the language, the structure or the literary techniques being used by the writer to communicate meanings and create effects. Sometimes you will be responding to a whole play or novel that you have studied in class and sometimes you will be writing about two previously unseen poems.

Explain and comment on writers' use of language

Learning objectives
You will learn how to
- identify the overall viewpoint in a text
- write about the effects of writers' language choices, linking them to the overall viewpoint.

Assessment objective
- English Language AO2

Why does it matter which words and phrases the writer chooses?

Getting you thinking

When reading a text for the first time, focus on these key questions: What is the writer's **viewpoint**? How does the writer want me to think or feel?

The writer's viewpoint will be communicated through their choice of language.

In *The Road to Wigan Pier*, George Orwell writes about a time of great change in the north of England following **industrialisation**.

> As you travel northward your eye, accustomed to the South or East, does not notice much difference until you are beyond Birmingham. [...] It is only when you get a little further north, to the **pottery towns** and beyond, that you begin to encounter the real ugliness of industrialism – an ugliness so frightful and so arresting that you are obliged, as it were, to come to terms with it.
>
> George Orwell, from *The Road to Wigan Pier*

1 What does Orwell describe in this extract?

2 What is Orwell's attitude to what he sees? Does he like it? Which words and phrases tell you this?

Explore the skills

Now you have worked out the main viewpoint of the text, you can begin to explore the ways in which Orwell communicates this to the reader.

In the next paragraph, Orwell describes what he sees when he visits a mining town.

Key term

viewpoint: an attitude, opinion or point of view

Glossary

industrialisation: the growth of the steel, coal, textiles and manufacturing industries in the late eighteenth and nineteenth centuries

pottery towns: towns like Stoke-on-Trent where pottery was manufactured

A slag-heap is at best a hideous thing, because it is so planless and functionless. It is something just dumped on the earth, like the emptying of a giant's dust-bin. On the outskirts of the mining towns there are frightful landscapes where your horizon is ringed completely round by jagged grey mountains, and underfoot is mud and ashes and overhead the steel cables where tubs of dirt travel slowly across miles of country. Often the slag-heaps are on fire, and at night you can see the red rivulets of fire winding this way and that, and also the slow-moving blue flames of sulphur, which always seem on the point of expiring and always spring out again. Even when a slag-heap sinks, as it does ultimately, only an evil brown grass grows on it, and it retains its hummocky surface. One in the slums of Wigan, used as a playground, looks like a choppy sea suddenly frozen; 'the flock mattress', it is called locally. Even centuries hence when the plough drives over the places where coal was once mined, the sites of ancient slag-heaps will still be distinguishable from an aeroplane.

3 Read the paragraph again and find examples of Orwell's language choices to complete the second column of the table.

Language choice	Example(s)	Effect: how it makes me feel and why
Adverbials	underfoot overhead ringed completely round	Create a feeling of claustrophobia because they suggest people are completely surrounded by the effects of industrialisation
References to colour		
Powerful adjectives		
Repetition		
Imagery or comparisons		

Key term

Adverbials: words or phrases used to modify a verb, adjective or adverb to tell you how, when, where something is happening. Adverbials modify meaning to give the reader more information. For example:

The boy ran *clumsily* across the road.

The boy ran *gracefully* across the road.

Resolutely, the boy ran across the road.

Without looking, the boy ran across the road.

Develop the skills

The next step is to explain the **effects** of the writer's language choices: how they make you feel and why.

Look at the way this student has commented on the effect of Orwell's use of colour.

Key term

effects: what a reader thinks, feels or pictures in their mind's eye as they read

> Orwell uses colour references to create a sense of danger or threat. He describes the fires as moving like 'red rivulets'. All the other colour references are 'grey' or 'brown' which creates a feeling of death and decay. The use of 'red' is a contrast to this and makes the fires caused by the slag heaps seem even more noticeable and dangerous. Orwell is suggesting that the industrial north of England is a dangerous, hellish place to live and work.

Identify the point, the evidence, and the explanation of the effect. Has the student thought about how certain words make the reader think, feel or imagine? How has the student linked this effect to Orwell's overall viewpoint?

5 Which other language choices from your table suggest living in the industrial north might be unpleasant or unnatural? Choose the two examples you can write most about. Make notes about their effects in the final column.

6 Now write a short paragraph about one of your examples explaining what effect you think it creates and how it helps to communicate Orwell's viewpoint to the reader.

Checklist for success

- Make a clear point.
- Use some appropriate evidence.
- Explain the effect on the reader and link this to Orwell's viewpoint.

Apply the skills

Now you have selected two or three specific examples of language to explain and comment on, you are ready to form a response to a question. Complete the following task.

How does Orwell use language to communicate his viewpoint about the industrial north of England?

7 Make a brief plan first of all. You might want to use the one below as a guide for each paragraph.

- Orwell is suggesting that the north of England has been completely taken over by industrialisation — clear overview of writer's viewpoint

- he uses adverbials to create a sense of how claustrophobic it is for the inhabitants — identification of a language feature

- examples of adverbials include 'round', 'underfoot', 'over-head', 'all round', 'between', 'covered with' — examples, using direct evidence

- this creates a sense of claustrophobia as he seems to be suggesting that the effects of industrialisation are surrounding the people who live there — explanation of the effect of the language used

8 Repeat the planning process for each point you want to make and write your response.

Check your progress:

▲▲ I can interpret the writer's viewpoint and make detailed comments about a range of carefully selected words and phrases to support my interpretation.

▲▲ I can clearly explain the writer's viewpoint, using some relevant examples to support my explanation.

▲ I can identify the writer's viewpoint and refer to one or two words and phrases from the text.

Explain and comment on writers' use of language techniques

Learning objectives

You will learn how to
- identify and explain the effects of some language techniques in a non-fiction text
- comment on these techniques in your own writing.

Assessment objective
- English Language AO2

How do writers use language techniques to influence the way you think about things?

Getting you thinking

Good writers use language techniques to get their viewpoints across.

1 Look at the first two lines of the following article and find an example of a **rhetorical technique** in action.

2 What effect is this technique designed to have on the reader?

3 What do you think is the writer's viewpoint?

Key term

rhetorical technique: a language technique used to persuade a reader to consider an idea from a different point of view

Explore the skills

4 Now read the first two paragraphs and answer the questions in the annotations.

Let's put the brakes on teen drivers and make them wait until they are older

A recent report has recommended that the age for probationary driving licences be raised to 18.

Would you give a child a loaded gun? Loaded guns are unbelievably dangerous, and children's brains not yet capable of properly understanding danger, or heeding warnings. Of course you wouldn't.

But would you allow a 17-year-old to drive a car? **1** We've **2** all been right behind it, for many years: or at least, no one I know has been out on the streets protesting about the threshold at which teenagers can apply for a provisional driving licence.

But now, at last, sanity is starting to prevail. A government report, by the Transport Research Laboratory, **3** has recommended raising the age at which kids can learn to drive to 18. My 15-year-old daughter, **4** who is counting the months until she's almost 17 (the application can go in three months before their birthday) will be devastated when she hears the news – and so will thousands of other teens, for whom getting a licence and learning to drive is seen as a rite of passage.

But I use the word 'kids' deliberately. Anyone who has older children – and I have two, aged 21 and 19 – knows they are really toddlers in an extraordinarily effective disguise. They look (especially if you don't currently have one) so adult! All grown-up! **5** But – and there's an increasing amount of research to back this up – until they're at least 21, their brains are still in formation. They don't yet 'think' like adults; in particular, they don't connect 'actions' and 'consequences'. If you're a driver, you know how bad that could be.

And yet we give them the car keys; we sit beside them as they learn the difference between the accelerator and the brake; we applaud when they pass their driving test; we pay the extortionate insurance premiums for them. **6** And still we don't twig how bonkers **7** it all is: unless your family is hit by tragedy when a teenager crashes, and suddenly it's all crystal clear. My husband's cousin crashed, fresh from her driving test. She survived for two years in a coma, but then she died. A young woman who would now be in her mid-30s, carried off way too soon, more by society's negligence than by her inexperience as a driver. **8**

And when it happens: wham. **9** Not just the impact – which is immeasurable, because road traffic deaths blight families for decades after people assume they're 'over it' – but the madness of it all. Why did that child have a loaded gun? **10**

Key term

colloquial: informal language

1 Here the writer uses a direct question. Who is the question addressed to and what response is expected?

2 The writer is using the first person here. How does this help the writer to get the reader on her side?

3 sounds official – she's got important research to back her ideas up

4 using personal details makes it sound like she really cares about and understands the issue

5 exclamation marks emphasising the idea that you are still young at 17

6 repetition of 'we' is reinforcing the point she is making

7 use of **colloquial** language making the tone seem relaxed and personal

8 personal anecdote really reinforcing her point

9 the punctuation here really emphasises that 'wham' – a bit like a car crash?

10 repetition of 'loaded gun' metaphor, reminding the reader of her main argument

Develop the skills

Now read paragraphs 3 and 4.

Look at the notes a student has made. They are quite basic.

> Purpose: to argue a viewpoint. She thinks the driving age should be raised to 18
>
> Language techniques: rhetorical techniques (questions / hyperbole), personal address and informal tone seem to be the strongest
>
> Effect: wants her reader to agree with her

5 Pick one of the techniques the student has identified and write a paragraph explaining what effect it has on the reader.

6 Now read the rest of the article and identify three things that the writer does to persuade you to share her point of view.

Sometimes it's not only themselves they kill either: they take their siblings, their friends, with them.

Once you've been hit by a road traffic death – and my family has, as well as my husband's – you know it's impossible to overestimate its toll. And the terrible reality is that road deaths are the most common tragedy in all our lives; and teenagers, the people we should be protecting, are four times as likely to die in a road accident than as a result of drink or drugs. Four times! And here's betting you've heard far more about the dangers of drink and drugs.

Today's government report urges more than just rowing back on the age threshold. It suggests a lot of hand-holding, as you would do for a young child. A night-time curfew, unless they have an over-30 with them (what a delightful idea that is – my taxi beckons, after all those years when it's been the other way round), and a learner phase when they drive under supervision.

Some people will call it the nanny state. But I bet you this: none of them are people who've ever watched a teenage driver's coffin being lowered into the earth. It's not a sight you easily forget; and nor should it be.

Apply the skills

7 Using your notes, write 200–300 words in response to the following task.

How does the writer use language techniques to help persuade the reader to agree with her point of view?

Checklist for success

- Be clear about the writer's overall viewpoint.
- Select two or three language techniques.
- For each one, make a clear point about how this technique links to the overall viewpoint and purpose of the article.

Check your progress:

I can understand the writer's ideas and can clearly explain how language techniques are used to communicate them to the reader.

I can understand the writer's ideas and can explain and comment in detail on how language techniques are used to communicate these to the reader.

I can identify the writer's ideas and can identify some language techniques.

Explain the way writers use language to create character

Learning objectives
You will learn how to
- notice particular details about the ways characters are described in novels
- look closely at how these details add to the overall effect being created.

Assessment objectives
- English Language AO2
- English Literature AO2

Do you have to pay close attention to every single word when you're writing about a fiction text? How do you choose what to write about?

Getting you thinking

As a discerning, analytical reader, one of your most useful tools is an imaginary magnifying glass. Imagine you are a detective or a forensic scientist, poring over the details in a text and inferring meaning from the choice of detail.

Charles Dickens is known for his vivid descriptions of characters. In the following extract from *A Christmas Carol*, the **omniscient narrator** is describing the character of Ebenezer Scrooge in the third person.

> Oh! But he was a tight-fisted hand at the grindstone, Scrooge! a squeezing, wrenching, grasping, scraping, clutching, covetous, old sinner! Hard and sharp as flint, from which no steel had ever struck out generous fire; secret, and self-contained, and solitary as an oyster.
>
> Charles Dickens, from *A Christmas Carol*

Key term

omniscient narrator: a narrator who writes in the third person, is 'outside' the story, not part of it, and is 'all knowing' having access to the thoughts and feelings of the characters as well as the plot of the whole story

1 What kind of person do you think Scrooge is? Select two details to support your view.

2 Why did you choose these details in particular? Explain why the details you have selected support your view of Scrooge.

An analytical reader selects the most useful detail. You don't have to write about every detail; you need to make careful selections.

Explore the skills

3 Read the extract again. Select a range of different techniques that create impressions of Scrooge, using a table like the one below.

Technique	Example	Connotation
Adjectives	grasping	*Suggests harshness and desperation, as if money is something that Scrooge feels very passionately about*
Imagery	**a tight-fisted hand at the grindstone**	
Narrator	Oh!	

Key term

Connotation: an idea or association suggested by a word in addition to its literal meaning

4 Choose one piece of description to look at more closely. This example shows you how to put your 'magnifying glass' onto one detail, in this case, a simile. Think about the connotations of the words in this phrase.

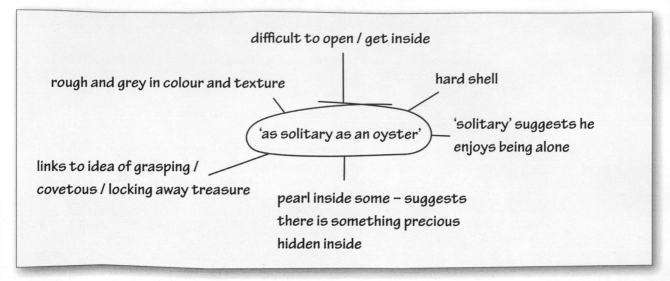

difficult to open / get inside

rough and grey in colour and texture

hard shell

'as solitary as an oyster'

'solitary' suggests he enjoys being alone

links to idea of grasping / covetous / locking away treasure

pearl inside some – suggests there is something precious hidden inside

Now choose a detail and create your own spider diagram.

As the passage continues, Dickens uses a **semantic field** in order to describe Scrooge.

> External heat and cold had little influence on Scrooge. No warmth could warm, no wintry weather chill him. No wind that blew was bitterer than he, no falling snow was more intent upon its purpose, no pelting rain less open to entreaty. Foul weather didn't know where to have him. The heaviest rain, and snow, and hail, and sleet, could boast of the advantage over him in only one respect. They often came down handsomely, and Scrooge never did.

Key terms

semantic field: a collection of words that have a similar meaning or create a similar idea in the mind of the reader

5 What is the semantic field here? How many words in this semantic field can you spot? What are they?

6 What is the effect of grouping all these words together in one paragraph?

Develop the skills

When you read a text for the first time, pay attention to the narrative perspective. Is it **first person** or **third person**? The writer will have deliberately selected a particular perspective – what effect does it have?

Key terms

first person: using 'I'
third person: using 'he/she'

Read this extract from *Mr Pip* by Lloyd Jones. Matilda, the narrator, does not have a good relationship with her mother, Dolores. Dolores has been invited to talk to Matilda's class.

I stood up and announced what everyone else already knew.

'This is my mum'.

'And does Mum have a name?'

'Dolores,' I said, and slid lower into my desk. 'Dolores Laimo'.

My mum smiled back at me. She was wearing the green scarf my dad had sent in the very last package we received. She wore it tied tight at the back of her head which was the same way the rebels wore their bandanas. Her hair was pulled back in a tight bun. It gave her an air of defiance. Her mouth clamped down, her nostrils flared. My father used to say she had the blood of righteousness running in her veins. She should have been a church woman, he'd say, because persuasiveness for my mum was not an intellectual exercise. Quality of argument was neither here nor there. It was all about the intensity of belief. And every part of her – from the whites of her eyes to her muscular calves – rallied on her behalf.

My mum didn't smile enough. When she did it was nearly always in victory. Or else it was at night-time when she thought she was all alone. When she was thinking she tended to look angry, as if the act of thinking was potentially ruinous, even ending in her humiliation. Even when she concentrated she looked angry. In fact, she appeared to be angry much of the time. I used to think it was because she was thinking about my dad. But she couldn't have been thinking about him all the time.

Lloyd Jones, from *Mr Pip*

---

7 **a** Why do you think the author has chosen to write from Matilda's perspective?

b Can you see anything to admire in Dolores that Matilda doesn't appreciate?

Apply the skills

8 Complete the following task.

Reread the extract from *Mr Pip*.

a Select two powerful details and explain how these details suggest that Matilda, the narrator, does not have a good relationship with her mother.

b Later in the novel, Matilda learns to admire and respect her mother. In this extract, how is the writer suggesting that there are aspects of Dolores that the reader should notice and admire?

Checklist for success

- Identify what you think the writer wants the reader to infer.
- Select a strong example and think about all the different connotations of that detail.
- Explain how this example works on the reader.

Check your progress:

 I can select and analyse particular methods in detail, linking them precisely to the overall effect being created.

I can choose clear supporting evidence to explain how one or more methods help to communicate the writer's ideas.

I can identify a method and I am aware of the effect the writer is trying to create.

Explain and comment on writers' use of structural features

Learning objectives

You will learn how to
- identify some ways writers use structural features and organise their writing
- explain the effects of structural features on the reader.

Assessment objectives
- English Language AO2
- English Literature AO2

What does 'structure' mean and why is it important?

> **Getting you thinking**

When we are thinking about the range of ways a writer communicates meaning to the reader, it is important to look at the organisation, order and sequence of the words, phrases and sentences as they appear in the text.

You probably already know more about structure and **cohesion** than you think.

Key term

cohesion: connected together to form a united whole

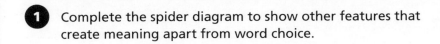

1 Complete the spider diagram to show other features that create meaning apart from word choice.

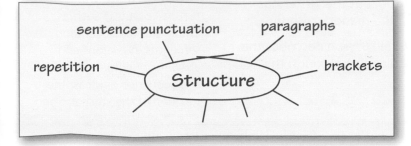

sentence punctuation   paragraphs

repetition   **Structure**   brackets

Explore the skills

The way the writer structures their text can shape our understanding of characters or setting and set up a mood or tone.

Read scene 1 of *DNA* by Dennis Kelly on the right.

2 Read the scene out loud with a partner, first quickly, with interruptions, then slowly with pauses.

Are there moments in this scene where it is more effective to slow down, or to speed up? Why is this?

3 Notice Kelly's use of question and answer in this scene. Which character knows something and which character (like the reader) is in the dark?

4 **a** Describe the relationship between Jan and Mark. How well do they know each other? Notice the minimal responses and how they finish each other's lines.

b Notice the use of repetition. What effect does it have? Do they sound relaxed or anxious?

5 How does Kelly use structure to suggest ideas about Jan and Mark to the audience?

6 This is the first scene in the play, so it is important in the mood of the whole play. How does it engage our interest? What questions does it open up for us? How does it make us feel?

Jan:	Dead?
Mark:	Yeah.
Jan:	What, dead?
Mark:	Yeah
Jan:	Like dead, dead
Mark:	Yes
Jan:	proper dead, not living dead?
Mark:	Not living dead, yes.
Jan:	Are you sure?
Mark:	Yes.
Jan:	I mean there's no
Mark:	No.
Jan:	mistake or
Mark:	No mistake.
Jan:	it's not a joke
Mark:	It's not a joke.
Jan:	coz it's not funny.
Mark:	it's not funny because it's not a joke, if it was a joke it would be funny.
Jan:	Not hiding?
Mark:	Not hiding, dead.
Jan:	not
Mark:	Dead.
Jan:	Oh.
Mark:	Yes.
Jan:	God.
Mark:	Yes.
Jan:	God.
Mark:	Exactly.

Pause.

Jan:	What are we going to do?

Dennis Kelly, from *DNA*

Develop the skills

The following text has a very different form, but the writer has also used **structural features** to influence the reader's response.

In this extract from *A Walk in the Woods*, Bill Bryson describes the potential dangers involved in a hike he's planning through the Appalachian Trail in America.

Key term

structural features: features of a text such as listing; use of short / long sentences; questions and answers; punctuation; order and sequence of ideas; the function of the start and end

Then there were all the diseases lurking in the woods – Giardia lamblia, Eastern equine encephalitis, Rocky Mountain spotted fever, Lyme disease, Helicobactor pylori, Ehrlichia chafeenis, schistosomiasis, brucellosis, and shigella, to offer but a sampling. Eastern equine encephalitis, caused by the prick of a mosquito, attacks the brain and central nervous system. If you are very lucky you can hope to spend the rest of your life propped in a chair with a bib around your neck, but generally it will kill you. There is no known cure. No less arresting is Lyme disease, which comes from the bite of a deer tick. If undetected, it can lie dormant in the human body for years before erupting in a positive fiesta of maladies. This is a disease for the person who wants to experience it all. The symptoms begin with headaches, fatigue, fever, chills, shortness of breath, dizziness and shooting pains in the extremities, then march onto cardiac irregularities, facial paralysis, muscle spasms, severe mental impairment, loss of control of body functions, and – not surprising in the circumstances – chronic depression.

Bill Bryson, from *A Walk in the Woods*

7 Use the table to describe the effects of the structural features.

Structural feature	Example	Effect on reader
List of possible diseases	Ehrlichia chafeenis, schistosomiasis, brucellosis, and shigella	So many technical terms – means he has read up on the diseases. Might suggest he is fixated with what he might catch and suggests he is afraid. However, it could also suggest he is determined to find out everything he can so he is prepared.
The use of short simple sentences that contain one idea		
The list of symptoms of Lyme disease		
The use of **dashes**		

Key term

dashes: punctuation marks used to add an aside or interjection

Structural features, just like language choices, are used to communicate meanings to the reader.

8 Look at the final phrase, 'chronic depression'. How does Bryson build up to this phrase through the paragraph?

9 **a** What is the **tone** of this extract? Does it appear to be serious, humorous, or somewhere in the middle? Remember that the trip is Bryson's idea – does it sound as if he wants to go?

b How do the structural features help to create the tone of the extract?

Read the following response.

Notice how the student is commenting on particular structural features.

Key term

tone: the mood, voice or feeling created by the writer's language choices: for example, humorous or sarcastic

Bill Bryson seems to be creating a humorous tone with the use of sentence structure in this extract. He starts off by giving a long list of diseases. This not only suggests that there are loads and loads of illnesses that you could catch from these woods, but also, because he has used their technical names, it implies that he has done lots of research and come up with a massive list of the things he could catch. This is amusing because it suggests that he is frightened and doesn't want to go on the trip, which is ironic because the trip is his idea in the first place.

— identifies writer's purpose

— identifies a structural technique

— explains one effect

— explains another effect of the same technique

— links back to the purpose of the text

Apply the skills

10 Using your notes and the student response as a model, answer the following question.

> How does Bryson use structural features to create a humorous tone in the extract from *A Walk in the Woods*?

Checklist for success

• Explain the overall tone Bryson is creating in the extract.

• Identify at least two different structural features.

• Explain how these features add to the overall effect.

Check your progress:

▲▲ I can comment in detail on the writer's use of structural features, linking these precisely to the overall effect being created.

▲ I can clearly explain the effects created by the writer through the use of particular structural features.

▲ I can identify one or more deliberate structural features and begin to explain what the effects of these might be.

Explain and comment on writers' use of openings

Learning objective
You will learn how to
• identify the ways writers introduce important ideas at the start of their texts.

Assessment objectives
• English Language AO2
• English Literature AO2

Why is the opening of a story important?

Getting you thinking

1 Think about your favourite story, novel or film. What is it about the start that got you hooked? What made you want to carry on reading or watching?

The way a writer structures their writing is vital. In a story opening, you might be given some clues about

- mood
- characters
- settings
- plot or story to come.

In the opening paragraph to the short story 'The Way the Pit Works', the writer gives clues about the story to follow.

> We went on holiday to the seaside every year, the three of us. Mum and me would wake up before it got light. Once we were in the car, I'd watch for the dawn through the gaps in the houses. I'd tell myself that the sky only looked grey because it was really still night-time, not because it was cloudy. Some years I was right, but the year I'm thinking of, the year I was nine, the sun didn't appear at all.
>
> Gaye Jee, from 'The Way the Pit Works'

2 **a** Look at one detail:

'I'd tell myself that the sky only looked grey because it was really still night-time'

— seems to be trying to convince herself

— mention of grey, sounds gloomy and dark

— mention of night-time also adds to the feeling of darkness

b Pick another detail and annotate it.

3 The second paragraph develops the mood. As you read, carry on collecting clues. The table below suggests some ideas you could use:

> By eight o'clock we were on the beach, Mum and me sitting on our macs huddled together under a blanket which still smelt of our dog, even though he'd been dead nearly a year. A thin, bad-tempered breeze blew sand into our faces and whipped up under my skirt. Dad was pacing up and down the beach looking for destroyers. I could picture them wading through the sea to smash the houses and caravans and people with their enormous sandalled feet.

'Eight o'clock'	Too early to be on a beach – suggests something is not right
'huddled together'	Implying the need for comfort / protection
'dead nearly a year'	

4 **a** What impact does the mood have on the reader at this point in the story? What details give you this impression?

b What do you imagine may happen later in the story?

c What questions does this opening raise for the reader?

Explore the skills

In the first few sentences of the novel *Jane Eyre* by Charlotte
Brontë, the reader is being invited to ask some questions and to
infer some meanings.

Read the first paragraph of *Jane Eyre*.

Key term

infer: to work out meanings
from clues given in the text;
to 'read between the lines'

5   What kind of mood or tone is being created? Which details
chosen, language used and structural features suggest this?

> There was no possibility of taking a walk that day. We had been wandering, indeed, in the leafless
> shrubbery an hour in the morning; but since dinner (Mrs. Reed, when there was no company, dined
> early) the cold winter wind had brought with it clouds so sombre, and a rain so penetrating, that
> further out-door exercise was now out of the question.
>
> Charlotte Brontë, from *Jane Eyre*

6   The table below gives some examples of **inferences**.
See what you can add.

Detail	Quotation	Inference
Negative start	'no possibility of taking a walk'	First sentence negative, suggests life is hard / miserable?
Verbs	'wandering'	Suggests …
Narrator	'we'	

Key terms

inferences: conclusions
formed from evidence

Narrator: the speaker in a
text; usually (although not
always) the central character
of the story

7   What inferences can we make about the narrator's
life and circumstances? Is she happy? How old do you
think she is? Does she like where she lives?

Develop the skills

Read the next extract and look carefully at how Brontë
describes Mrs Reed.

8   What can we infer about Mrs Reed from how she is
described? What clues is Brontë giving us? Are we
meant to like or dislike this character?

9   What more do we learn about the narrator in the
following section of text?

The said Eliza, John, and Georgiana were now clustered round their mama in the drawing-room: she lay reclined on a sofa by the fire-side, and with her darlings about her (for the time neither quarrelling nor crying) looked perfectly happy. Me, she had dispensed from joining the group; saying, 'She regretted to be under the necessity of keeping me at a distance; but that until she heard from Bessie, and could discover by her own observation, that I was endeavouring in good earnest to acquire a more sociable and child-like disposition, a more attractive and sprightly manner – something lighter, franker, more natural, as it were – she really must exclude me from privileges intended only for contented, happy, little children.'

Apply the skills

10 In the novel, we will learn that Jane is sensitive, imaginative, independent and strong-willed. We will also learn that Mrs Reed is an unpleasant woman. Find clues about each character in the next section of text and add them to your evidence table.

Glossary

cavillers: people who raises trivial or annoying objections or questions

'What does Bessie say I have done?' I asked.
'Jane, I don't like **cavillers** or questioners: besides, there is something truly forbidding in a child taking up her elders in that manner. Be seated somewhere; and until you can speak pleasantly, remain silent.'
A breakfast-room adjoined the drawing-room: I slipped in there. It contained a book-case: I soon possessed myself of a volume, taking care that it should be one stored with pictures. I mounted into the window-seat: gathering up my feet, I sat cross-legged, like a Turk; and, having drawn the red moreen curtain nearly close, I was shrined in double retirement.

11 Now you can put all of your findings together to complete the following task.

How does Brontë use details in the first few paragraphs of *Jane Eyre* to introduce the characters of Jane and Mrs Reed to the reader?

Checklist for success

- Make clear statements about both characters.
- Select useful quotations to support your statements.
- Make clear inferences about what that evidence might suggest about either Jane or Mrs Reed.
- Comment on what is revealed about Jane and Mrs Reed from the opening section.

Check your progress:

▲▲ I can interpret the subtle inferences a writer is making in the introduction to a text and use precise references to support my interpretations.

▲ I can infer some meaning from details in the opening to a text and use some relevant examples to support my interpretations.

▲ I can identify some ideas from the opening of a text and refer to one or more direct examples.

12 Look back at your notes and responses. Write another paragraph explaining what elements of this opening might be successful in engaging a reader's interest and why.

Explain and comment on the ways writers create meanings and effects with structure and form

Learning objective
You will learn how to
• identify and explain some of the ways that writers use structural techniques to create meanings.

Assessment objective
• English Literature AO2

What is the difference between structure and form, and why do they matter?

Getting you thinking

'Structure' refers to the ways in which ideas are organised and sequenced, and to how ideas link together in order to create **cohesion**.

'Form' refers to the overall shape and conventions of a text. It is particularly useful to think about when you are looking at how ideas are communicated in poetry.

Key term

cohesion: connecting together to form a united whole

1 What is the difference between these forms? Imagine you had to describe each of them to someone who didn't know the difference: what would you say?

A newspaper article   A short story   A novel

A play   A poem

These forms tend to have lots of 'mini-forms' as well! For example, there are lots of different poetic 'forms'.

2 How many different forms of poetry do you already know? Describe:

a limerick   an acrostic

a haiku   a ballad.

Acrostic on the Queen's Jubilee.

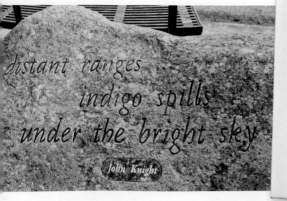

distant ranges
indigo spills
under the bright sky

John Knight

THE BALLAD OF READING GAOL

I

HE did not wear his scarlet coat,
  For blood and wine are red,
And blood and wine were on his hands
  When they found him with the dead,
The poor dead woman whom he loved,
  And murdered in her bed.

He walked amongst the Trial Men
  In a suit of shabby gray;
A cricket cap was on his head,
  And his step seemed light and gay;
But I never saw a man who looked
  So wistfully at the day.

I never saw a man who looked
  With such a wistful eye
Upon that little tent of blue
  Which prisoners call the sky,
And at every drifting cloud that went
  With sails of silver by.

There was an old man of Dumbree,
Who taught little owls to drink tea;
  For he said, "To eat mice,
  Is not proper or nice,"
That amiable man of Dumbree.

Explore the skills

Read the following poem by William Shakespeare.

Sonnet 17

Who will believe my verse in time to come,
If it were fill'd with your most high deserts?
Though yet, heaven knows, it is but as a tomb
Which hides your life, and shows not half your parts.
If I could write the beauty of your eyes
And in fresh numbers number all your graces,
The age to come would say 'This poet lies;
Such heavenly touches ne'er touch'd earthly faces'.
So should my papers, yellowed with their age,
Be scorn'd, like old men of less truth than tongue;
And your true rights be term'd a poet's rage,
And stretched metre of an antique song.
But were some child of yours alive that time,
You should live twice – in it, and in my rhyme.

William Shakespeare

3 **a** The poet says that future generations will not believe his poem's description of how amazing his true love is. Pick out all the ways he says his readers will respond.

b Now look at the last two lines of the poem. How does the poet think he could offer proof that his love is so beautiful?

4 Now look at the form of this poem.

a How many lines does it have?

b How many beats and how many syllables can you count in each line?

c Does it rhyme? Can you describe the pattern of the rhyme?

d What do you notice about the last two lines? How are they different to the rest of the poem?

This poem is a sonnet. A Shakespearean sonnet is made up of 14 lines of **iambic pentameter** with a strict rhyme scheme ABAB, CDCD, EFEF, GG. The sonnet form is very tight and organised. It is used to explore big abstract concepts like love.

/Who **will** /be**lieve** /my **verse** /in **time** /to **come**,
/If **it** /were **fill'd** /with **your** /most **high** /de**serts**?

Key term

iambic pentameter: line of poetry with ten syllables, five stressed and five unstressed, creating five 'di dums' or heartbeats (iambs)

Develop the skills

In the following modern poem, Carol Ann Duffy takes the voice of Shakespeare's wife, Anne Hathaway.

Anne Hathaway

*'Item I gyve unto my wife my **second best bed**...'*
(from Shakespeare's will)

The bed we loved in was a spinning world
of forests, castles, torchlight, clifftops, seas
where we would dive for pearls. My lover's words
were shooting stars which fell to earth as kisses
on these lips; my body now a softer rhyme
to his, now echo, assonance; his touch
a verb dancing in the centre of a noun.
Some nights, I dreamed he'd written me, the bed
a page beneath his writer's hands. Romance
and drama played by touch, by scent, by taste.
In the other bed, the best, our guests dozed on,
dribbling their prose. My living laughing love –
I hold him in the casket of my widow's head
as he held me upon that next best bed.

Carol Ann Duffy

Glossary

second best bed: in Elizabethan England, the 'best bed' in the house was the one reserved for guests; the 'second best bed' would be the marital bed, shared by the husband and wife

5 Read the poem a few times. What is this actually about? Who is Anne Hathaway talking about in this poem?

Look at this line from the poem:

'Some nights, I dreamed he'd written me, the bed'

If you mark out the syllables, it looks like this:

'Some **nights/**, I **dreamed** / he'd **wri**/tten **me/**, the **bed**'

Look back at the definition of a sonnet. Does 'Anne Hathaway' conform to all the rules of a sonnet? Which of the following does it have?

- fourteen lines
- a rhythm of iambic pentameter in each line
- an ABAB, CDCD, EFEF, GG rhyme scheme
- a clear structure of three four-line stanzas and one final rhyming **couplet**

Key term

couplet: pair of lines that rhyme

So, why is this interesting? Well, the answer is that once you have noticed *what* Duffy is doing with the structure in this poem, you can start to think about *why* she has done it... or what you can make it *mean*.

6 Why do you think Duffy uses a sonnet form? What might she want the reader to infer about the relationship between Anne Hathaway and her husband?

When you are writing about structure / form, it is really important to focus on the effect being created by a technique rather than just to identify what the technique is.

7 What does Duffy want us to understand about Anne Hathaway's feelings in this poem? How might this be connected to her choices of form and structure? Make notes about:

- why Shakespeare's wife might choose to write a sonnet about her marriage to William Shakespeare
- why sometimes the rhyme scheme is very strong and sometimes it is weaker, and what that might suggest about Anne Hathaway, or about her feelings towards her husband
- the effect of the strong final rhyming **couplet**.

Apply the skills

8 Now you are ready to put all your ideas together into a piece of writing. Complete the following task.

Explore the ways Duffy uses structure and form to present ideas about a relationship in 'Anne Hathaway'.

Checklist for success

- Give a clear explanation of the poet's ideas.
- Use relevant supporting evidence about Duffy's choices of structure and form.
- Give a clear explanation of the effects of Duffy's choice of structural techniques or form.

Check your progress:

▲▲ I can analyse particular features of structure and form in detail, linking them precisely to the overall effect being created and use technical vocabulary as a precise shorthand to explain effects.

▲ I can explain some features of structure and form, and make clear links to the effects being created. I can make accurate use of technical vocabulary.

▲ I can identify at least one structural feature and comment on the effect it creates.

Apply your skills to English Language and English Literature tasks

Learning objectives
You will learn to
- apply the key skills from this chapter to two unseen English Language tasks
- apply the key skills from this chapter to one English Literature task
- reflect on your progress through looking at different responses to all three tasks.

Assessment objectives
- English Language AO2
- English Literature AO2

Responding to an English Language task about language

1 This extract is the prologue (introductory chapter) of a novel. As you read it, think about the following questions.

- What is this extract about?
- What are we learning about the boy?
- How has the writer used language and structure to communicate ideas to the reader?

The wide avenue with its big white-washed houses set well back in their own lush gardens was an insult. The plush white Lexus was an insult. Shadow knelt by the car's fuel tank, the perspiration glistening on his brow and arms. Like rain on dark glass, a drop of sweat ran down his left cheek, over his short muscular neck and into the cotton of his worn T-shirt. For a fifteen-year-old boy, Shadow was built big and solid. At his side were the tools of his trade: a rag, a can of gasoline. In his pocket was the means to a magical end: a box of matches.

[...]

Shadow drank the smell from the gas tank. Sheer bliss. The smell alone could transport him to paradise. Quickly, he stuffed the rag into the wound in the side of the car, letting a few inches hang out like a wick. To make sure there was enough food for the fire, Shadow splashed gasoline over the cloth and down the side of the car. Slowly, working his way backwards, away from the Lexus, he laid a trail of gasoline. In the warmth of the night, the fuel evaporated and filled the air with its sweet hungry smell. Twenty metres from the car, the shiny liquid fuse leading to the Lexus, Shadow stopped.

He was eager to see the greedy flames and yet he wanted to linger, to savour the moment that was about to make him important once more. He called it Shadowtime. His fingers gripped that little box, slowly extracted a match. Such a tiny thing, like an exclamation mark. One simple strike, a quick twist of the wrist, and the cleansing began with a graceful yellow plume like a candle in a church. Shadow's spine tingled, his heartbeat raced. He was about to see the most beautiful show on Earth. He dropped the lighted match and the eager fuel reached up and embraced Shadow's gift of life.

The seductive flame danced silently, slickly down the road towards the white car. The itchy yellow fingers clawed up the side of the Lexus, blistering the paint, and loitered for a few seconds on the wick before worming their way into the interior.

[…]

Fluttering yellow birds flew out into the darkness and sucked the oxygen from the night air. Some of the flames flashed beneath the Lexus and baked the car as if it were on a gas cooker. After a delicious delay, the windows blew out and the vehicle leapt a metre off the road in an exquisite explosion, engulfed by a fiery yellow sheath as if it were being carried to heaven by a host of shining angels. The flame shot upwards into the night, pushing aside the darkness, illuminating the sky.

The shock wave rushed past Shadow, pushing him backwards and roaring in his ears. A split-second later, Shadow felt an extra ripple of unnatural heat wafting over him, sensing it most on his bare skin. He did not even blink. This is what he lived for. Forget school. This was what life was all about.

Only when he detected movement in the street was it time to retreat. At first, Shadow jogged backwards so that he could keep an eye on the still burning wreck, so he could keep the image on his retina for as long as possible. In the coming days he would replay it many times – until he ached for a different image. But the next one would also be that magnificent combination of yellow and black. Street-lamps at night, gold on skin, flame scavenging among charred ruins. For now, he could see it whenever he looked. The flickering flower was reflected in every window of every house and every parked car. It was like a dream that the whole world was on fire. Paradise.

Malcolm Rose, from *Bloodline*

Your task

Look in detail at this part of the extract.

He was eager to see the greedy flames and yet he wanted to linger, to savour the moment that was about to make him important once more. He called it Shadowtime. His fingers gripped that little box, slowly extracted a match. Such a tiny thing, like an exclamation mark. One simple strike, a quick twist of the wrist, and the cleansing began with a graceful yellow plume like a candle in a church. Shadow's spine tingled, his heartbeat raced. He was about to see the most beautiful show on Earth. He dropped the lighted match and the eager fuel reached up and embraced Shadow's gift of life.

The seductive flame danced silently, slickly down the road towards the white car. The itchy yellow fingers clawed up the side of the Lexus, blistering the paint, and loitered for a few seconds on the wick before worming their way into the interior.

How does the writer's use of language create a picture of the boy's excitement?

Checklist for success

A successful response should include:

- reference to particular words and phrases
- comments on the effects of language features and techniques
- comments on the effects of sentences and punctuation.

Reflecting on your progress

 2 Read the following response to this task. As you read, think about what the student has done well and what advice they might need in order to make more progress.

Response 1

The writer uses language to show that the boy is excited in this extract. It is clear that the boy is excited because it says that he was 'eager'. This suggests that he is excited to see the fire starting. It also uses the word 'savour'. This suggests that he is really looking forward to this moment and wants to take his time over it, as if it is something he has been building up to.

The writer describes him as being excited because it says that 'his spine tingled and his heartbeat raced'. This also suggests that he is excited.

The writer uses lots of imagery to suggest that the boy is excited. The fire is described as if it is alive. This creates the idea that the boy thinks it is beautiful. He describes it as 'graceful' and that it 'danced' as if the flame is a living thing. He also says it is 'the most beautiful show on earth' which also suggests that it is something he has been really looking forward to and is excited to see.

The writer uses short sentences and commas to create the effect of the boy being excited – 'Shadow's spine tingled, his heartbeat raced'. This creates the effect of the boy being excited because it is as if there isn't time to say any more, he keeps it short and simple.

an example and simple comment on the effect of a language choice

clear explanation of the effect on the reader of the choice of language

another example and simple comment on effect

simple comment on the effect of a language technique

clear examples to support the comment

a better explanation of the effects of the language, but not really linked to the technique

simple, clear comment on the effect of short sentences

Comments on Response 1

This response focuses on the task and gives several clear examples of language being used for effect. The explanations are clear but rather undeveloped. The student has identified a technique by saying 'the flame is described as a living thing' but not said what the technique is or really explained what the effect of this technique is.

3 How could this sample response be improved? Using the middle rung of the Check your progress ladder at the end of this chapter, think about what advice you might give to this student in order to improve their work.

4 Now read Response 2. As you read, think about what the student has done that is an improvement on Response 1, and what advice this student might need in order to make even more progress.

Response 2

The boy's excitement to set the car on fire is shown at the start of the extract with the contrast between 'eager' and 'linger' – as if the boy is desperate to start the fire but also wants to slow down and take his time. This is intensified with the word 'savour', which reinforces the idea that he has looked forward to this moment and wants to take his time over it in order to get the maximum amount of excitement from it. This creates a sense of anticipation. His physical excitement is shown in 'his spine tingled and his heartbeat raced', as if his body is reacting to the anticipation as well as his mind.

The writer uses personification throughout the extract to compare the flames to a living thing; 'itchy yellow fingers', 'danced' and 'eager'. Perhaps this suggests that the idea of the fire is a companion to the boy – it is something alive, something he can relate to. The comparison to 'a candle in a church' creates the idea of worship, as if the flame is something that the boy values so highly that it should be in a holy place like a church. The reference to 'the most beautiful show on earth' reminds the reader that the central character is only young – this phrase is used to describe a circus, so this creates the impression that for the boy, setting fire to things gives him the same feeling of excitement that a young child would have if they were going to the circus.

Sentencing and punctuation are also used to increase the pace and suggest the boy is excited. 'Shadow's spine tingled, his heartbeat raced', is short and purposeful, as if the description of the boy is not as important as the description of the flames, which are described in longer more complex sentences.

really clear explanation of how language has been used to create the sense of excitement

developing the explanation with another example

very clear comment on the effect of the language choices

understanding of the effect of the language technique, clearly explained

thoughtful idea about the use of imagery

really interesting interpretation of the effect of this image, clearly linked to a detailed understanding of the ideas in the extract

another very interesting interpretation of the effect of sentence structure on meanings and ideas

Comments on Response 2

This is a really thoughtful and detailed response to the task, with lots of relevant examples used to examine the ways language has been used to create a picture of the boy's excitement. Several of the points have been developed in detail and it is clear that the student has a sound understanding of the ideas in the extract and is linking them to the ways in which the writer has used language to communicate them.

5 How might this response be improved even further? Using the top rung of the Check your progress ladder at the end of this chapter, decide what feedback and advice you might give to this student.

Responding to an English Language task about structure

6 Now look at this practice task and think about how you would approach it.

Your task

You now need to think about the whole extract and the ways the writer has shaped and structured their writing.

This extract is from the opening to a novel. How has the writer used structure within the extract to interest the reader?

Checklist for success

You could write about:

* what the writer focuses your attention on at the very start
* what else the writer draws your attention to as the extract develops
* any other structural features that interest you as a reader.

Reflecting on your progress

 7 Read the following response to this task. As you read, think about what the student has done well and what advice they might need in order to make more progress.

Response 1

> The first paragraph of the extract sets the scene for the reader, and shows us where the story is set. The writer does this so that the reader can picture where we are. The first paragraph also describes the boy and what he is doing. This adds the effect of drawing the reader in and making us wonder what the boy is doing and why he is there.
>
> As the extract develops, the writer describes the boy and what he is doing in more detail, rather than the place. This shows the reader that the boy is the focus of the story and he is the one we should be interested in. He 'stuffed the rag' and 'splashed gasoline'. The writer focuses the attention of the reader on what the boy is doing to suggest that setting the car on fire is going to be very important later on in the story.
>
> The writer ends the extract with the boy moving away from the fire and thinking about it. It also shows that this is going to be important later because it says that 'in the coming days' which suggests that this is the start of the story rather than the end. It also says 'the next one' which gives a hint that this is going to happen again.

— clear focus on the task and appropriate comment on the start of the extract

— clear explanation of how the structure is communicating meaning to the reader

— relevant use of embedded evidence

— explanation of effects of the use of structure on the reader

— moving towards the end of the extract; good focus on the task still

— another purposeful use of embedded evidence with a clear explanation of effect on meaning

Comments on Response 1

This is a clear and well-explained response to the task, with a good focus on the ways the extract starts, develops and ends. Examples are relevant and are used to clearly illustrate the points being made. There is a definite focus on the effect of structure on the reader, and on the meanings.

8 How could this sample response be improved? Using the middle rung of the Check your progress ladder at the end of this chapter, think about what advice you might give to this student in order to improve their work.

9 Now read Response 2. As you read, think about what the student has done that is an improvement on Response 1, and what advice this student might need in order to make even more progress.

Response 2

The first paragraph of the extract sets the scene for the reader, describing 'big' houses and 'lush' gardens, as if the story is set in an expensive, rich environment. However, the writer says that these things were an 'insult', which makes the reader wonder straight away who they are insulting and why. The writer then introduces the boy by describing where he is and what he is doing, but not explaining why; he has 'gasoline' and 'matches' which creates tension straight way, but without any more information to go on. Again, this sets up questions in the mind of the reader.

As the extract develops, the writer focuses more on the boy and the act of setting the car on fire. There are lots of descriptions of his actions and reactions; he 'drank the smell' and 'was eager to see', suggests that he is the central character of the story and his reactions are going to be important to the rest of the story.

The short sentences are used to add even more emphasis to the boy's reactions; 'He did not even blink. This is what he lived for. Forget school. This was what life was all about.' The effect of these four simple sentences together reinforces the idea that the fire is the most important thing in the boy's life.

The writer indicates, towards the end of the extract, that this is just the beginning of the story, and that the boy and lighting fires are going to be central to the plot.

It refers to the 'coming days' and 'the next one', suggesting that this is just an introduction, giving some kind of close explanation of the effect of lighting fires on this boy. Perhaps the writer wants to introduce the feelings of the boy straight away, showing his perspective and reactions, either because the reader needs to understand this from his point of view or perhaps because he is going to be the central character. The

a clear focus on the start of the extract, using detail to support the explanation of the effect

another clear explanation with well-chosen evidence

good explanation of how the structure guides the reader and suggests ideas

this is a lovely comment on internal structure, explaining the effect of the sentences on the reader

close focus on how structure links to overall purpose and ideas

starting to really examine and consider writer's use of structure here writer makes the reader look forward into the future with 'until he ached for a different image', suggesting that there are more situations like this to come in the rest of the book. The single word sentence 'Paradise.' reinforces the idea that this is what the boy lives for.

— develops the focus on writer's purpose and intention

Comments on Response 2

This is a very confident response with a clear focus on the ways the writer has used structure to have a deliberate effect on how the extract will be read. There are lots of relevant examples used to illustrate the points being made, and the student has started to consider the effects of structure with some lovely thoughtful comments on possible meanings.

10 How might this response be improved even further? Using the top rung of the Check your progress ladder at the end of this chapter, decide what feedback and advice you might give to this student.

Responding to an English Literature task

1 Read the poem, 'First Love'. As you read, think about the following questions:

- What is this poem about?
- What ideas and feelings do you think the writer is communicating?
- What do you notice about the ways language and structure have been used to communicate these ideas and feelings to the reader?

2 Now look at this practice task and think about how you would approach it.

Your task

How does the writer present ideas about love in 'First Love'?

First Love

I ne'er was struck before that hour
    With love so sudden and so sweet,
Her face it bloomed like a sweet flower
    And stole my heart away complete.
My face turned pale as deadly pale,
    My legs refused to walk away,
And when she looked, what could I ail?
    My life and all seemed turned to clay.

And then my blood rushed to my face
    And took my eyesight quite away,
The trees and bushes round the place
    Seemed midnight at noonday.
I could not see a single thing,
    Words from my eyes did start—
They spoke as chords do from the string,
    And blood burnt round my heart.

Are flowers the winter's choice?
    Is love's bed always snow?
She seemed to hear my silent voice,
    Not love's appeals to know.
I never saw so sweet a face
    As that I stood before.
My heart has left its dwelling-place
    And can return no more.

John Clare

Checklist for success

A successful response should:

- demonstrate your understanding of the ideas and feelings in the poem
- include some well-selected evidence to support your points
- analyse the effects of particular words, techniques and structural features, linking them to the ideas and feelings in the poem.

Reflecting on your progress

3 Read the following section of a response to this task. As you read, think about what the student has done well and what advice they might need in order to make more progress.

Response 1

This poem is written about a falling in love with someone for the first time. The speaker in the poem seems to be completely in love with the girl he is describing.

The writer uses nature imagery to make it seem that this is the first time he has fallen in love because it makes it sound innocent. He uses words like 'sweet' and 'flower' to make it seem like it is a natural thing to fall in love.

shows awareness of the ideas in the poem

use of relevant quotation with simple explanation of the effect being created

The repetition of 'sweet' and the alliteration of 'sudden and so sweet' emphasise the idea that this is a shock for him. He also links these words with alliteration with the word 'struck' in the first line.

As the poem goes on, it starts to sound darker and more dangerous.

In the second verse, he uses the word 'blood' which is associated with danger. It is as if he is aware that falling in love can be hurtful if the other person doesn't feel the same. He then talks about his 'heart' which is linked with the word 'blood' at the end of the poem. He says that his 'heart has left its dwelling place' as if nothing can ever be the same again. The last line also shows that his life has changed for ever now he has fallen in love, 'can return no more'.

— correct use of literary terms with example and simple comment on effect created

— correct identification of a conscious decision made by the writer

— use of relevant quotation with simple explanation of what it might mean

— clear focus on the meanings and ideas in the poem with a further clear use of direct quotation to support the point being made

Comments on Response 1

The examples are well chosen and explained, although the explanations could have been more developed. The comments on the 'nature imagery' are relevant, with appropriate examples from the poem. These comments could have been more developed, by linking them to the ideas and feelings in the poem. By the end of the response, there is a sense that the student is aware of the main ideas in the poem, but again, they don't offer an interpretation that is particularly developed or clearly explained.

4 How could this sample response be improved? Using the middle rung of the Check your progress ladder at the end of this chapter, think about what advice you might give to this student in order to improve their work.

5 Now read Response 2. As you read, think about what the student has done that is an improvement on Response 1, and what advice this student might need in order to make even more progress.

Response 2

The speaker in this poem seems to be very deeply affected by falling in love for the first time. The use of first person makes the poem seem very personal and honest, as if the speaker is

— clear explanation of ideas and feelings with a clear response to the effects of a technique

pouring his heart out on the page. The first verse uses a mixture of positive and dangerous language to suggest how confused and overwhelmed the speaker is: the repetition of 'sweet' and the imagery of 'bloomed like a sweet flower' contrast with images of danger suggested by 'struck', 'sudden' and 'deadly'.

correct use of literary term with relevant references to the poem

'My life and all seemed turned to clay' could suggest that the speaker feels unformed, as if he could be moulded into a new person by this experience. However, it could also suggest ideas about death, as the idea of 'clay' links to the idea of being dead and buried.

use of relevant quotation with some developed explanation of the possible effects being created

This idea of danger is developed with references to 'blood', 'burnt' and 'heart' in the second stanza. On the one hand, it is as if the speaker has come alive for the first time and the blood is rushing around his body. However, there are also clear connotations of danger with the alliteration and repetition of 'blood' and 'burnt', reinforcing the idea that this situation is potentially dangerous for him.

develops the explanation of the effect of imagery with another relevant example clearly linked to ideas

The use of questions in the third stanza could imply that the speaker feels unsure of everything, as if his experience has made him question everything he thought he knew about the world. However, they could also suggest him demanding to know the answers, as if he is interrogating life. 'Is love's bed always snow?' suggests that he feels that love can be cold, perhaps linked to the idea of death or just fear that his love will not be returned to him.

focus on the effect of a particular technique with good interpretation of effect

details used to support the explanation of the metaphor

Comments on Response 2

There is a very clear understanding of the point of the poem, with well-chosen evidence throughout. There is a clear focus on the ideas and feelings and how these have been communicated to the reader in a range of ways.

The response focuses on the ways the poem has been written from the start, with a good explanation of the use of address. There are some clear explanations of the effect of particular language choices and imagery, and the evidence has been quite skilfully embedded into the response. Overall, this candidate seems to be clear and confident about their understanding of the poem, and is also trying out ways of offering alternative interpretations and meanings.

Check your progress

- I can interpret writers' viewpoints and ideas.
- I can make careful, precise selections of words and phrases to support my interpretations of viewpoints and ideas.
- I can interpret subtle implications writers are making through their use of particular details.
- I can explain and comment in detail on how language techniques are used to communicate ideas to the reader.
- I can comment in detail on writers' use of structural features, linking these precisely to the overall effect being created.
- I can use technical vocabulary as a precise shorthand to explain effects.

- I can clearly explain writers' viewpoints and ideas.
- I can choose useful and appropriate examples from the text to support my explanations of viewpoints and ideas.
- I can infer meanings from details in texts and use some relevant examples to support my interpretations.
- I can clearly explain how language techniques are used to communicate ideas to the reader.
- I can clearly explain the effects created by the writer through the use of particular structural features.
- I can use appropriate technical vocabulary to describe language techniques or structure to support my explanations.

- I can identify writers' viewpoints and ideas.
- I can make clear references to some relevant details from the text to support the points I make.
- I can comment on the effects of particular words and phrases and how they have been used to present a particular idea or viewpoint.
- I can identify some of the language techniques that writers use and begin to explain what the effects of these might be.
- I can identify some of the structural features writers use and begin to explain what the effects of these might be.
- I can make relevant reference to some techniques used by writers.

Chapter 5

Working with context

What's it all about?

In this chapter, you will learn about what context means and how different types of context can be used to help understand and analyse a range of texts for English Literature. Context should never be seen as separate from a writer's language, ideas or techniques, but as an integral part of all three.

In this chapter, you will learn how to

- understand and define context
- relate themes and language to context
- relate context to language
- explore setting as context
- explore the same context from different perspectives
- apply your skills to an English Literature task.

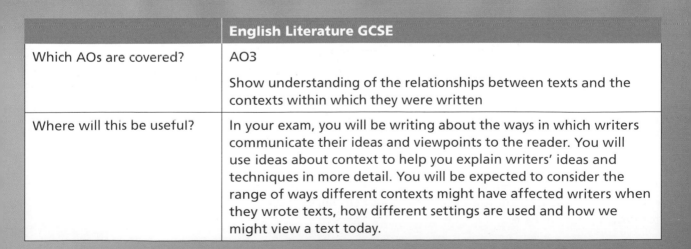

	English Literature GCSE
Which AOs are covered?	AO3 Show understanding of the relationships between texts and the contexts within which they were written
Where will this be useful?	In your exam, you will be writing about the ways in which writers communicate their ideas and viewpoints to the reader. You will use ideas about context to help you explain writers' ideas and techniques in more detail. You will be expected to consider the range of ways different contexts might have affected writers when they wrote texts, how different settings are used and how we might view a text today.

Understand and define context

Learning objectives
You will learn how to
- define what context can mean
- understand how thinking about context can deepen understanding of ideas in a text.

Assessment objective
- English Literature AO3

What is context and how can it help you to understand literary texts?

Getting you thinking

1 Look at these statements and decide which one you agree with most.

A You cannot understand what a text means unless you know exactly what the writer meant when they wrote it.

B It doesn't matter at all what the writer meant when they wrote a text; all that matters is what I think about it when I read it.

C It sometimes helps to know about a writer's ideas and viewpoints. It can also help to know something about what was happening when the text was written. Having said this, our own experiences and ideas will mean that every reader will have a slightly different interpretation of a text. A great work of literature will be valuable at any time because its ideas remain relevant.

Think about some stories you know already:
- Cinderella
- The Boy who Cried Wolf
- The Hare and the Tortoise
- Little Red Riding Hood.

These stories are **allegories**: they are designed to teach children moral lessons about the world in a non-threatening way.

2 What lessons might these four stories teach children?

Key term

allegories: stories which can be interpreted to have a hidden meaning, usually moral or political

Explore the skills

The subtitle of *Animal Farm* by George Orwell is 'A Fairy Story'. *Animal Farm* has remained extremely popular across the world for over 70 years. We also know a great deal about Orwell's reasons for writing *Animal Farm*.

3 Read the following summary of *Animal Farm* and decide what moral lessons might come from the story.

Manor Farm is run by a cruel drunken farmer called Mr Jones. One day the animals, encouraged by the teachings of Old Major (a very clever pig), attack Mr Jones and chase him from the farm. The animals rename the farm Animal Farm and set up Seven Commandments to live by, the most important of which is 'All animals are equal'. Things start well and the animals enjoy their new freedom and equality. However, the pigs, the cleverest animals, become more and more powerful and discover that they enjoy being in power and that they enjoy the luxuries of living like a human. Led by Napoleon, the pigs take control of Animal Farm and use the other animals to make their lives easier. Napoleon uses the vicious dogs he has trained to chase his rival, Snowball, from the farm. In the end, the pigs end up living in the farmhouse like humans while the other animals work harder and harder for less and less food until they are worse off than they were under Mr Jones. The Seven Commandments are replaced with one: 'All animals are equal but some animals are more equal than others'.

Develop the skills

4 Now look at this summary of twentieth-century events. What similarities can you find between Orwell's story and real-life events?

In 1917, Russia was governed by an extremely wealthy Tsar and his family. Most Russians were very poor and had few rights. The Bolsheviks (a Communist party inspired by the ideas of Karl Marx) took over Russia. They changed the name of Russia to the USSR (Union of Soviet Socialist Republics) and Lenin became the first leader. The USSR became a fairer and more equal country at first. Lenin died in 1924 and Stalin became the undisputed ruler of the USSR by ruthlessly removing any opposition. Stalin's rival Trotsky fled in fear of Stalin's secret police. Important members of the Communist Party led privileged lives while many ordinary Russians were as poor or poorer than they had been under the Tsar's rule. Stalin is believed to be personally responsible for the deaths of 22 million Russians, making him the most effective mass murderer of all time.

Apply the skills

It is important to remember that you are studying English Literature, not History. Begin with the text and think about how a writer explores ideas through the ways they tell the story.

In the preface of the 1947 edition of *Animal Farm*, Orwell said:

> I do not wish to comment on the work (Animal Farm);
> if it does not speak for itself, it is a failure.

Now read this extract from the novel.

At this there was a terrible baying outside, and nine enormous dogs wearing brass-studded collars came bounding into the barn. They dashed straight for Snowball, who only sprang from his place just in time to escape their snapping jaws. In a moment he was out of the door and they were after him. Too amazed and frightened to speak, all the animals crowded through the door to watch the chase. Snowball was racing across the long pasture that led to the road. He was running as only a pig can run, but the dogs were close on his heels. Suddenly he slipped and it seemed certain that they had him. Then he was up again, running faster than ever, then the dogs were gaining on him again. One of them all but closed his jaws on Snowball's tail, but Snowball whisked it free just in time. Then he put on an extra spurt and, with a few inches to spare, slipped through a hole in the hedge and was seen no more.

Silent and terrified, the animals crept back into the barn. In a moment the dogs came bounding back. At first no one had been able to imagine where these creatures came from, but the problem was soon solved: they were the puppies whom Napoleon has taken away from their mothers and reared privately. Though not yet full-grown, they were huge dogs, and as fierce-looking as wolves.

They kept close to Napoleon. It was noticed that they wagged their tails to him in the same way as the other dogs had been used to do to Mr Jones.

Napoleon, with the dogs following him, now mounted on to the raised portion of the floor where Major had previously stood to deliver his speech. He announced that from now on the Sunday morning Meetings would come to an end. They were unnecessary, he said, and wasted time. In future all questions relating to the working of the farm would be settled by a special committee of pigs, presided over by himself. These would meet in private and afterwards communicate their decisions to the others.

George Orwell, from *Animal Farm*

5 Read the task and then use the Checklist for success to help you write a response.

How does Orwell use this extract to warn about the power of Napoleon and other dictators like him?

Aim to write 200–250 words.

Checklist for success

Think about:

* why Napoleon would want to chase Snowball, the bravest and cleverest pig, from Animal Farm
* the importance of the dogs and what they might represent in the wider world
* why Napoleon chooses this moment to end the 'Sunday morning Meetings'
* the effect of the events on the other animals
* how Orwell is suggesting that Napoleon is becoming like Mr Jones.

Check your progress:

I can link the story closely to contextual ideas.

I can explain how contextual ideas influenced the story.

I can explain contextual ideas and give one or two examples from the story.

Relate themes and language to context

Learning objectives
You will learn how to
- understand how Shakespeare presents a key theme in Macbeth
- be able to explain themes, ideas and language by referring to context.

Assessment objectives
- English Literature AO2, AO3

How can understanding ideas and attitudes from the time in which a text was written help us to understand the story and its themes?

Getting you thinking

In today's society, it is usually seen as a good thing to be ambitious. You go to school to get good qualifications and try to achieve as highly as possible so you can do what you want when you leave school. Parents want children to have a better life than they did. Having said this, we still understand ideas of class and status; they are all around us.

1 Try putting the following occupations into a hierarchy or order:

- Doctor
- Police officer
- Managing director
- Shop assistant
- Teacher
- Premier league footballer
- Pop singer
- Nurse
- Film actor
- Refuse collector
- Taxi driver

How did you decide?

King

The most important position in the hierarchy was the king or queen. In Shakespeare's time, many people believed in the divine right of kings: that the king or queen got their power straight from God and therefore had to be obeyed in all matters.

Serf

If you were a boy and your father was a ploughman, you were almost certainly going to be a ploughman; you were not expected to try to be anything different.

Explore the skills

In Shakespeare's time, many people believed in a strict hierarchy or order. Everybody and everything had a position in this hierarchy and, by and large, people stayed in their position.

2 What advantages or disadvantages can you see in this system compared to today's society?

In the play *Macbeth*, Shakespeare tells the story of a brave and ambitious Scottish soldier called Macbeth. Tempted by witches and spurred on by his wife, Macbeth murders the noble King Duncan and becomes king himself. However, nothing goes right for Macbeth after that. He sees threats to his power everywhere and murders anyone he suspects. He becomes a tyrant and, eventually, the people of Scotland turn against him. Macbeth is killed in a battle and Malcolm, Duncan's eldest son and the rightful king, is restored to the throne.

People in Shakespeare's time also believed that things like storms, plagues, poor harvests and earthquakes could be punishments for sinful and wicked human acts. Shakespeare showed this to the audience in many different ways.

Look at this extract from Act 2 Scene 3 where Lennox describes the night of Duncan's murder.

> **LENNOX** The night has been unruly. Where we lay,
> Our chimneys were blown down; and, as they say, 60
> Lamentings heard i' th' air, strange screams of death,
> And prophesying, with accents terrible,
> Of dire combustion and confus'd events
> New hatch'd to th' woeful time; the **obscure bird**
> Clamour'd the livelong night. Some say, the earth
> Was feverous and did shake.
>
> William Shakespeare, from *Macbeth*, Act 2 Scene 3

Lennox does not yet know about Duncan's death. He clearly thinks something bad is about to happen though.

3 What events does Lennox describe?

4 Which words and phrases add to the idea that the events are extreme and unnatural?

5 Do any words or phrases suggest a link between the 'unruly' night and the human world? Which ones?

Glossary

obscure bird: an owl – owls were linked with death in Shakespeare's time

Develop the skills

In the following scene, Ross discusses events of the same night. Here, Ross and the old man know about the murder of King Duncan and the events they describe are even more strange and unnatural.

ACT II SCENE IV   *Outside Macbeth's castle.*

[Enter ROSS and an old Man]

Old Man	Threescore and ten I can remember well;	
	Within the volume of which time I have seen	
	Hours dreadful and things strange; but this sore night	
	Hath trifled former knowings.	
ROSS	Ah, good father,	5
	Thou seest, the heavens, as troubled with man's act,	
	Threaten his bloody stage. By th' clock, 'tis day,	
	And yet dark night strangles the travelling lamp.	
	Is't night's predominance, or the day's shame,	
	That darkness does the face of earth entomb,	10
	When living light should kiss it?	
Old Man	'Tis unnatural,	
	Even like the deed that's done. On Tuesday last,	
	A falcon, tow'ring in her pride of place,	
	Was by a mousing owl hawk'd at and kill'd.	15
ROSS	And Duncan's horses– a thing most strange and certain –	
	Beauteous and swift, the minions of their race,	
	Turn'd wild in nature, broke their stalls, flung out,	
	Contending 'gainst obedience, as they would make	
	War with mankind.	20
Old Man	'Tis said they eat each other.	
ROSS	They did so, to the amazement of mine eyes	
	That look'd upon't.	

---

6   Make a list of any unnatural events the characters describe.

7   Ross says that the 'heavens' are 'troubled with man's act'. What do you think he is suggesting?

Apply the skills

8   Now read the following task.

> How does Shakespeare use events in the natural world to highlight the importance of a king's death?

9   Look at this student's answer and the accompanying notes. Write a sentence explaining why this is a good response.

Shakespeare shows that the murder of a king is extremely serious by describing massive disturbances to the natural world. Lennox describes an 'unruly night' where 'chimneys were blown down'. The word 'unruly' suggests that the natural world is out of control and actually attacking people. This is backed up by the old man who says 'this sore night hath trifled former knowings'. The fact that two different characters agree with each other makes Shakespeare's message more powerful. Also, Shakespeare emphasises how bad the storm was by making an old man say that he has never seen a worse night so it must be the worst storm for a very long time. The word 'unruly' suggests that the night is out of control and the word 'sore' suggests that the night has caused pain and suffering. The audience in Shakespeare's time would infer that these events were caused by Macbeth's unnatural killing of a king and would maybe also infer that his time as king will be painful for everyone.

— clear topic sentence shows understanding of question

— embedded quotation shows clear understanding of language

— connective helps to develop the point in more detail

— clear comment on effects of language

— paragraph ends by developing the point with information about context

10 Now have a go at answering the task. Use the paragraph above as a model and refer back to your notes to help you. This time, try to choose your own evidence.

Checklist for success

- Begin with a sentence which gives a clear overview of what you are going to say.
- Embed short quotations in your answer.
- Comment on the effects of language choices.
- Develop your comments with some of the information about context you have learned.
- Use both extracts to help you answer.

Check your progress:

- I can use context to help me examine ideas and language choices in detail.

- I can explain ideas and language choices clearly and make links to context.

- I can write about some ideas and back them up with evidence. I can show that I understand something about context.

Relate context to language

Learning objectives
You will learn how to
- identify and analyse aspects of language
- develop your analysis of language using contextual factors.

Assessment objectives
- English Literature AO2, AO3

How do the ideas of the time affect the language of the text?

Getting you thinking

Imagine hearing this news report:

...The alien spacecraft hovering over the English Channel has begun communications with the human race. What they have revealed is staggering and has shaken all humanity to the core. The aliens created life on earth 10,000 years ago as an experiment. They planted fossils and other clues to see how intelligent their creations were. Life on Earth has been a very popular entertainment programme on their planet...

1 How would you feel if you heard this news? What beliefs about our life on earth would it change?

Many scientific discoveries were made in the 19th century which forced people to question beliefs they had held for a long time.

2 How might Darwin's ideas have affected people in the 19th century?

Charles Darwin published *The Origin of Species* in 1859. This book outlined the theory of evolution in a scientific way. Darwin argued that all life on earth had evolved over millions of years from the same primitive organisms. This upset many people because it went against their religious beliefs. Most people believed that God had created humans in his own image and that humans were different from other animals because they had a soul. This led to fear and distrust of science from some people who felt that humans were beginning to 'play God'.

Explore the skills

When writing about context, it is important to link your ideas to the text and the writer's language.

Dr Jekyll and Mr Hyde was published in 1886. In the following extract, Robert Louis Stevenson describes Mr Hyde, the evil alter ego of Dr Henry Jekyll. Jekyll has created a potion which transforms him into Mr Hyde and separates the good and evil sides of his personality.

Glossary

troglodytic: like a primitive cave-dweller

Dr. Fell: a type of person you dislike but can't think exactly why

clay continent: the body

Mr. Hyde was pale and dwarfish, he gave an impression of deformity without any nameable malformation, he had a displeasing smile, he had borne himself to the lawyer with a sort of murderous mixture of timidity and boldness, and he spoke with a husky, whispering and somewhat broken voice; all these were points against him, but not all of these together could explain the hitherto unknown disgust, loathing, and fear with which Mr. Utterson regarded him. 'There must be something else,' said the perplexed gentleman. 'There is something more, if I could find a name for it. God bless me, the man seems hardly human! Something **troglodytic**, shall we say? or can it be the old story of **Dr. Fell**? or is it the mere radiance of a foul soul that thus transpires through, and transfigures, its **clay continent**? The last, I think; for, O my poor old Harry Jekyll, if ever I read Satan's signature upon a face, it is on that of your new friend.'

Robert Louis Stevenson, from *Dr Jekyll and Mr Hyde*

3 What are your first impressions of Mr Hyde from this extract?

4 What words or phrases does Stevenson use to create this impression?

Develop the skills

Later in the novel, Stevenson describes the vicious and unprovoked murder of Sir Danvers Carew by Mr Hyde. It was witnessed by a maid watching from an upstairs window.

The table below contains some short quotations from the book describing how Mr Hyde carried out the murder.

5 Look closely at Stevenson's use of language in each quotation and make some notes in the table about how you might link them to ideas about context.

Quotation	Notes
And then all of a sudden he broke out in a great flame of anger	
stamping with his foot	
brandishing the cane	
clubbed him to the earth	The word 'clubbed' instantly makes us think about cavemen and perhaps how when Jekyll changes into Hyde, he is evolving backwards into a more primitive, irrational and violent form.
with ape-like fury	
he was trampling his victim under foot	
hailing down a storm of blows	The words 'hailing' and 'storm' are both powerful natural images of violence. Perhaps they show that Hyde's violence is inevitable and unstoppable, like the weather.
bones were audibly shattered	

Apply the skills

6 Now look at this student's writing. Choose two things this student has done well and use them as your writing targets.

> Stevenson makes Hyde sound extremely shocking and frightening. One way he does this is by making him

— clear opening sentence shows understanding

sound inhuman. Firstly Hyde is 'pale and dwarfish' which — well-chosen quotation with comment on language

suggests that he is like a fairy tale monster but unwell at the same time. — developing the idea

He is also 'troglodytic' which means like a caveman and Stevenson could be suggesting that he is evolving backwards because he is so evil. — idea about context

Stevenson could also be saying that science is dangerous and Jekyll was playing around with forces he did not really understand. — idea about context linked to writer's ideas

Also, Hyde does not shoot or stab Carew, he batters him to death with 'ape-like fury' and uses his 'heavy cane' — well-chosen evidence embedded in sentence

like a caveman might use a club. This might have made people feel uncomfortable at the time because they might have felt that this animal violence existed in them too.

Stevenson also uses religious ideas to show that Hyde is more dangerous than an animal. — idea about context

He links him to 'Satan' and says he has a 'foul soul' — quotations link religious idea to text

which makes him worse than an animal because he is doing things on purpose.

7 You are now going to answer the following task yourself.

How does Stevenson use language to portray Hyde? What might this tell us about attitudes and ideas at that time?

Use the extract, the quotations from the table and your notes to help you answer the questions.

Checklist for success

- Analyse the effects of language choices, using quotations and analysis vocabulary like 'implies' and 'suggests'.
- Develop your analysis by exploring how Stevenson portrays Hyde as a primitive, inhuman, animal-like creature.
- Refer to evidence from both the extract and the table.
- Write about how the extract and the quotations in the table might reflect ideas about evolution.
- Aim to write 200–250 words.

You could begin:

> *Stevenson portrays Hyde as a violent, inhuman, primitive creature...*

Check your progress:

⏶⏶ I can examine language choices in some detail and use ideas about context to help me develop my ideas.

⏶ I can clearly explain the effects of some language choices and sometimes link them to context.

⏶ I can pick out some interesting choices of language and explain what they might mean. I can refer to some ideas about context to help.

Explore setting as context

Learning objective
You will learn how to
- consider the effects of setting a work of literature in the past.

Assessment objective
- English Literature AO3

If you want to write a political play to change people's attitudes in the modern world, why set it in the past?

Getting you thinking

1 Find out when these events took place and make a timeline.

- World War 2 ends
- *Titanic* sinks on its maiden voyage
- The National Health Service is created in England and Wales
- World War 1 begins
- *An Inspector Calls* is first performed in Russia
- World War 1 ends
- World War 2 begins
- *An Inspector Calls* is first performed in the UK
- The first Labour Majority Government is elected in the UK with the aim of creating the Welfare State

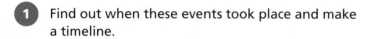

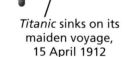

Titanic sinks on its maiden voyage, 15 April 1912

This timeline gives you some context to the play *An Inspector Calls*. In other words, it gives you some information about the world Priestley's audience was living in.

Explore the skills

Dramatic irony is a technique often used by playwrights. It is when the audience know something that the characters on the stage do not know.

You might know about dramatic irony from pantomimes.

Look at this extract from *An Inspector Calls*, a play first performed in 1945. Arthur Birling, who is a rich factory owner, gives his views on the state of the world in 1912. You are going to explore what Arthur says and work out how the writer, J.B. Priestley, uses dramatic irony.

I'm talking as a hard-headed, practical man of business. And I say there isn't a chance of war. The world's developing so fast that it'll make war impossible. Look at the progress we're making. In a year or two we'll have aeroplanes that will be able to go anywhere. And look at the way the automobile's making headway – bigger and faster all the time. And then ships. Why, a friend of mine went over this new liner last week – the Titanic – she sails next week – forty-six thousand eight hundred tons – forty-six thousand eight hundred tons – New York in five days – and every luxury – and unsinkable, absolutely unsinkable. That's what you've got to keep your eye on, facts like that, progress like that – and not a few German officers talking nonsense and a few scaremongers here making a fuss about nothing. Now you three young people, just listen to this – let's say, in 1940 – you may be giving a little party like this – your son or daughter might be getting engaged – and I tell you by that time you'll be living in a world that'll have forgotten all these Capital versus Labour agitations and all these silly little war scares. There'll be peace and prosperity and rapid progress everywhere – except of course in Russia, which will always be behindhand, naturally.

J.B. Priestley, from *An Inspector Calls*

2 Complete the table below.

Facts we know	Things Arthur says	Dramatic Irony
Aeroplanes were used in WW1 and WW2 to destroy cities and kill civilians.	'In a year or two we'll have aeroplanes that will be able to go anywhere.'	Arthur sees aeroplanes as a sign of progress. The audience might see this differently as over 40,000 British civilians were killed in the Blitz during WW2. So, maybe Priestley is saying that Capitalism just creates more efficient ways of killing innocent people.
Titanic sank on its maiden voyage.		
WW1 broke out two years later in 1914.		
In 1940, Britain was involved in WW2.		
The 1920s and 1930s were marked by strikes and conflict between trade unionists and capitalists, especially the General Strike in 1926.		
The Russian army entered Berlin in 1945 leading to the final defeat of Germany in WW2.		

3 How has Priestley used the historical setting of 1912 to discredit the views of Arthur Birling?

Develop the skills

In the play, Inspector Goole arrives at the Birlings' house to quiz the Birling family about the death of Eva Smith. Eva Smith was a young woman who used to work at the Birlings' factory. All the family were responsible in one way or another for Eva's death.

Now look at this extract. It is the last speech from Inspector Goole.

> But just remember this. One Eva Smith has gone – but there are millions and millions and millions of Eva Smiths and John Smiths still left with us, with their lives, their hopes and fears, their suffering, and chance of happiness, all intertwined with our lives, with what we think and say and do. We don't live alone. We are members of one body. We are responsible for each other. And I tell you that the time will soon come when, if men will not learn that lesson, then they will be taught it in fire and blood and anguish. Good night.

Glossary

capitalist: a person who owns a large business and employs a workforce

socialist: someone who believes in a more equal society, and wants to improve the lives of the poorest people and who values the community over the individual

4 What are the Inspector's views about how people should be treated? Do you think he is a **capitalist** like Birling or a **socialist**?

5 What might the Inspector be referring to when he says 'fire and blood and anguish'? What happened between 1912 and 1945?

Apply the skills

6 Read the following task.

How does Priestley use a historical setting to explore ideas about how people should behave towards one another?

First, look at this student's answer.

Priestley sets the play in 1912 which allows him to use dramatic irony. He can then use real historical events to show whether characters are right or wrong in what they say. — opening two sentences give a clear overview and show clear understanding

Arthur Birling calls the *Titanic* 'absolutely unsinkable' — well-chosen evidence

which shows that he believes that capitalism leads to — clear explanation with some detail

progress. However, the audience would know that the *Titanic* does sink. This would make them begin to doubt everything else that Arthur says. They might also think that he is arrogant to believe that humans can build something more powerful than the ocean. On the other hand, the Inspector talks about how selfish attitudes — well-chosen evidence

will lead to 'fire and blood and anguish' and this seems to come true because WW1 starts only two years after he says this. This makes the audience more likely to believe — clear explanation

other things he says like 'we are responsible for one another'. This helps Priestley to get across his message — final sentence returns to the question and concludes the topic of the paragraph effectively

of socialism showing how people should behave towards one another.

7 Choose two things this student has done well and use them as your writing targets.

8 Find two places where they could have developed their ideas in more detail.

9 Now write your own answer to the task. Aim for 250–300 words.

Checklist for success

- Use examples from both extracts.
- Focus on Priestley's point of view and how he shows it.
- Use information about context to help you write a more detailed and more thoughtful response.

Check your progress:

▲▲ I can use context about historical settings to help me develop ideas in detail.

▲ I can explain ideas about context clearly and link them to the text and the writer's ideas.

▲ I can refer to some aspects of context when explaining things.

Explore the same context from different perspectives

Learning objectives
You will learn how to
- identify and explain writers' viewpoints
- write about the effects of writers' language choices, linking them to the overall viewpoint.

Assessment objectives
- English Literature AO2, AO3

How can two writers see such different things in the same setting?

> **Getting you thinking**

Think about the place where you live. Would everybody agree about its good points and bad points?

1　**a**　What are the pros and cons of the place where you live?

　　b　How might somebody else see it differently?

2　Discuss with a partner and, after your discussion, list three advantages and three disadvantages of the place where you live.

The context in this case is not just the place, but the person who sees it – and the attitudes they bring to it.

Explore the skills

In the following poem, Wordsworth is portraying the City of London at the beginning of the nineteenth century. The speaker is standing on Westminster Bridge looking at the City of London at dawn. As you read, think about whether the speaker appears to like London or not.

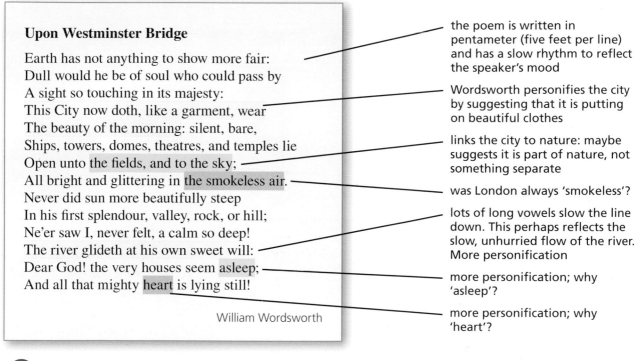

Upon Westminster Bridge

Earth has not anything to show more fair:
Dull would he be of soul who could pass by
A sight so touching in its majesty:
This City now doth, like a garment, wear
The beauty of the morning: silent, bare,
Ships, towers, domes, theatres, and temples lie
Open unto the fields, and to the sky;
All bright and glittering in the smokeless air.
Never did sun more beautifully steep
In his first splendour, valley, rock, or hill;
Ne'er saw I, never felt, a calm so deep!
The river glideth at his own sweet will:
Dear God! the very houses seem asleep;
And all that mighty heart is lying still!

William Wordsworth

the poem is written in pentameter (five feet per line) and has a slow rhythm to reflect the speaker's mood

Wordsworth personifies the city by suggesting that it is putting on beautiful clothes

links the city to nature: maybe suggests it is part of nature, not something separate

was London always 'smokeless'?

lots of long vowels slow the line down. This perhaps reflects the slow, unhurried flow of the river. More personification

more personification; why 'asleep'?

more personification; why 'heart'?

3 What is the speaker's overall view of the city and how do you know?

4 What details does he use to show us his view?

5 How does Wordsworth present and develop his ideas about London? Think about his choice of language and other poetic techniques, and use the annotations to help you.

Develop the skills

Here is another poem about London. This one was written by George Eliot in 1879, in the same century as Wordsworth wrote 'Upon Westminster Bridge'. The speaker has a very different **perspective** of the same setting: she is looking through a window and therefore has a more enclosed and limited view of the city. Her perspective is part of the context you need to consider.

> **Key term**
>
> **perspective:** another word for viewpoint or attitude

In a London Drawingroom

The sky is cloudy, yellowed by the smoke.
For view there are the houses opposite
Cutting the sky with one long line of wall
Like solid fog: far as the eye can stretch
Monotony of surface & of form
Without a break to hang a guess upon.
No bird can make a shadow as it flies,
For all is shadow, as in ways o'erhung
By thickest canvass, where the golden rays
Are clothed in hemp. No figure lingering
Pauses to feed the hunger of the eye
Or rest a little on the lap of life.
All hurry on & look upon the ground,
Or glance unmarking at the passers by
The wheels are hurrying too, cabs, carriages
All closed, in multiplied identity.
The world seems one huge prison-house & court
Where men are punished at the slightest cost,
With lowest rate of colour, warmth & joy.

George Eliot

yellow is normally a bright colour but here is made to sound dirty by the smoke

birds often represent freedom but the shadows seem to prevent this view of them

again, 'golden' would normally suggest brightness but here it is 'clothed in hemp', a dull brown material. Compare with Wordsworth's clothing simile

Eliot's speaker has a much more negative view of London than Wordsworth's.

6   What do we learn about the speaker's opinion of London?

7   What details does the speaker focus on? What can we learn about life in London at that time?

8   Why do you think the speaker concludes that 'the world seems one huge prison-house'?

Apply the skills

You are going to write a response to this task, using the annotations on both poems and your own ideas.

What do we learn about the two speakers' different attitudes to London from these two poems?

Checklist for success

- Show a clear understanding of each poet's viewpoint about London.
- Link your ideas closely to how the poets use language to describe the city.
- Develop your ideas in as much detail as you can.
- Aim to write 250–300 words.

Before you start, look at this student's answer.

Wordsworth describes London as a beautiful place and you can tell that he really likes it. He is standing on a bridge in the early morning watching the river flow by and the sunrise over the peaceful city. You can tell he likes it because he uses words like 'majesty', 'bright', 'glittering', 'calm' and 'sweet'. Eliot thinks London is a horrible place because there is nothing beautiful in her description of it. She looks through a window but finds her view blocked by 'the houses opposite' which she thinks are 'like solid fog'. She sees people hurrying everywhere, not noticing the people around them and looking 'upon the ground'.

Everybody she sees and hears is 'closed' and shut up in their own little world and so she sees London as a miserable place whereas Wordsworth really likes it. Wordsworth describes nice buildings like 'towers, domes, theatres and temples' to show how beautiful the city is. On the other hand, Eliot describes the buildings in a depressing way saying things like 'monotony of surface and of form without a break' which makes the view from the window sound very boring.

9 Imagine you are marking this student's work. They have some good ideas and they can back up their ideas with evidence. The problem is that the student does not comment in detail about the effects of the poets' language choices. For example, the student could have written:

When Wordsworth uses the word 'majesty', It makes the city sound royal like a king or queen and emphasises how grand and beautiful the city is.

Show how the student could have gone into more detail about some of Eliot's language choices.

10 Now write your own answer to the question. Remember to refer to the Checklist for success.

Check your progress:

- I can link ideas about the poets' viewpoint closely to the poems and comment in detail on how the poets get those ideas across.

- I can make clear points about the poets' viewpoint, find evidence in the poem to back up what I'm saying and explain the effects of some words or phrases.

- I can say something about the poets' viewpoints and find some evidence in the poems to back up what I'm saying.

Apply your skills to an English Literature task

Learning objectives
You will learn how to
- apply the key skills from this chapter to a new text
- reflect on your progress by looking at different responses to a task.

Assessment objectives
- English Literature AO1, AO2, AO3

Views of nature

In this section, you are going to look at poems which explore views on nature from the Romantic period to modern times. You will look at how people's responses might have been affected by Romantic ideas. It is important to remember that ideas about context must always be linked to a close analysis of the text.

Romanticism

Romanticism was an important artistic and cultural movement which started in the late eighteenth century. It can be seen as a reaction against the Industrial Revolution which had started a little earlier. The Industrial Revolution led to massive changes in society. Fewer people worked in agriculture and had to find employment in factories, often moving from the countryside to live in crowded and dirty cities. Traditional trades died out as human skills were increasingly replaced by machines.

The Romantics hated these changes and felt they led to people becoming unhappy because they were not living in 'natural' conditions. The table opposite sums up some important Romantic ideas in very general terms.

Romantic ideas		
The Romantics liked	**The Romantics hated**	**Example**
art and poetry	rationalism	Wordsworth thought that rationalism, including science, was the opposite of poetry. Science could not explain everything. Poetry was a better way of explaining deeper meaning.
childhood	adulthood	Romantics associated childhood with innocence and this was the 'natural' state for humans. People lost this innocence as they became adults.
the countryside and nature	towns and cities	The countryside is a 'natural' place for humans to live. Towns and cities are 'unnatural' and make people unhappy, often without them realising.
the past	the present	In the past, people lived in a 'state of nature'. Too much civilisation destroys this. Romantics are often nostalgic and see the past as a golden age.
the power of the imagination and strong feeling	precise observation and logic	The imagination is the most important part of being human. The imagination can see things in a way which science can't explain.
the individual	society	Romantics did not like rules and felt that society often prevented individual people from fulfilling their potential.
freedom (literal and metaphorical)	slavery (literal and metaphorical)	Freedom of thought and expression was very important for Romantics. A person could be a slave to ideas, rules, their job, a city, poverty or anything which prevented their imagination being free.

John Clare

John Clare is often known as 'the peasant poet' because he came from an ordinary rural family and had little formal education, which was very unusual for poets at that time. He lived in the countryside and many of his poems are about the things he observed around him, often focusing on their beauty.

His first volume of poetry was published in 1820 and was extremely popular. One reason for this might be that it reminded people of a simpler rural life and helped them to escape from the pressures of everyday life in towns and cities. He remains one of the most popular Romantic poets.

> **The Swallow**
> Swift goes the sooty swallow o'er the heath,
> Swifter than skims the cloud-rack of the skies;
> As swiftly flies its shadow underneath,
> And on his wing the twittering sunbeam lies,
> As bright as water glitters in the eyes
> Of those it passes; 'tis a pretty thing,
> The ornament of meadows and clear skies:
> With dingy breast and narrow pointed wing,
> Its daily twittering is a song to Spring.
>
> John Clare

1. What makes this a Romantic poem rather than just a description of some flowers? Refer back to the table about the Romantics to help you.

2. Write your own response to the poem, but develop your ideas using some of the information you have learned about the Romantics.

   You could use some of these sentence stems to help you:

   - Clare chooses a typical Romantic setting for the poem...

   - Clare explores the Romantic idea of freedom...

   - Clare describes the swallow using powerful imaginative language...

   - Clare is impressed by the sublime power of the swallow's flight...

   - Clare's poem is important because it helped people to escape from their everyday lives...

Ted Hughes

Ted Hughes is one of the most famous and respected British poets of the twentieth century. Nature is important in his work. Some of his most famous poems like 'Jaguar' and 'Hawk Roosting' explore the often-savage beauty of nature. 'The Thought-Fox' uses nature to explore poetic inspiration and the imagination. It is easy to see how these ideas can be linked to Romanticism.

In 'Work and Play', Hughes contrasts the freedom of swallows with holidaymakers 'enjoying' a day at the beach.

Work and Play

The swallow of summer, she toils all the summer,
A blue-dark knot of glittering voltage,
A whiplash swimmer, a fish of the air.
     But the serpent of cars that crawls through the dust
     In shimmering exhaust
     Searching to slake
     Its fever in ocean
     Will play and be idle or else it will bust.

The swallow of summer, the barbed harpoon,
She flings from the furnace, a rainbow of purples,
Dips her glow in the pond and is perfect.
     But the serpent of cars that collapsed on the beach
     Disgorges its organs
     A scamper of colours
     Which roll like tomatoes
     Nude as tomatoes
     With sand in their creases
     To cringe in the sparkle of rollers and screech.

The swallow of summer, the seamstress of summer,
She scissors the blue into shapes and she sews it,
She draws a long thread and she knots it at the corners.
     But the holiday people
     Are laid out like wounded
     Flat as in ovens
     Roasting and basting
     With faces of torment as space burns them blue
     Their heads are transistors
     Their teeth grit on sand grains
     Their lost kids are squalling
     While man-eating flies
     Jab electric shock needles but what can they do?

They can climb in their cars with raw bodies, raw faces
     And start up the serpent
     And headache it homeward
     A car full of squabbles
     And sobbing and stickiness
     With sand in their crannies
     Inhaling petroleum
     That pours from the foxgloves
     While the evening swallow

The swallow of summer, cartwheeling through crimson,
Touches the honey-slow river and turning
Returns to the hand stretched from under the eaves –
A boomerang of rejoicing shadow.

Ted Hughes

3 Complete the following table to help you explore how Hughes portrays the freedom and beauty of the swallows.

Quotation	Exploration
A blue-dark knot of glittering voltage	Hughes uses 'blue-dark' to precisely capture the colour of the swallows. The word 'knot' perhaps suggests a mystery that needs to be solved or unravelled – one that is not straightforward and takes time and careful thought. 'Glittering' links the swallows to the sun and 'voltage' suggests the power, speed and excitement of electricity.
A whiplash swimmer, a fish of the air	
the barbed harpoon	
She flings from the furnace, a rainbow of purples	
Dips her glow in the pond and is perfect	
the seamstress of summer	This could link to the 'Work' mentioned in the title. Hughes could be ironically contrasting the 'work' of the swallows which mainly seems to be enjoying flying freely with the 'play' of the people as they endure a hot day at the crowded beach.
She scissors the blue into shapes and she sews it, She draws a long thread and she knots it at the corners	
cartwheeling through crimson	
Touches the honey-slow river	
Returns to the hand stretched from under the eaves	
A boomerang of rejoicing shadow	

4 Now make a similar table to explore how Hughes portrays the people 'enjoying' their day at the beach. This time, choose your own quotations.

Quotation	Exploration
the serpent of cars that crawls through the dust	The 'serpent' immediately has negative connotations. It makes us think of the serpent from the Garden of Eden. The serpent 'crawls' which reflects the slow movement of the traffic jam but also contrasts with the free 'cartwheeling' movement of the swallows. The choking 'dust' contrasts with the clear, blue sky.

5 What Romantic ideas might Hughes be exploring? Refer to the Romantic ideas table to help you.

6 It might sound like a day at the seaside would be a Romantic way of leaving behind the hustle and bustle of everyday life and enjoying the beauty of nature. What might be wrong with this interpretation?

Responding to an English Literature task

1 Look at this practice task and think about how you would approach it.

Your task

How does the poet explore ideas about humans and nature in 'Work and Play'?

Checklist for success

A successful response should:

- have strong focus on the question
- include some well-selected evidence
- analyse the effects of particular words, literary techniques and structural features, linked to the ideas and themes in the text
- recognise the writer as the 'maker' of the text
- use ideas about context, especially Romantic ideas, to help develop explorations.

Reflecting on your progress

2 Read the following section of a response to this task. As you read, think about what the student has done well and what advice they might need in order to make more progress.

Response 1

Hughes portrays the swallows positively. Hughes recognises the beauty of the swallows as they fly. He compares them to 'a boomerang of rejoicing shadow' as they return to their nests. The swallows are very different to the people 'roasting and basting' at the beach or

— a good start with focus on the question

— excellent use of embedded quotations as evidence

'sobbing' and 'squabbling' in their cars. Hughes could be using nature to show how humans have become separated from their true selves and cannot see the difference between the true beauty of nature and a stressful visit to the beach. In fact, they are actually portrayed as victims of the flies and the hot sun.

— excellent use of embedded quotations as evidence

— starting to explore the writer's ideas

— beginning to use ideas about context to develop response

Comments on Response 1

This student clearly knows the poem very well and has good understanding of the main ideas. The student recognises that the writer sees something positive in the swallows and in nature. Points are backed up effectively with embedded quotations. However, the student clearly knows more than they write down. There is not enough detail about how the poet gets his ideas across using language, structure or form and instead there is too much description of what happens in the poem. The student begins to explore the writer's ideas and links to ideas about context at the end of the response.

3 How could this sample response be improved? Using the middle rung of the Check your progress ladder at the end of this chapter, think about what advice you might give to this student in order to improve their work.

4 Response 2 is by a different student. Again, as you read, think about what the student has done well and what advice they might need to make further progress.

Response 2

Hughes portrays the beauty of nature in a Romantic way. Hughes has a less than positive view of people in the modern world. He portrays the sublime beauty and power of the swallows comparing them to a 'barbed harpoon' to help us imagine their shape and saying that they 'fling' a 'rainbow of purples' suggesting the way they reflect the rays of the sun into many beautiful shades. While all this is going on, holidaymakers are arriving at the beach in a 'serpent of cars' which creates a negative mood straight away and shows that the people will already be stressed when they arrive at

— focus on writer straight away

— context is identified explicitly

— consistently well-chosen evidence embedded in response

— comments on effects of language

the beach because they have been in a traffic jam. The word 'serpent' suggests evil and this is linked to the people. Many other words suggest that the 'holiday people' do not enjoy their day. Hughes mentions 'headaches', 'squabbles', 'sobbing' and 'stickiness' as he describes the people. Each stanza is split into two parts to help Hughes show the difference between the swallows and the people and the fact that the people are so preoccupied with their holiday that they fail to notice the power and beauty of nature around them. Hughes could be saying that, in the modern world, people have become separated from nature and their true identities and have become slaves to modern ideas about how we should enjoy ourselves. He also shows that this kind of holidaymaking does not work and leads to frustration and unhappiness and, like the Romantics, concludes that many people are not free in the modern world.

nice comment on structure

brave exploration of writer's ideas

concluding sentence links context to ideas and returns to the question

Comments on Response 2

The student keeps a clear focus on the task throughout. Evidence is well chosen and embedded into the answer. The student has a high level of understanding of the writer's themes and ideas and explores them in some detail.

There is some analysis of language with a comment on the effects of some of Hughes's vocabulary choices but this could have been done with some of the other quotations as well to show a more in-depth understanding of the poet's technique. There is a good point about stanza structure emphasising the difference between humans and nature but this could also have been developed.

The student has begun to show how the poem might have been influenced by some Romantic ideas and makes some good points about the power of nature and freedom. If handled more skilfully, context could have been used as an overview to hold the whole response together.

Check your progress

- I can understand how a range of contexts, such as setting, historical period, social / cultural attitudes and literary movements and the writer's own attitudes and perspective, can affect what texts are like.
- I can explain in detail how context can influence a writer's themes and ideas.
- I can explain in detail how context can influence how a writer uses language, structure and form to create a range of meanings.

- I can explain different contexts, such as setting, historical period, social / cultural attitudes and literary movements and the writer's own attitudes and perspective, and what they might suggest about a text.
- I can explain the writer's themes and ideas using ideas about context.
- I can explain how context can affect the ways a writer uses language, structure and form to create meanings.

- I can recognise some types of context, such as setting, historical period, social / cultural attitudes, literary movements and the writer's own attitudes and perspective.
- I can sometimes write about how context is linked to what a writer is trying to say.
- I can sometimes show that context is linked to the way a writer is doing deliberate things to create a particular effect.

Chapter 6

Forming a critical response

What's it all about?

In this chapter, you will learn how to construct longer essay-style responses to unseen and studied texts. You will learn how to build on your comprehension skills and your knowledge about analysing language and structure. You will learn how to put those elements together to answer longer essay-style tasks in a methodical way, showing the best of all your skills.

In this chapter, you will learn about

- critical evaluation: form an interpretation
- critical evaluation: gather and present evidence about language
- critical evaluation: gather and present evidence about structure
- critical evaluation: gather and present evidence about mood

- critical evaluation: construct a convincing response to literary texts
- critical evaluation: construct a convincing response to non-fiction texts
- apply your skills to English Language and English Literature tasks.

	English Language GCSE	English Literature GCSE
Which AOs are covered?	AO4 Evaluate texts critically and support this with appropriate textual references	AO1 Read, understand and respond to texts. You should be able to maintain a critical style and develop an informed personal response using textual references, including quotations, to support and illustrate interpretations
How will this be tested?	All the texts you will be responding to will be previously unseen. You will be given longer essay-type texts that expect you to look at significant areas of texts or whole texts, and 'evaluate critically'. 'Critical' reading is a step up from basic comprehension questions and expects you to respond to a text in detail, to work almost like a detective, exploring clues or inferences and gathering evidence from the text's language, structure or tone and mood. 'Evaluating' means weighing up those inferences to piece together the meaning of the text.	Sometimes you will be responding to a whole play or novel that you have studied in class and sometimes you will be writing about two previously unseen poems. You will be given longer essay-type texts that expect you to look at significant areas of texts or whole texts. A 'critical' task expects you to respond to a text in detail, to work almost like a detective, exploring clues or inferences and gathering the evidence from the text's language, structure, tone and mood.

Critical evaluation: form an interpretation

Learning objective
You will learn how to
• explore the nature of critical evaluation and consider how we build an interpretation of a text.

Assessment objectives
• English Language AO4
• English Literature AO1

How is this different from doing basic comprehension work?

Getting you thinking

Critical evaluation is not what you might expect it to be. 'Critical' reading does not mean being negative or picking faults. Instead, you examine and respond to a text in detail, working like a detective to explore clues, draw **inferences** and gather evidence.

'Evaluating' means weighing up those inferences to piece together the meaning of the text.

In evaluating a text critically you:

• think about what the writer wants you to see from the clues they have left behind in their use of language, structure and tone

• think about what else you see that may not have been in the writer's mind when they wrote the text

• present your response – your **interpretation** – in an essay style.

① Look at the opening of the following poem, 'A Case of Murder' by Vernon Scannell. Answer the questions in the annotations to gather your first clues. These will help you to make inferences about the text. Make a note of your inferences.

Key terms

inferences: short explanations of what you have been able to read between the lines at certain points in a text. This confirms your understanding of key ideas

interpretation: your overall detailed response to a text made up of all the clues and evidence you have gathered

A Case of Murder

They should not have left him there alone, — Who is being referred to here?

Alone that is except for the cat.

He was only nine, not old enough — Why use the word 'only' before the age?

To be left alone in a basement flat, — What does the place make you think of?

Alone, that is, except for the cat. — Why has the word 'alone' been used four times already?

Vernon Scannell

2 Look at the inferences you have made. What does the writer seem to want us to think about the boy and his situation? What's your evidence?

3 Do you have any different thoughts of your own about the boy and his situation?

Explore the skills

4 Now look at these annotations that a student has made on the next section before answering the questions below.

He hated that cat; he watched it sit, — these are strong feelings to use against your pet!

A buzzing machine of soft black stuff,

He sat and watched and he hated it, — the cat doesn't sound real here – maybe like a ticking time bomb

Snug in its fur, hot blood in a muff,

And its mad gold stare and the way it sat — this sounds evil – like something from a horror film

Crooning dark warmth: he loathed all that.

again, the cat doesn't seem normal – it has evil eyes and you wouldn't want to be on your own with it – you can't trust it

5 What does the writer seem to want you to think of the cat? What's your evidence? Do you agree with the inferences the student has made?

6 Have you changed your opinion of the boy? Why?

7 Now it's time to do some detective work of your own.

Look at the next section of the poem, then focus on the highlighted sections.

a Make a note of the inferences you make about the boy from the yellow sections.

b Make a note of the inferences you make about the cat from the blue sections.

So he took Daddy's stick and he hit the cat.

Then quick as a sudden crack in glass

It hissed, black flash, to a hiding place

In the dust and dark beneath the couch,

And he followed the grin on his new-made face,

A wide-eyed, frightened snarl of a grin,

And he took the stick and he thrust it in,

Hard and quick in the furry dark.

The black fur squealed and he felt his skin

Prickle with sparks of dry delight.

Then the cat again came into sight,

Shot for the door that wasn't quite shut,

But the boy, quick too, slammed fast the door:

The cat, half-through, was cracked like a nut

And the soft black thud was dumped on the floor.

8 Now what do you think of the boy? What's your evidence?

9 Have you changed your opinion of the cat? Why?

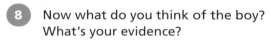
Develop the skills

This final section of the poem creates a puzzle for the reader.

If you have been reading the poem literally or 'on the surface' as being about a boy who was scared of his pet cat, then the ending seems unrealistic and absurd.

To solve the puzzle you need to think less literally and decide how else you might interpret the text. What other possible ways of reading and understanding the text are there?

He dared not touch the thing with his hands

So he fetched a spade and shovelled it

And dumped the load of heavy fur

In the spidery cupboard under the stair

Where it's been for years, and though it died

It's grown in that cupboard and its hot low purr

Grows slowly louder year by year:

There'll not be a corner for the boy to hide

When the cupboard swells and all sides split

And the huge black cat pads out of it.

Here are the thoughts of two students.

Student A

> I think this poem is like a horror story, where in the end the cat becomes the monster the little boy thinks it is.

Student B

> *I think this poem is about bullying – the boy is like a victim at the beginning and then he becomes the bully. The ending shows this just gets worse over time and shows that bullying is always wrong and always gets out of hand.*

10 What evidence can you find in the poem to support the way each student has interpreted the text?

11 Can you think of a different interpretation? What is your evidence?

In this way, you could conclude that there are several ways of reading a text and several ways of interpreting it. The piece of writing you produce pulling together all of the evidence for your interpretation is a **critical evaluation**.

Apply the skills

12 Complete the following task.

The black cat in Vernon Scannell's poem can be 'read' or interpreted in many different ways. Which interpretation convinces you the most:

- Student A's
- Student B's
- your own?

Write two to three paragraphs setting out your detective work on 'A Case of Murder' following the method in the Checklist for success.

Checklist for success

- **Look** for the clues the writer has left behind.
- Ask **questions**.
- Make your deductions or **inferences**.
- Present your ideas as clear **statements**.
- Use **quotations** from the text to support those ideas.
- Explain the **inferences** you have made to reach your **interpretation**.

Check your progress:

- I can read texts and present all of the clues I have gathered in an organised way to show my own interpretation.

- I can read texts and ask myself questions to build up more of a picture of the writer's meaning.

- I can read texts and pick up on some of the clues left by the writer.

Critical evaluation: gather and present evidence about language

Learning objective
You will
- explore how following clues in the choices of words and phrases can help us to build an interpretation.

Assessment objectives
- English Language AO2, AO4
- English Literature AO2, AO4

Do you need your knowledge about language in evaluative essay-type questions too?

Getting you thinking

You have already learned that in evaluating a text critically, you think about what the writer wants you to see from the clues they have left behind.

The writer's choice of words, phrases and language features provide a lot of clues to meaning.

However, you have to be **selective**. That means choosing to analyse the aspects of a text that definitely add something to your own interpretation.

1 A student is considering this task:

> Evaluate critically how Wilfred Owen has presented the soldiers in the World War 1 poem 'Dulce et Decorum est'.

The student has **selected** these three words from the poem, which is about World War 1 to help them present their evaluation:

> 'hags'   'cursed'   'haunting'

a Do these words belong in the same **semantic field**?

b What are the connotations of these words?

c Using your detective skills, think about why the writer might have used them in a poem about war. Jot down your initial thoughts.

Key term

semantic field: a collection of words that have a similar meaning or create a similar idea in the mind of the reader

Explore the skills

Now read the opening of the poem for yourself.

> Bent double, like old beggars under sacks,
>
> Knock-kneed, coughing like hags, we cursed through sludge,
>
> Till on the haunting flares we turned our backs
>
> And towards our distant rest began to trudge.
>
> Men marched asleep. Many had lost their boots
>
> But limped on, blood-shod. All went lame; all blind;
>
> Drunk with fatigue; deaf even to the hoots
>
> Of tired, outstripped **Five-Nines** that dropped behind.
>
> Wilfred Owen, from 'Dulce et Decorum est'

Glossary
....
Five-Nines: explosive shells

2 The student considering the task has made these notes. Can you see the links the student is making? Consider how this will help the student to present a clear interpretation of the poem.

> 'Hags' – reminds me of the witches in Macbeth/old women, not young men like I imagine soldiers in WW1 to be
>
> 'Cursed' – I think in the poem it means the soldiers are swearing and cursing as they are trying to march through 'sludge' but cursed also links to witches – like putting a curse on someone
>
> 'Haunting' – this is usually linked to ghosts and the supernatural but here it's the flares going up that haunt them.

3 You are going to work on an interpretation of your own. Look at the words highlighted in yellow. What language feature has been used in both examples? What do you see in your mind's eye? Is this what you would usually think of when you imagine soldiers? Make a note of your ideas.

4   Look at the words highlighted in pink. What do all of these references have in common? Again, do they imply a strong and effective fighting force?

5   Collect your ideas together – perhaps in a table like this one.

Selected quotations	Language feature	My detective work **Connotations** of the words: what they suggest to the reader My inferences
'Like old beggars' 'Coughing like hags'		
'Bent double' 'Knock-kneed' 'Lame' 'Blind' 'Deaf'		

Develop the skills

6   Now look closely at the task:

> Evaluate critically how Wilfred Owen has presented the soldiers in the World War 1 poem 'Dulce et decorum est'.

How would the language points you have collected help you to tackle this question?

What image do you have in your mind's eye as to what a fighting force should look like?

How might Wilfred Owen want you to see the soldiers?

What might Wilfred Owen want you to understand about the soldiers?

By considering these questions, you are getting ready to present your own interpretation of the poem.

7   Look at this paragraph that the student wrote presenting their **language evidence** in response to the task.

Remember this is not a complete evaluation – just **one** aspect of it.

What can you note about the way the student has presented their ideas? Use the checklist below it to identify which skills the student has shown.

Key term

Connotations: what we see in our mind's eye when we think of a particular thing or idea; our associations; what is suggested to us

The poet uses three words from a ghostly and supernatural semantic field. The use of the noun 'hags' reminds us of witchcraft and we might associate this more readily with old women, not young, active men in combat. This suggests how decrepit the young soldiers have become, how they seem to have aged and what a terrible mess they are in, not smart or well-equipped. The poet tells us they 'cursed through sludge'. On the surface, the verb 'cursed' suggests they are swearing, but also implies they have had a curse put on them, to be in this situation. The soldiers are marching towards their 'distant rest' but even though they are marching away from the flares, they are still 'haunting' the soldiers. Again, this word connects to the supernatural and suggests the horror of the war will stay with the soldiers.

✓ or ✗

- the paragraph focuses on language analysis right the way through
- uses language terminology with examples
- blends in supporting quotations from the poem so they still make sense within the sentences
- considers what the poet is doing and what he wants us to see
- makes inferences about the key ideas, building their own interpretation of the poem
- presents work clearly in Standard English.

Apply the skills

8 Look back at your notes from Activities 3, 4 and 5.

Look carefully again at the task.

> Evaluate critically how Wilfred Owen has presented the soldiers in the World War 1 poem 'Dulce et Decorum est'.

You are going to write one paragraph of a response to this task which focuses on language.

Checklist for success

- Decide what **Wilfred Owen** wanted you to see about the soldiers.
- Decide what **you** see.
- Aim to practise setting out your work in the style of the example in Activity 7.

Check your progress:

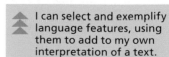

I can select and exemplify language features, using them to add to my own interpretation of a text.

I can select key language features and use examples of them in my answers.

I can recognise language features in texts and mention them in my answers.

Critical evaluation: gather and present evidence about structure

Learning objective
You will
- explore how following clues in how a writer has structured a text can help us to build an interpretation.

Assessment objectives
- English Language AO2, AO4
- English Literature AO1, AO2

What else can you say apart from: 'it's got a beginning, a middle and an end and it's made up of long sentences'?

Getting you thinking

Once you've considered the language clues the writer has left you, you should also consider the **structure** of the text.

The structure of a text includes all of the ways in which it has been 'built' and put together. You might think of structure as being the building blocks of a text.

Asking yourself why the writer made the decisions to structure the piece as they have will help you to build your critical evaluation.

Key term

structure: the way in which a writer chooses to organise a text; this may include the order of ideas or topics; paragraphing; sentence structure; narrative perspective (first person or third person); chronology (sequencing of events); pace; patterns within the writing such as repetition, contrasts

1 Look at where this extract begins. It is from the novel *If Nobody Speaks of Remarkable Things* by Jon McGregor.

> In the flat upstairs, an old man is looking for a box of matches to light the gas under the kettle, he turns to the table and he sees an envelope lying there, his name scratched across it in wavering handwriting. He smiles, he turns and opens the cutlery drawer of the Welsh dresser, he takes out an envelope with his wife's name on it, his own handwriting as newly unreliable as hers.
>
> He places the two cards side by side, he thinks about opening his for a moment and decides not to. He looks for the matches and thinks about that day.
>
> Jon McGregor, from *If Nobody Speaks of Remarkable Things*

2 What special event do you think the old man in the extract is celebrating? When might a husband and wife send a card to each other?

How does the structure of the text help you to work this out?

- What tense is used?
- Is this happening in the past or present?
- Why are there only two paragraphs?
- Is there a fast pace here, or a slow pace?
- What is it about the sentences that creates the pace?
- Think about the sequence of events with the cards and why he waits to open his card.

3 Look closely at the final sentence. It is a **compound sentence** joining two ideas together. What two ideas are joined? What is implied by 'that day'.

4 The final sentence gives the writer the opportunity to create a 'story within the story'. Where do you think the story could go next?

Key term

compound sentence: when two ideas (which could be simple sentences) are joined together. They are joined with conjunctions such as *for, and, nor, but, or, yet, so*

Explore the skills

Now read the next extract from the same novel.

It wasn't a spectacular wedding. It happened in a hurry, and they only spent one night together before he went away again, went away properly.
[…]
But it was a wedding, and they looked each other in the eyes and said the words, they made their vows and they have kept them all these years.
[…]
And they took the wedding certificate back to their new house, propped it up on the chest of drawers at the foot of the bed, and spent the whole evening looking at it.
[…]
She said, tell me the story of us, tell me it the way you'll tell our children, when they ask.
[…]
And he'd always say it the same way, starting with once upon a time there was a handsome soldier boy with a smart uniform…

5 A student has made the following notes on the key structural features of the extract. Add your own ideas to these notes, exploring the impact of the features on meaning and thinking about what they help the writer to communicate to you.

- starts with a simple sentence – seems to be the only one
- tense changes
- loads of paragraphs here
- there's speech in it but no speech marks – indirect
- another of those 'story within a story' things
- his story tells me what time in history this is and why he's leaving because...

Develop the skills

We know now that the following structural features are important in this text:

- past and present
- paragraph structure
- sentence structure
- story within a story
- indirect speech.

6 Using a copy of this final extract, identify and annotate for yourself the structural features that make an impact on the meaning of the story.

And that first time he'd told the story, that night, lying side by side on the bed, fully clothed, neither of them said anything when he finished, they just lay there looking at the official type, the formal words.

And she'd whispered it's a good story isn't it? And the last thing she'd said to him, just before she went to sleep that night, quietly, almost as though she thought he was asleep, she said you will come back won't you, you will keep safe, please, you will come home?

---

7 Look again at the first extract you read in Activity 1.

   a What do we now know about the young soldier in the final extract?

   b What do we know about the marriage that took place?

   c What has Jon McGregor managed to communicate to you about the relationship between the old man and his wife through his interesting structure?

Apply the skills

8 You're now going to tackle this task.

> Evaluate critically how Jon McGregor has presented the relationship of the elderly couple.

You are going to write one paragraph of a response to this task which focuses on structure.

Checklist for success

- **Decide** what Jon McGregor wanted you to realise about the elderly man and his relationship with his wife.
- Think about how his **structural choices** have helped you to see that.
- Aim to include **three separate features** and explore how they help us to interpret the meaning of the text.

You could begin:

> Part of the way Jon McGregor presents this relationship is through the structural choices he makes in the extract. For example, the use of time is important. He begins by using a setting in the present, where we see an elderly man, who is pleased to see his wife has remembered their wedding anniversary. He emphasises that this is happening 'now' by using the present tense, for example...

Check your progress:

⬆⬆ I can identify and exemplify structural features and comment on how they add to the meaning of the text.

⬆ I can identify and give examples of some of the structural features a writer uses.

▲ I can identify some of the ways a writer structures or organises their text.

Critical evaluation: gather and present evidence about mood

Learning objective
You will
- explore how following clues about mood can help us to build an interpretation.

Assessment objectives
- English Language AO4
- English Literature AO1, AO2

Why is mood important in critical evaluation?

Getting you thinking

Creative writing which presents scenes, events or relationships can create a particular **mood** or atmosphere that you can almost 'feel'.

Checklist for success

In putting together a critical evaluation, it is important to:

- look at the clues in the language of a text
- look at the clues in the structure of a text
- then consider what **tone** or **mood** the writer has created for you.

1 Look at the following ingredients for a story below. What kind of **mood** or atmosphere would you expect from a story with these ingredients?

thunder	forest	howling
lightning	isolation	candle
ruined castle	scream	cloaked figure
night		

Explore the skills

2 Read the following extract from the opening chapter of a famous Victorian novel. The narrator is on a journey by coach and horses.

> By-and-by, however, as I was curious to know how time was passing, I struck a match, and by its flame looked at my watch. It was within a few minutes of midnight.
>
> This gave me a sort of shock, for I suppose the general superstition about midnight was increased by my recent experiences. I waited with a sick feeling of suspense.

Then a dog began to howl somewhere in a farmhouse far down the road, a long, agonized wailing, as if from fear. The sound was taken up by another dog, and then another and another, till, borne on the wind which now sighed softly through the Pass, a wild howling began, which seemed to come from all over the country, as far as the imagination could grasp it through the gloom of the night.

Then answer these questions.

a How does the choice of time help to create the atmosphere of this piece? Is there anything stereotypical about its use?

b How does the addition of the howling dogs add to the atmosphere? Does this make you link the piece to a particular genre?

c What detail is given to you about the weather? How does this use of **pathetic fallacy** add to the atmosphere?

d Note down five different words that you would use to describe the atmosphere or mood in the story at this point.

e List the words and phrases that contribute to this atmosphere / mood.

Key term

pathetic fallacy: when the writer describes the conditions of the natural world to add to the atmosphere of the story

3 Look at the extract from a student's essay about the **mood** of this extract. Do you agree with their ideas and interpretation? Add your own ideas in a bullet-pointed list.

The extract creates a spooky atmosphere by using the semantic field of horror with references to 'midnight', 'fear' and 'howling' and 'agonised wailing'. There is a ghostly feel and this is increased because of the reference to midnight – the stereotypical time when bad things happen. The use of pathetic fallacy adds to the atmosphere as we know the wind 'sighed softly' like a ghost. The narrator is clearly frightened as he describes having a 'sick feeling of suspense'. He doesn't know what is going to happen and neither do we, which adds to that feeling of suspense.

Develop the skills

The extract you read in Activity 2 is from the novel *Dracula* by Bram Stoker, a famous vampire novel in the **gothic horror genre**.

4 Now go on to read the remainder of the extract.

Find and note down quotations that show:

- the **semantic field** of entrapment
- the use of pathetic fallacy
- the emotions of the narrator
- a mysterious character
- any other stereotypical conventions of the gothic horror genre.

Now note down any which add to the mood the text is creating.

Key terms

gothic horror genre: a genre that became popular in the late eighteenth and early nineteenth century, featuring characters trying to solve mysteries, often in danger in frightening settings and sometimes involving the supernatural

semantic field: a cluster of words in a text which all link to the same topic, for example, love, war, nature

Soon we were hemmed in with trees, which in places arched right over the roadway till we passed as through a tunnel. And again great frowning rocks guarded us boldly on either side. Though we were in shelter, we could hear the rising wind, for it moaned and whistled through the rocks, and the branches of the trees crashed together as we swept along. It grew colder and colder still, and fine, powdery snow began to fall, so that soon we and all around us were covered with a white blanket. The keen wind still carried the howling of the dogs, though this grew fainter as we went on our way. The baying of the wolves sounded nearer and nearer, as though they were closing round on us from every side. I grew dreadfully afraid, and the horses shared my fear. The driver, however, was not in the least disturbed. He kept turning his head to left and right, but I could not see anything through the darkness.

But just then the moon, sailing through the black clouds, appeared behind the jagged crest of a beetling, pine-clad rock, and by its light I saw around us a ring of wolves, with white teeth and lolling red tongues, with long, sinewy limbs and shaggy hair. They were a hundred times more terrible in the grim silence which held them than even when they howled. For myself, I felt a sort of paralysis of fear. It is only when a man feels himself face to face with such horrors that he can understand their true import.

We kept on ascending, with occasional periods of quick descent, but in the main always ascending. Suddenly, I became conscious of the fact that the driver was in the act of pulling up the horses in the courtyard of a vast ruined castle, from whose tall black windows came no ray of light, and whose broken battlements showed a jagged line against the sky.

Apply the skills

5 In the style of the original, write the next paragraph of the story, describing the narrator entering the castle for the first time and his first impressions.

Checklist for success

Think carefully about:

- the choice of words you will use to describe the castle

- the techniques you can use to help create the atmosphere such as: semantic fields, pathetic fallacy, introducing another mystery character.

6 Go on to write a paragraph explaining how you have made your writing match the mood and atmosphere of the original.

Check your progress:

▲▲ I can identify and comment on the different techniques that writers use to create mood in their work.

▲▲ I can understand that writers use different techniques to create different moods and I can recognise some of them.

▲ I can understand that different texts can have different moods or atmospheres.

Critical evaluation: construct a convincing response to literary texts

Learning objective
You will learn to
- understand how to put your evidence together clearly and effectively.

Assessment objectives
- English Language AO4
- English Literature AO1

You have gathered a lot of clues and quotations, but how do you put it all together?

Getting you thinking

1 Look at the task below and think about how you might tackle it.

- What are the key words in the task?
- What words in particular give you a clue as to how to interpret a text that you haven't seen before?

> Write a critical evaluation of the poem 'Ozymandias', exploring how the poet P.B. Shelley seems to view the abuse of power.

You know now that to put together a critical evaluation means you need to use:

- your comprehension skills
- your language skills
- your structuring skills.

Then you need to:

- work out the mood of the text
- decide on an interpretation of the text.

Your final piece of work is therefore going to be a longer response – pulling everything together.

You will present a complete picture, like a finished jigsaw puzzle.

However, you can't write about everything!

Selection is the key.

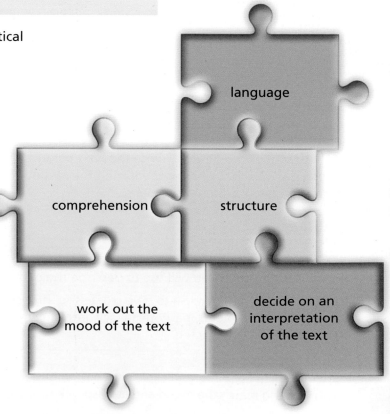

Explore the skills

A student has highlighted the poem 'Ozymandias' by P.B. Shelley in different colours to help them organise the following ideas:

- language
- structure
- mood
- the poet's view

2 Read the poem through twice. Then use the student's initial thoughts and questions to compile your own more detailed notes on the poem. You could do this in a series of spider diagrams or a chart like the one below.

Ozymandias
I met a traveller from an antique land
Who said: 'Two vast and trunkless legs of stone
Stand in the desert. Near them, on the sand,
Half sunk, a shattered visage lies, whose frown,
And wrinkled lip, and sneer of cold command,
Tell that its sculptor well those passions read
Which yet survive, stamped on these lifeless things,
The hand that mocked them and the heart that fed.
And on the pedestal these words appear –
"My name is Ozymandias, king of kings:
Look on my works, ye Mighty, and despair!"
Nothing beside remains. Round the decay
Of that colossal wreck, boundless and bare
The lone and level sands stretch far away.'

P.B. Shelley

what is the poet saying about past civilisations – they are all dead and gone. A warning? When was Shelley writing? Need to check. Is this message still/more important today? Why end with the sand – that image quite frightening somehow.

'antique land' makes me think of old civilisations – the past – powerful empires /person in statue not happy! Sounds fierce. Like a dictator – 'cold command' alliteration/harsh

ideas about the poet's message

language ideas

'Ozymandias'

mood ideas

structure ideas

Doesn't sound great – there is no civilisation here anymore/everything dead and gone/decayed/in ruins

tricky – a narrator/big quotation from the traveller/we get to see the inscription from the statue so must be important. This poem has got 14 lines and some rhyming – is this a sonnet? Need to check

Develop the skills

Reread the task.

> Write a critical evaluation of the poem 'Ozymandias',
> exploring how the poet P.B. Shelley seems to view the abuse
> of power.

3 Now look carefully at all of your notes. Which points seem
key or most important? Which ones link most logically to
each other? Decide which points you would like to keep
and use in your response and which, if any, you would like
to reject.

4 How will you open your response with a clear statement
linked to the question?

5 Look at the approach taken by Student A. Are they actually
answering the question in their introduction? Are they
evaluating the text?

Student A

> Percy Shelley was born in 1792 and he was a Romantic poet. He was married to
> Mary Shelley who wrote Frankenstein. Romantic poets were sometimes a bit
> radical and they protested a lot about things that were going on in society at
> the time, like the industrial revolution, which they were against.

6 By comparison, look at this stronger opening to the task by
Student B.

Student B

> Shelley's poem Ozymandias explores how a leader of a past civilisation imposed power. The noun
> phrase 'an antique land' makes us think of past civilisations such as the Romans, the Ancient
> Greeks or the Aztecs — all powerful empires with powerful leaders. The description of the statue of
> Ozymandias with his 'frown' and 'sneer of cold command' implies this leader was harsh — it is even
> reflected in his statue. The alliteration of 'cold command' suggests to us that . . .

What is Student B's opening paragraph doing that Student
A's did not?

7 Using your notes on language from Activity 2, complete the paragraph on language in the poem.

8 Look at the following concluding paragraph from Student B.

   a How does this bring together the student's interpretation of the poem?

   b How does it consider the poet's key ideas and message?

   c How does it link clearly to the task?

   d How does it use context more usefully than Student A's response?

Checklist for success

- Once all of your ideas are selected, gathered and organised get straight into the question.
- Don't waste time on lengthy introductions or passages about the context or the author.
- Make a strong statement summarising your interpretation and linking it to the question.

> It would seem that overall the poet is giving us a strong message about the abuse of power by leaders and empires. It is interesting that Shelley was writing this poem at the time when the British Empire was growing and growing and it seems he is giving a sharp reminder that all past empires have nothing left of them but 'decay'. It's also a sharp reminder that no matter how powerful one person might be in their lifetime, they end up as nothing but dust: 'the lone and level sands stretch far away'. There is a clear moral in the poem that I think is just as relevant today as different countries and different powerful leaders still try to impose control over others and oppress them.

Apply the skills

9 Now complete the following task.

Continuing from your opening paragraph on language, go on to write paragraphs two and three of this task:

- paragraph two should be about structure
- paragraph three should be about mood.

Find a way to ensure that the end of your third paragraph will link usefully to the concluding paragraph you have been given as an example in Activity 8.

If you wish, you may write your own strong concluding paragraph incorporating your interpretation of the poet's ideas and key message.

Check your progress:

 I can plan, write and support a response to a literary text which shows my own convincing interpretation of the text.

 I can read a literary text, plan and use supporting evidence to back up my ideas when I write my response.

I can read a literary text and plan some things to write about its ideas, language, structure and mood.

Critical evaluation: construct a convincing response to non-fiction texts

Learning objective
You will learn how to
- understand how to put your evidence together clearly and effectively for non-fiction texts.

Assessment objective
- English Language AO4

You can write up your ideas about poems and stories, but you find it harder with non-fiction texts. How do you improve?

Getting you thinking

The same method you use for evaluating literary texts applies to non-literary ones too. This involves using:

- your comprehension skills
- your structure skills.
- your language skills

Then you need to:

- work out the tone of the text
- decide on an overall interpretation of the text.

1 Write some short revision notes for yourself, reminding yourself of these key elements for writing about texts critically. Include a glossary or definitions of all the key terms you need to remember.

Explore the skills

You are going to look at a complete text and practise the skills that you learned in 6.5. Think about the following task.

Evaluate how Jessica Ennis has presented the experience of competing in the Olympic Games.

2 Read the following extract from the autobiography of athlete Jessica Ennis. In it she describes the moments before her first big event in the London 2012 Olympics. This time you have colour-coded questions to think about the writer's use of the following:

- language
- structure
- tone
- key messages

Key term

tone: links to the idea of 'tone of voice'; it suggests a sound quality or a 'voice' in the text that is 'speaking' to you in a particular way

This is the day that I have dreamt about for years. This has been what all that dying on the side of a track has been about. This is the end of the raging pain. This is my one opportunity. My one shot. Walking into this arena is an assault on the senses – the purple and green and red, the crescendo of noise and the haze at the end of the straight where the Olympic flame is burning bright. This is it. This is my chance. I cannot help thinking that if it goes wrong I will never get this opportunity again. I might make another Olympics, but it won't be at home and I won't be touted as the face of the Games again. This combination of circumstances will never arise again. It is my first time and my last chance. Finally I realize just how big and scary the Olympic Games are. I follow the other girls to the start and we get into our blocks. It's like that Eminem song goes: one opportunity to seize everything you want. Will I capture the moment or let it slip?

It has taken me sixteen years to get here. Now I have seven events and two days to make it all worthwhile. There have been countless times when I have wondered if it would happen. I have been down, broken and almost out, but I have dragged myself back from the brink. Part of me wonders how this has happened. I am just an ordinary girl from a run-of-the-mill street in Sheffield and yet I have been plucked out of that normality and plunged into this melting pot of hopes and dreams and fierce competition. It is what I have wanted when I have been training every day, but it is frightening.

I feel adrenaline, excitement and fear. I have lost my crowns in the last year and there are bigger, stronger girls ready to push me around. Tatyana Chernova is the world champion. Nataliya Dobrynska is the Olympic champion. I have no titles, just one shot. We crouch and the roar drops to total silence. It is that special moment of bated breath and possibility. And then suddenly, in those seconds before the gun, I feel a strange calmness wash over me and I am ready. It is now or never.

Jessica Ennis, from *Unbelievable*

What seems to be important about the use of pronouns in this paragraph? Is there a metaphor used for effect?

What do you notice about repeated patterns in this paragraph? What is the impact of the short, **simple sentences** and the **minor sentences**? Can you see any examples of listing or **rhetorical questions**? Can you see any uses of contrast?

Do you get the sense of Jessica Ennis's nervousness in this paragraph? What is creating that for you in the language and the structure?

What does she want you to realise about this experience?

Why do you think she uses so many numbers here?

What does she want you to realise about her as a person?

How does the writer try and convey the atmosphere in the stadium? How many words connected to feelings and atmosphere are mentioned here?

What is the impact of the simple sentences in this final paragraph?

Key terms

simple sentences: these will contain one idea; they will have one verb or verb phrase as the sentence will only have one action, event, or state within it

minor sentences: sentences that don't contain a main clause, for example, 'Run!' or 'My one shot.'

rhetorical questions: questions addressed directly to an audience in order to make a point

3 Now **select** and gather the evidence you would like to use in your response to the task:

> Evaluate how Jessica Ennis has presented the experience of competing in the Olympic Games.

Use a grid similar to this one. Remember, you can't write about everything.

Language points	Structure points	Points about tone	Key messages

4 Think back to what you learned in 6.5 about how to open your piece of work strongly. Write up your first paragraph, zooming in on two or three language points to aid your overall interpretation. You could start in the following way:

> Jessica Ennis presents us with a vivid account of how significant and important a personal achievement it was for her to compete in the Olympics. One of the ways she conveys this is through her repeated use of personal pronouns...

Apply the skills

5 Go on to complete the task by adding in paragraphs on structure and tone.

You could begin each in the following ways:

> Jessica Ennis uses patterns of strong declarative sentences in the opening. She states 'This is', 'This is' and repeats the same structure. This makes her sound definite and determined as though she is strongly convincing herself that she can win the event...

> The tone of the piece changes throughout. Despite sounding definite and determined in the first paragraph, Jessica sounds less self-assured in the second when she describes herself as...

Write a concluding paragraph explaining what you feel are Jessica's key messages for you as a reader and how you feel about the experience she shares with us.

Check your progress:

▲▲ I can plan, write and support a response to a non-fiction text which shows my own convincing interpretation.

▲ I can read a non-fiction text, plan and write my response and use supporting evidence to back up my ideas.

▲ I can read a non-fiction text and plan and write some things to say about its ideas, language, structure and tone.

Apply your skills to English Language and English Literature tasks

Learning objectives
You will learn how to
- apply the key skills from this chapter to one unseen English Language task
- apply the key skills from this chapter to one English Literature task
- reflect on your progress through looking at different responses to both tasks.

Assessment objectives
- English Language AO4
- English Literature AO1

Responding to an English Language task

1 This extract is from the novel *The Great Gatsby* by F. Scott Fitzgerald, about a mysterious millionaire living in New York in the 1920s. The story is narrated by his neighbour, Nick Carraway. As you read it, think about the following questions.

- What is this extract about?
- How has the writer used descriptive language and an interesting structure to communicate ideas to the reader?

There was music from my neighbour's house through the summer nights. In his blue gardens men and girls came and went like moths among the whisperings and the champagne and the stars. At high tide in the afternoon I watched his guests diving from the tower of his raft, or taking the sun on the hot sand of his beach while his two motor-boats slit the waters of the Sound, drawing aquaplanes over cataracts of foam. On week-ends his Rolls-Royce became an omnibus, bearing parties to and from the city between nine in the morning and long past midnight, while his station wagon scampered like a brisk yellow bug to meet all trains. And on Mondays eight servants, including an extra gardener, toiled all day with mops and scrubbing-brushes and hammers and garden-shears, repairing the ravages of the night before.

Every Friday five crates of oranges and lemons arrived from a fruiterer in New York — every Monday these same oranges and lemons left his back door in a pyramid of pulpless halves. There was a machine in the kitchen which could extract the juice of two hundred oranges in half an hour if a little button was pressed two hundred times by a butler's thumb.

At least once a fortnight a corps of caterers came down with several hundred feet of canvas and enough colored lights to make a Christmas tree of Gatsby's enormous garden. On buffet tables, garnished with glistening hors-d'oeuvre, spiced baked hams crowded against salads of harlequin designs and pastry pigs and turkeys bewitched to a dark gold. In the main hall a bar with a real brass rail was set up, and stocked with gins and liquors and with cordials so long forgotten that most of his female guests were too young to know one from another.

By seven o'clock the orchestra has arrived, no thin five-piece affair, but a whole pitful of oboes and trombones and saxophones and viols and cornets and piccolos, and low and high drums. The last swimmers have come in from the beach now and are dressing up-stairs; the cars from New York are parked five deep in the drive, and already the halls and salons and verandas are gaudy with primary colors, and hair bobbed in strange new ways, and shawls beyond the dreams of Castile. The bar is in full swing, and floating rounds of cocktails permeate the garden outside, until the air is alive with chatter and laughter, and casual innuendo and introductions forgotten on the spot, and enthusiastic meetings between women who never knew each other's names.

The lights grow brighter as the earth lurches away from the sun, and now the orchestra is playing yellow cocktail music, and the opera of voices pitches a key higher. Laughter is easier minute by minute, spilled with prodigality, tipped out at a cheerful word. The groups change more swiftly, swell with new arrivals, dissolve and form in the same breath; already there are wanderers, confident girls who weave here and there among the stouter and more stable, become for a sharp, joyous moment the centre of a group, and then, excited with triumph, glide on through the sea-change of faces and voices and colour under the constantly changing light.

F. Scott Fitzgerald, from *The Great Gatsby*

Your task

F. Scott Fitzgerald creates a real sense of wealth and glamour in his description.

To what extent do you agree?

In your response you should:

- consider your own impressions of Gatsby's parties
- evaluate the effects the descriptions have on you
- support your opinions with quotations from the text.

Checklist for success

A successful response should include:

- statements and inferences about the party, supported by quotations
- comments on the effects of descriptive language features and techniques, supported by examples
- comments on the effects of structure, supported by examples
- comments on the mood, tone or atmosphere.

You should create your own interpretation of the text in order to answer the question.

Reflecting on your progress

2 Read Response 1 below. Think about what the student has done well and what advice they might need in order to make more progress.

Response 1

The writer gives a sense of wealth and glamour by telling us how very busy Gatsby's parties were 'cars are parked five deep in the drive' which suggests that people came from miles around to the parties. They seem like they are very lively, with a lot of cocktails and music because he tells us 'the air is alive with chatter and laughter'. This tells us everyone enjoyed the parties. The parties must have cost a lot of money as there is gorgeous food there such as 'salads of harlequin designs' and 'turkeys bewitched to a dark gold' and also things like an orchestra for the music. The writer makes us think only a very wealthy person could afford to have parties like this.

some clear comments showing understanding of the parties with relevant quotations to support

The writer makes the parties sound very beautiful by using description like 'The lights grow brighter' and 'the champagne and the stars'. He makes the place seem bright and colourful by using phrases like 'gaudy with primary colours ' and 'blue gardens' and 'yellow cocktail music'. There is a semantic field of happiness with words like 'cheerful', 'joyous' and 'excited' which give the effect that everyone is having a great time. He uses very long sentences to give the impression that the party is like never-ending fun.

there is some selection of descriptive language using quotations

another example of language, this time trying some terminology

attempts a comment on structure but no examples

The tone is very exciting and very glamorous as the writer tells us about the Rolls Royce picking up the guests and how the party gets livelier as it goes along.

attempts to comment on tone but no real detail or examples that link to atmosphere

Overall, I think the writer gives a very good impression of the wealth and glamour of the parties and uses a lot of detail effectively to make me visualise all of the excitement and people and how big the parties were.

a useful summarising comment at the end linked back to task, but not really showing the student's own interpretation.

Comments on Response 1

This response focuses on the task and makes several comments with inferences, as well as touching on all the key areas necessary for a good critical evaluation. The explanations are clear but rather undeveloped. For example, the student has identified some aspects of language but not shown much knowledge of language or structural terminology.
They have attempted to comment on effect but not in any great detail. The conclusion does not really present a very convincing interpretation.

3 How could this sample response be improved? Using the middle rung of the Check your progress ladder at the end of this chapter, think about what advice you might give to this student in order to improve their work.

4 Now read Response 2. As you read, think about what the student has done that is an improvement on Response 1, and what advice this student might need in order to make even more progress.

Response 2

F. Scott Fitzgerald gives an amazing sense of how glamorous his parties were by telling us about the scale of them and the preparation that went into them 'his Rolls Royce became an omnibus, bearing parties to and from the city between nine in the morning and long past midnight'. This suggests these were more than just parties; they were big, extravagant events. Fitzgerald also creates a sense of wealth by mentioning not just the 'Rolls Royce' but all of the food, cocktails and luxury that his guests had, such as 'the crates of oranges and lemons', 'the turkeys bewitched to a dark gold' and the 'orchestra' for the music. This tells us that the parties were all about wealth and showing it off. We know the parties are pretty wild as it takes 'eight servants ... repairing the ravages of the night before' suggesting someone can afford this not just once but all through the summer.

This is shown too in the language and the description. The writer uses phrases such as 'enormous garden' and 'a corps of caterers' to communicate the scale of the parties to us.

really clear impression of the party, supported by relevant quotations and with a number of clear inferences made

uses language point to back up the ideas in the first paragraph and selects useful quotations

He uses listing such as 'the whisperings and the champagne and the stars' to make the party seem magical. Interesting verbs like 'dissolve and form', 'weave' and 'glide' also make the people seem magical and like they are in some kind of fairytale.

The extract is very organised though, with each paragraph almost representing a different part of the party — 'Every Friday', 'By seven o' clock' — such as the getting ready, the arrival of the guests, the party itself and the clearing up. Even though the party seems very lively and informal, it also seems very organised.

The tone is a lively and busy one but it's also a little bit sad. No one actually seems to know each other as people are 'forgotten on the spot', 'women who never knew each other's names' and there is a lot of coming and going, a 'sea-change of faces.'

We clearly get a real sense of wealth and glamour but it also seems a bit fake and false and like no one really cares. They have lots of money but leave the 'servants' to do all the hard work and the clearing up.

considers the writer's choices and uses some subject terminology. Interesting idea regarding effect

comments on structure in a clear and useful way with relevant examples

comments on the effect of this choice by the writer

really interesting interpretation linked to the tone or mood of the piece and backed up with a good choice of quotation

another very interesting interpretation in the conclusion

Comments on Response 2

This is a well-organised and detailed response which has a good understanding of the text and the task. There are lots of relevant examples used to back up ideas on both the party and the methods the writer has used to describe it. The first paragraph is detailed and secure and uses quotation in a skilful way. There are some nice effects touched on in both the comments on language and structure. The conclusion shows the student is starting to 'think outside the box' and build their own interpretation of the text, not just accept what's on the surface. They are clearly beginning to 'read between the lines'.

Responding to an English Literature task

1 Read the following extract from 'The Adventure of the Speckled Band', a Sherlock Holmes short story by Arthur Conan Doyle. As you read, think about the following questions:

- What is this extract about?
- What impressions of different characters do you think the writer is communicating?
- What do you notice about the ways language and structure have been used to communicate those impressions to the reader?

A lady dressed in black and heavily veiled, who had been sitting in the window, rose as we entered.

'Good morning, madam,' said Holmes cheerily. 'My name is Sherlock Holmes. This is my intimate friend and associate, Dr. Watson, before whom you can speak as freely as before myself. Ha, I am glad to see that Mrs. Hudson has had the good sense to light the fire. Pray draw up to it, and I shall order you a cup of hot coffee, for I observe that you are shivering.'

'It is not cold which makes me shiver,' said the woman in a low voice, changing her seat as requested.

'What, then?'

'It is fear, Mr. Holmes. It is terror.' She raised her veil as she spoke, and we could see that she was indeed in a pitiable state of agitation, her face all drawn and grey, with restless frightened eyes, like those of some hunted animal. Her features and figure were those of a woman of thirty, but her hair was shot with premature grey, and her expression was weary and haggard. Sherlock Holmes ran her over with one of his quick, all-comprehensive glances.

'You must not fear,' said he soothingly, bending forward and patting her forearm. 'We shall soon set matters right, I have no doubt. You have come in by train this morning, I see.'

'You know me, then?'

'No, but I observe the second half of a return ticket in the palm of your left glove. You must have started early and yet you had a good drive in a dog-cart, along heavy roads, before you reached the station.'

The lady gave a violent start and stared in bewilderment at my companion.

'There is no mystery, my dear madam,' said he, smiling. 'The left arm of your jacket is spattered with mud in no less than seven places. The marks are perfectly fresh. There is no vehicle save a dog-cart which throws up mud in that way, and then only when you sit on the left-hand side of the driver.'

'Whatever your reasons may be, you are perfectly correct,' said she. 'I started from home before six, reached Leatherhead at twenty past, and came in by the first train to Waterloo. Sir, I can stand this strain no longer; I shall go mad if it continues. I have no one to turn to – none, save only one, who cares for me, and he, poor fellow, can be of little aid. I have heard of you, Mr. Holmes; I have heard of you from Mrs. Farintosh, whom you helped in the hour of her sore need. It was from her that I had your address. Oh, sir, do you not think that you could help me too, and at least throw a little light through the dense darkness which surrounds me?'

Arthur Conan Doyle, from 'The Adventure of the Speckled Band'

Your task

How does the writer present the woman who has come to ask for help from Holmes in this extract? Refer closely to details from the extract in your answer.

Checklist for success

A successful response should:

- demonstrate your ideas about the character of the woman
- include some well-selected evidence
- analyse the effects of particular words, literary techniques and structural features, linked to the character of the woman.

Reflecting on your progress

2 Read the following response, thinking about what the student has done well and what advice they might need in order to make more progress.

Response 1

The writer presents the woman in a mysterious way as he tells us she is 'dressed in black and heavily veiled'. This immediately makes it look like she does not want to be recognised. She is also mysterious when she speaks and says, 'It is not cold which makes me shiver', suggesting she is frightened of something or some body. She is frightened all the way through the extract but we don't know why which is a good way to intrigue the reader.

The writer uses words like 'fear' and 'terror' and adjectives like 'weary and haggard' to describe her which makes us think she has a big problem or something she is worried about. He uses a simile 'like those of some hunted animal' which makes us want to know just what it is she is so frightened about.

The woman is presented as being a bit suspicious because she 'gave a violent start' when Holmes says his clues about her journey. However, she seems to feel she can trust Holmes as he was recommended to her.

some ideas about the woman are given with useful supporting quotations and inferences which show understanding

a simple effect on the reader is considered

examples of language and language features with examples. Considers effect but rather undeveloped

more ideas about the character of the woman with evidence and a useful inference

In the last paragraph the woman becomes really dramatic and desperate to tell Holmes her problem. The writer uses dialogue and presents what the woman says in long sentences, like she is talking very fast. She calls him 'Sir' like she looks up to him and is really relying on him to help her.

— attempts to make an evaluative comment on tone

— attempts a structural idea but with no examples

— offers a final idea about the woman with inference

Comments on Response 1

This response is on task and sticks to the focus of how the woman is presented all the way through. The student has several ideas about the woman's character, all of which have some textual support, and many have useful inferences which show understanding. There are some ideas about language and structure, but they are not particularly detailed or well organised. There is only a fairly simple use of subject terminology. The student has attempted to comment on effect, but not in any great detail or in a very thoughtful way.

3 How could this sample response be improved? Using the middle rung of the Check your progress ladder at the end of this chapter, think about what advice you might give to this student in order to improve their work.

4 Now read Response 2. As you read, think about what the student has done that is an improvement on Response 1, and what advice this student might need in order to make even more progress.

Response 2

Conan Doyle presents us with a mystery figure by having the woman, 'dressed in black and heavily veiled', so that at first her identity and personality are hidden. As she begins to speak, the sense of mystery increases and the mention of her 'low voice' emphasises the mystery surrounding her.
However, as she removes her veil and begins to speak, she is shown to be a figure who is more of a victim than a mystery. She uses adjectives such as 'fear' and 'terror' in her dialogue to communicate how she is feeling.

— very clear impression of the woman, supported by embedded quotation and with clear inferences made

— links in a point regarding change to the structure and chronology of the extract

The description of the woman also emphasises how she is feeling, using noun phrases such as 'restless frightened eyes' and 'hunted animal' which makes her seem more vulnerable and trapped. Her hair is described as 'streaked with premature grey' which suggests that whatever is frightening her has been going on for a long time and has been a constant worry, making her 'weary and haggard'.

Conan Doyle uses dialogue and the clues Sherlock picks up about her to create even more of a sense of her nervousness: 'a violent start' and 'bewilderment' show this. *She seems fearful, even of Holmes, who she has come to see for help.*

In the final paragraph the woman is presented as speaking in long complex sentences, 'Sir, I can stand this strain … I shall go mad …', and seems to suggest her increasing panic and desperation. She is almost pleading with Holmes at this point, 'Oh Sir' and she finishes by describing her problem as 'the dense darkness'.

By using this melodramatic metaphor we are left intrigued as to what the issue might be and what Holmes will do to solve it.

some secure language points made with concise examples. Sensible comments on effect

uses language as an opportunity to make a further inference and begins own interpretation

reflects on what the writer is doing

more inference linked to concise quotations

a useful point on structure and effect with an example

makes a final language point and sets up a useful bridge to deal with the remainder of the text

Comments on Response 2

This is very clear response which makes use of quotations and textual references effectively. There is a good understanding of the text and the task and crisp organisation of ideas throughout. A strength is the concise use of quotation and the embedded quotation. There is a clear consideration of a number of ideas and strong inferences suggest a good, clear understanding throughout. The response considers a number of methods used by the writer, exemplifies them and makes sensible comments on effect which move beyond the surface. The work is organised and well expressed and concludes in a useful way ready to move on to the whole text question.

Check your progress

- I can read texts and present all of the clues I have gathered in an organised way to show my own interpretation.
- I can select and exemplify language features, using them to add to my own interpretation of a text.
- I can identify and exemplify structural features and comment on how they add to the meaning of the text.
- I can identify and comment on the different techniques that writers use to create mood in their work.
- I can plan, write and support a response to a literary text which shows my own convincing interpretation of the text.
- I can plan, write and support a response to a non-fiction text which shows my own convincing interpretation.

- I can read texts and ask myself questions to build up more of a picture of the writer's meaning.
- I can select key language features and use examples of them in my answers.
- I can identify and give examples of some of the structural features a writer uses.
- I can understand that writers use different techniques to create different moods and I can recognise some of them.
- I can read a literary text, plan my response and use supporting evidence to back up my ideas.
- I can read a non-fiction text, plan my response and use supporting evidence to back up my ideas.

- I can read texts and pick up on some of the clues left by the writer.
- I can recognise language features in texts and mention them in my answers.
- I can identify some of the ways a writer structures or organises their text.
- I can understand that different texts can have different moods or atmospheres.
- I can read a literary text and plan some things to say about its ideas, language, structure and mood.
- I can read a non-fiction text and plan some things to say about its ideas, language, structure and tone.

Chapter 7

Comparing texts

What's it all about?

In this chapter, you will learn to make meaningful comparisons across texts by considering ideas, meanings and viewpoints. You will also learn to make comparisons between the ways these meanings are conveyed to the reader.

In this chapter, you will learn how to

- compare views and perspectives in non-literary non-fiction from the twentieth century
- compare non-fiction prose texts
- compare the ways viewpoints are presented in texts from the early twentieth century
- structure a comparative response to poetry
- apply your skills to English Language and English Literature tasks.

	English Language GCSE	English Literature GCSE
Which AOs are covered?	AO3 Compare writers' ideas and perspectives, as well as how these are conveyed, across two or more texts	AO2 Analyse the language, form and structure used by a writer to create meanings and effects, using relevant subject terminology where appropriate
How will this be tested?	You will be asked to compare viewpoints in two texts and also to think about the ways these viewpoints have been presented. All the texts you will be reading and responding to will be previously unseen.	You will make comparisons between poems. To do this you will be considering the ideas, the language, structure and form of the poems. Sometimes you will be responding to poems that you have studied in class and sometimes you will be writing about two poems that are unseen.

Compare views and perspectives in non-literary non-fiction from the twentieth century

Learning objective
You will learn how to
- identify different viewpoints on the same subject.

Assessment objective
- English Language AO3

How do you compare two different viewpoints?

Getting you thinking

Whether we are thinking about climate change or status updates, people often have very different viewpoints.

1 What different viewpoints can you think of about whether or not schools should have a uniform? Think about price, quality, individuality, and a sense of belonging.

2 Which viewpoint do you think might be held by a student, by a teacher, and by a parent? Explain why.

Explore the skills

Read the following article.

Why I'm taking my child out of school for a holiday

This half-term, my family and I are leaving the country for a much-needed break. To save around £800, I will be taking my child out of school before the term officially ends. I have not sought permission from the head teacher. Nor will I.

[…]

Firstly, I genuinely don't feel my child (aged 4) will be disadvantaged by one or two days out of school. Second, and controversially, I don't feel the school will be disadvantaged either. I know how the argument goes – if everyone behaved like me we'd be in a sorry state with half-empty classrooms. But, really, would we? Aren't those who shout the loudest about the need for attendance the ones who are rich enough for term-time holidays never to be an issue?

I do feel guilty, but only for families who don't have the same financial resources as we do, so can't have a holiday at all, term time or not. I can't imagine any teacher devaluing the chance to learn a few words of a foreign language in situ, to see geology in action by playing on black sand, or start to understand basic engineering principles by looking at how planes fly. For us, the physical, intellectual and social advantages of travel would not be financially possible if we waited until the school holidays. Of course, I agree that attendance (most of the time) is vital but so is family harmony, unfrazzled parents, time to read or explore the world without the pressures of day-to-day life. Until travel companies offer more reasonable prices during school holidays, families like mine will continue to take their children out of school. Perhaps we should go easy on parents who value spending time with their children in a new and stimulating environment over Ofsted attendance targets.

Anonymous, *The Guardian*, 29 January 2014

3 Make a list of the reasons this writer gives to explain their viewpoint. For each one:

- find the point in the text
- find a quotation to support it
- explain what you infer about the writer's viewpoint from this evidence.

The structure **statement, quotation, inference** is useful for combining your ideas about viewpoint with your evidence:

This writer thinks that it is fine to take your child out of ——— Statement
holiday during term-time. They say that there are 'physical, ——— Quotation
intellectual and social advantages' to going on holiday.
This suggests that they think that missing a few days of ——— Inference
school is balanced by what a child learns from travelling to
a new place.

4 Write a short paragraph of your own explaining what you think the writer's viewpoint is at this point and using the statement, quotation, inference structure.

Now read the following article.

5 Using the statement, quotation, inference structure, write a short paragraph explaining this parent's viewpoint.

Why I'll never take my children out of school for a holiday

As chief holiday-planner in our household of six, I could be a lot richer – and/or my children could have seen a lot more of the world – if I'd fished them out of school, or even just shaved a few days off the beginning or end of term here and there. **1** Instead, over the last 16 years while we've had school-age kids, we've kept our holidays religiously within the vacation dates: and as my youngest child is still only 11, we've got another seven years of the same ahead. **2**

It's irksome, because there are huge financial savings to be made. Also, who wants to be on the beach in August, when it's packed and baking hot, when June and September (which is when my husband and I always holidayed in those dim and distant days before our eldest was born) are so less crowded, and the temperature more agreeable?

So why not just flout the system? Well, it all comes down to respect. Like all parents, I have occasional issues with aspects of my children's education: but on the whole, I aim to support the primary and comprehensive schools where they are, and have been, pupils. And part of the way I show my respect and support is by following the rules: and rule number one is, make sure your child is in school when he or she should be there. **3**

So many parents seem not to realise that the reason their kids don't work hard, or play truant, or get into trouble with their teachers, is connected to the fact that they have an a la carte attitude to rules themselves. **4** If you want your child to stick two fingers up at their teachers, to think education doesn't matter, or to skimp on revising for an exam, then go ahead and take them out of school so you can jet off on an exciting holiday for a fortnight. What you are role-modelling by your behaviour is your belief that rules are for other people, not for you; and your kids will pick up on that very, very quickly.

And here's another thing. My eldest, post-uni, is currently saving up to go to Asia on a gap year. Because travel is for life; but school is only for childhood, and as holiday-loving parents we need to remember that. **5**

Joanna Moorhead, *The Guardian*, 29 January 2014

1 What could the writer have done?

2 What did the writer decide to do?

3 What is the writer's main reason for keeping their child in school?

4 How does this statement develop their argument?

5 What is the overall viewpoint?

Develop the skills

When you are comparing viewpoints, the words **both**, **however** and **whereas** are very useful:

> Both writers have strong views about taking children out of school for holidays.
>
> However, one writer feels that it is fine to take your child out of school, whereas the other feels it is wrong.

6 **a** What similarities can you find between the viewpoints of the two texts?

b What differences can you find?

c Using 'both/however/whereas', create three statements about the two viewpoints.

Find evidence in the text.

Apply the skills

7 These two articles give different viewpoints about the same subject. You are now going to write a short comparison of these viewpoints. Use the structure, statement, quotation, inference.

Compare the writers' different views of taking their child out of school in term time.

Check your progress:

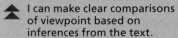

⬆⬆ I can present a detailed comparison between the viewpoints expressed in two texts, inferring meaning from a range of evidence.

⬆ I can make clear comparisons of viewpoint based on inferences from the text.

▲ I can identify the different viewpoints and explain what the similarities or differences are.

Compare non-fiction prose texts

Learning objective
You will learn how to
* compare viewpoints and perspectives on the same subject.

Assessment objective
* English Language AO3

How do you know what to compare when you're comparing two different texts?

Getting you thinking

1 Think about these famous sayings:

> * 'they're like chalk and cheese'
> * 'it's like comparing sugar and sand'.

Chalk and cheese have nothing in common, but what about sugar and sand?

2 List the things sugar and sand have in common, and what's different about them. Think about:

* their physical properties
* their appearance
* their purpose.

Sugar and sand appear to have some things in common, but are actually totally different.

When you are comparing two texts, find the link or connection between them. This becomes your starting point for a meaningful comparison.

Explore the skills

3 Read the extract from an article about 'The Hole in the Wall', a project designed to study the educational ability of children living in poverty. Think about the following question as you read:

> What does the writer do to test the slum children's learning?

4 **a** What is the main point the writer is making about learning?

b Make notes in response to the following questions:

* Do the children want to learn?
* Do they find learning easy?
* Does their poverty prevent them from learning?

In early 1999, some colleagues and I sunk a computer into the opening of a wall near our office in Kalkaji, New Delhi. The area was located in an expansive slum, with desperately poor people struggling to survive. The screen was visible from the street, and the PC was available to anyone who passed by. The computer had online access and a number of programs that could be used, but no instructions were given for its use.

What happened next astonished us. Children came running out of the nearest slum and glued themselves to the computer. They couldn't get enough. They began to click and explore. They began to learn how to use this strange thing. A few hours later, a visibly surprised Vivek said the children were actually surfing the Web.

We left the PC where it was, available to everyone on the street, and within six months the children of the neighborhood had learned all the mouse operations, could open and close programs, and were going online to download games, music and videos. We asked them how they had learned all of these sophisticated maneuvers, and each time they told us they had taught themselves.

[…] The children seemed to learn to use the computer without any assistance. Language did not matter, and neither did education […] Each time, the children were able to develop deep learning by teaching themselves.

Sugata Mitra, www.edutopia.org/blog/self-organized-learning-sugata-mitra

5 Complete the table. What inferences can you draw from these statements and quotations?

Statement	Quotation	Inference
The project deliberately chose a very deprived area.	'desperately poor people struggling to survive'	It would be an assumption that the deprivation would also lead to intellectual deprivation.
The children were interested in the computer.		
The children learned how to use it very quickly.		

6 What is the writer's viewpoint on this subject?

Develop the skills

Now read the article opposite, written by Charles Dickens more than 100 years before the first article.

Charles Dickens can be hard to access if you're not used to his writing style.

When you are reading a text like this for the first time:

- skim-read the text first to get an overall idea of what it seems to be about

- then take it slowly

- read one sentence at a time

- <u>underline</u> any unfamiliar words and see if you can work out what they mean from the context

- see if you can list the main points being made.

7 Look at the following statements. Find a piece of evidence to support each one.

  a The first paragraph is all about the terrible conditions and behaviour in the school.

  b The second paragraph is all about the fact that the students cannot be trusted.

  c There is a change in direction half way through the second paragraph.

The close, low chamber at the back, in which the boys were crowded, was so foul and stifling as to be, at first, almost insupportable. But its moral aspect was so far worse than its physical, that this was soon forgotten. Huddled together on a bench about the room, and shown out by some flaring candles stuck against the walls, were a crowd of boys, varying from mere infants to young men; sellers of fruit, herbs, lucifer-matches, flints; sleepers under the dry arches of bridges; young thieves and beggars--with nothing natural to youth about them: with nothing frank, ingenuous, or pleasant in their faces; low-browed, vicious, cunning, wicked; abandoned of all help but this; speeding downward to destruction; and UNUTTERABLY IGNORANT.

[...]

This was the Class I saw at the Ragged School. They could not be trusted with books; they could only be instructed orally; they were difficult of reduction to anything like attention, obedience, or decent behaviour; their benighted ignorance in reference to the Deity, or to any social duty (how could they guess at any social duty, being so discarded by all social teachers but the gaoler and the hangman!) was terrible to see. Yet, even here, and among these, something had been done already. The Ragged School was of recent date and very poor; but **he had inculcated some association with the name of the Almighty,** which was not an oath, and had taught them to look forward in a hymn (they sang it) to another life, which would correct the miseries and woes of this.

Charles Dickens, 'A Sleep to Startle Us', *Household Words*, 13 March 1852

Glossary

he had inculcated some association with the name of the Almighty: introduced the children to ideas about being a good Christian person

8 This article is also about learning and education in deprived circumstances. Make some notes on the same questions as before:

a Do the children want to learn?

b Do they find learning easy?

c Does their poverty prevent them from learning?

Find evidence to support your answers.

9 What connects this article with the one before? Finish these sentences:

Both articles are about...   Both articles are set in...

Both writers feel...

10 What are the differences between the two articles? Using **however** and **whereas**, finish these sentences.

a However, the first article presents the view that children can learn easily, whereas the second article...

b However, the tone of the first article seems very positive and optimistic, whereas the second article...

c However, the first article works through the story chronologically, whereas the second article...

Apply the skills

11 Now pull your findings and evidence together. Write a plan to answer the task below.

> Compare the viewpoints and perspectives of these two writers towards education for people living in deprived circumstances.

- What points will you include?
- What evidence will you select?
- What similarities and differences can you present?

Checklist for success

- Understand and explain the key connections between the two texts.
- Use the SQI structure (Statement, Quotation, Inference).
- Use the **both/however/whereas** key words to structure your comparison.

Check your progress:

 I can present a detailed comparison between the viewpoints expressed in two texts, inferring meaning from a range of evidence.

 I can make clear comparisons of viewpoint based on inferences from the text.

 I can identify the different viewpoints and explain what the similarities or differences are.

Compare the ways viewpoints are presented in texts from the early twentieth century

Learning objective
You will learn how to
* compare the ways viewpoints are presented to the reader in texts from the early twentieth century.

Assessment objectives
* English Language AO2, AO3

What kinds of things are you looking for when you're thinking about how writers present their viewpoints to the reader?

Getting you thinking

There is often a huge difference between recounting information and expressing a viewpoint.

1 **a** Think about a typical newsreader: do we have any idea of how they feel about the information they recount, or do they just give us the facts?

b Both of these statements provide the same information:

> The people were killed.

> The defenceless victims were mercilessly slaughtered in cold blood.

How does the choice of words in the second example enable the reader to understand the writer's viewpoint?

The second example uses **emotive language**:

> The defenceless **1** victims **2** were mercilessly **3** slaughtered **4** in cold blood. **5**

2 Choose one of the following sentences and rewrite it using **emotive language** in order to express a viewpoint.

* Lots of big supermarkets are making some of their employees redundant.
* One man hit another man for two minutes.
* A child was hurt in the park by another child.

Key term

emotive language: a deliberate choice of words to elicit an emotional response from the reader and enable the reader to infer the writer's viewpoint

1 adjective to describe the situation of the people

2 emotive synonym for the noun subject 'people'

3 adverb to describe the attitude towards their killers

4 emotive synonym for the verb 'killed'

5 extra information to show the writer's attitude towards the killers

Explore the skills

Read the following account, written by a survivor of the *Titanic* disaster.

3   **a**   What is this account about?

Harry Senior, a fireman on the Titanic, said last night:

I was in my bunk when I felt a bump. One man said. 'Hello, she has been struck.' I went on deck and saw a great pile of ice on the well deck below the forecastle, but we all thought the ship would last some time, and we went back to our bunks. Then one of the firemen came running down and yelled, 'All muster for the lifeboats!' I ran on deck, and the Captain said:

'All firemen keep down on the well deck. If a man comes up I'll shoot him.'

Then I saw the first boat lowered. Thirteen people were on board, eleven men and two women. Three were millionaires and one was Ismay.

Then I ran up on the hurricane deck and helped to throw one of the collapsible boats on to the lower deck. I saw an Italian woman holding two babies. I took one of them and made the woman jump overboard with the baby, while I did the same with the other. When I came to the surface the baby in my arms was dead. I saw the woman strike out in good style, but a boiler burst on the Titanic and started a big wave. When the woman saw that wave she gave up. Then, as the child was dead, I let it sink, too.

I swam around for about half an hour, and was swimming on my back when the Titanic went down. I tried to get aboard a boat, but some chap hit me over the head with an oar. There were too many in her. I got around to the other side of the boat and climbed in. There were thirty-five of us on board, including the second officer, and no women. I saw any amount of drowning and dead around us. We picked one man off an overturned boat and he died just as he was pulled over the side.

New York Times, 19 April 1912

b   How does the writer feel about his experience?

c   Is the account written in an emotional or unemotional way?

d   Do we get a strong viewpoint from reading this text?

This account is very impersonal; it provides a list of information without any emotive language to enable the reader to infer a viewpoint. However, the information itself is potentially very emotive.

 4
   a Select two or three sentences that have emotive content but are presented very factually.

     For example:

> 'When I came to the surface the baby in my arms was dead'

   b What is the effect of this factual presentation?

Develop the skills

Now read the following account written by the commander of a German U-boat in the World War 1.

> The steamer appeared to be close to us and looked colossal. I saw the captain walking on his bridge, a small whistle in his mouth. I saw the crew cleaning the deck forward, and I saw, with surprise and a slight shudder, long rows of wooden partitions right along all decks, from which gleamed the shining black and brown backs of horses.

'Oh heavens, horses! What a pity, those lovely beasts!'

'But it cannot be helped,' I went on thinking. 'War is war, and every horse the fewer on the Western front is a reduction of England's fighting power.' I must acknowledge, however, that the thought of what must come was a most unpleasant one, and I will describe what happened as briefly as possible.

'Stand by for firing a torpedo!' I called down to the control room.

'FIRE!'

A slight tremor went through the boat – the torpedo had gone.

The death-bringing shot was a true one, and the torpedo ran towards the doomed ship at high speed. I could follow its course exactly by the light streak of bubbles which was left in its wake.

I saw that the bubble-track of the torpedo had been discovered on the bridge of the steamer, as frightened arms pointed towards the water and the captain put his hands in front of his eyes and waited resignedly. Then a frightful explosion followed, and we were all thrown against one another by the concussion, and then, like Vulcan, huge and majestic, a column of water two hundred metres high and fifty metres broad, terrible in its beauty and power, shot up to the heavens.

'Hit abaft the second funnel,' I shouted down to the control room.

All her decks were visible to me. From all the hatchways a storming, despairing mass of men were fighting their way on deck, grimy stokers, officers, soldiers, groom, cooks. They all rushed, ran, screamed for boats, tore and thrust one another from the ladders leading down to them, fought for the lifebelts and jostled one another on the sloping deck. All amongst them, rearing, slipping horses are wedged. The starboard boats could not be lowered on account of the list; everyone therefore ran across to the port boats, which in the hurry and panic, had been lowered with great stupidity either half full or overcrowded. The men left behind were wringing their hands in despair and running to and fro along the decks; finally they threw themselves into the water so as to swim to the boats.

Then – a second explosion, followed by the escape of white hissing steam from all hatchways and scuttles. The white steam drove the horses mad. I saw a beautiful long-tailed dapple-grey horse take a mighty leap over the berthing rails and land into a fully laden boat. At that point I could not bear the sight any longer, and I lowered the periscope and dived deep.

Adolf von Spiegel, from 'U-Boat Attack'

5 **a** What happens in this account?

   b How does the writer feel about his experience?

   c Is the account written in an emotional or unemotional way?

   d Do we get a strong viewpoint from reading this text?

6 Find one example of each of the following techniques this writer uses to paint an emotive picture.

Technique	Example
description to paint a picture of the events	
first-person account	
direct speech	
a range of complex punctuation	
description of his feelings and attitudes	
hyperbole	
emotive language to describe the emotions and behaviour of the people	

> **Key term**
>
> **hyperbole:** exaggeration used for emphasis or effect

7 Like the first text, this one deals with some very emotional events. How does the presentation of these events in each text differ? Look at these two sentences:

- **A:** 'When I came to the surface the baby in my arms was dead.'
- **B:** 'Oh heavens, horses! What a pity, those lovely beasts!'

What is the difference between these two sentences? How have the writers presented emotive information differently?

Apply the skills

You are now going to compare the ways in which these two writers have presented their viewpoints to the reader. Use **both/whereas/however** to link your ideas.

You could structure your comparison like this:

- Both of these accounts are of traumatic events.
- Both of the writers are giving first-person accounts.
- Both give a chronological account of the events as they occur.
- However, whereas the first one is very dispassionate and factual, the second one is full of description and is very emotive in the way the viewpoint is expressed.

8 **a** Read this paragraph from a student's response. How has the student structured the comparison?

> Both of these accounts are of traumatic events. The first one is a first-person account of the Titanic disaster, and the other text, although first person, isn't as immediately involved because the eye-witness is watching the disaster rather than being part of it. Both events seem dangerous and very dramatic, however. Both contain lots of description; however, the first account tells the reader lots of things, whereas the second one comments on the feelings as they go through their account.

b Rewrite this paragraph, adding some direct quotation to support the ideas the student has already begun to present.

9 Now answer the task yourself.

> Compare the ways these two writers use language to present their viewpoints on a dramatic event.

Use the following plan to help structure your ideas:

- What are the two texts about?
- What is the purpose of the two texts?
- What viewpoint are they written from?
- Do they tell a chronological account of their experience?
- Which one is more emotive and which one is more dispassionate?

Checklist for success

- Comment on the similarities and/or differences between the ways the writers have used language to present their viewpoints, and the effect of this on the reader.
- Remember to use evidence to support your comments.

Check your progress:

▲▲ I can present a detailed comparison between the ways the writers use language and structure to express their viewpoints.

▲ I can make clear comparisons of the ways writers use language and structure to express their viewpoints.

▲ I can identify the different viewpoints and explain what the similarities or differences are.

Structure a comparative response to poetry

Learning objectives
You will learn how to
- compare the ways poets present a similar idea
- structure a written comparison to two poems.

Assessment objectives
- English Literature AO1, AO2

How do you know what to compare when you're comparing poems?

Getting you thinking

1 See what comparisons you can make between the following items. Which have got the most potential to compare? Which items have nothing in common?

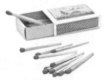

2 Choose two items from the list and write a **both/however/ whereas** paragraph comparing the similarities and differences between them.

Comparing literary texts works in exactly the same way. You have to find a starting point, a connection between the texts.

Think of forming a comparative argument like a coat rack.

Your hooks are your connections between the poems. The best connections of all are the subject matter or ideas in the poems.

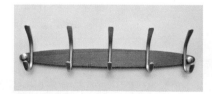

Explore the skills

The following poem gives the reader a very clear description of a place. The speaker is walking through a former **shanty town** in South Africa, remembering his childhood under **Apartheid**.

3 As you read the poem, make a note of all the details the writer is using to help create a picture of the place for the reader.

Glossary

shanty town: poor housing settlement on the outskirts of a city

Apartheid: system of racial segregation in South Africa

Nothing's Changed

Small round hard stones click
under my heels,
seeding grasses thrust
bearded seeds
into trouser cuffs, cans,
trodden on, crunch
in tall, purple-flowering,
amiable weeds.

District Six.
No board says it is:
but my feet know,
and my hands,
and the skin about my bones,
and the soft labouring of my lungs,
and the hot, white, inwards turning
anger of my eyes.

Brash with glass,
name flaring like a flag,
it squats
in the grass and weeds,
incipient Port Jackson trees:
new, up-market, haute cuisine,
guard at the gatepost,
whites only inn.

No sign says it is:

but we know where we belong.

I press my nose
to the clear panes, know,
before I see them, there will be
crushed ice white glass,
linen falls,
the single rose.

Down the road,
working man's cafe sells
bunny chows.
Take it with you, eat
it at a plastic table's top,
wipe your fingers on your jeans,
spit a little on the floor:
it's in the bone.

I back from the
glass,
boy again,
leaving small mean O
of small mean mouth.
Hands burn
for a stone, a bomb,
to shiver down the glass.
Nothing's changed.

Tatamkhula Afrika

4 What do we learn about this place from the way the speaker describes it?

Here are one student's notes on the first stanza in response to the following task:

Explore the ways attitudes to a place are presented in 'Nothing's Changed' by Tatamkhula Afrika.

connotations of being on the ground, underneath... downtrodden?

uncared for, 'gone to seed' idea

alliteration highlights the word 'crunch', idea of being 'trodden on' links to 'heels'

means 'friendly' – the only positive feeling, linked to 'purple' perhaps?

Small round hard stones click under my heels,
seeding grasses thrust bearded seeds
into trouser cuffs, cans,
trodden on, crunch
in tall, purple-flowering,
amiable weeds.

lots of monosyllables, harsh words, mention of stones, onomatopoeia makes the place seem harsh and unwelcome

another harsh word – implies a lack of control

back to negative idea again – weeds = in the wrong place.

5 Which features does the student comment on?

- ideas
- attitudes and feelings
- ways the writer has used language
- structure

6 Choose another stanza and make notes in the same way.

7 How many words can you find suggesting there are angry, resentful or bitter feelings towards this place?

Develop the skills

8 Now read another poem about a place. The speaker in this poem has also left her childhood home.

Make a note of all the details the writer uses to build a picture of the place that is different from the one in 'Nothing's Changed'.

Homeland

For a country of stone and harsh wind
For a country of bright perfect light
For the black of its earth and the white of its walls

For the silent and patient faces
Which poverty slowly etched
Close to the bone with the detail
Of a long irrefutable report

And for the faces like sun and wind

And for the clarity of those words
Always said with passion
For their colour and their weight
For their clean concrete silence
From which the named things spring
For the nakedness of awed words

Stone river wind house
Lament day song breath
Expanse root water –
My homeland and my centre

The moon hurts me the sea weeps me
And exile stamps the heart of time

Sophia de Mello Breyner

9 How many words can you find that suggest that the feelings for this place are warm, nostalgic or full of longing?

Now you need to find some connections (or hooks) to hang a comparison onto. For example:

Hook 1: **Both** poems are about places.

Hook 2: **Both** poems describe strong feelings about a place.

Hook 3: **However,** one poem is presenting an angry/bitter/resentful view, **whereas** the other poem presents a warmer/more nostalgic view.

10 What other 'hooks' can you find? Make some more **both** and **however** statements about the two poems.

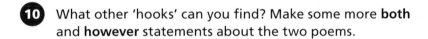

Apply the skills

11 Now put your ideas together into a piece of comparison by completing the following task.

Compare the ways writers present attitudes towards a place in 'Nothing's Changed' and 'Homeland'.
Aim to write 250–300 words.

Checklist for success

- Use **both/whereas/however**.
- Use evidence from both poems to support your comparison.
- Focus on the ideas/attitudes/feelings about the places being described.
- Include comments on language, or literary techniques, or structure.

Check your progress:

- I can analyse the similarities and differences between the ways a similar idea or topic is presented in two poems.

- I can compare the ways a similar idea or topic is presented in two poems.

- I can find some connections between two poems and make some links between how the ideas have been presented.

Apply your skills to English Language and English Literature tasks

Learning objectives
You will learn how to
- apply the key skills from this chapter to an English Language task
- apply the key skills from this chapter to an English Literature task
- reflect on your progress through looking at different responses to these tasks.

Assessment objectives
- English Language AO3
- English Literature AO1, AO2

Responding to an English Language task

1 Read Source 1, which is a biographical account by a young girl written in the nineteenth century. As you read it, think about the following questions:

- What are you learning about the girl and her experience?
- What are you learning about the girl's viewpoint on her experience?

Source 1

My father was a glass blower. When I was eight years old my father died and our family had to go to the Bristol Workhouse. My brother was sent from Bristol workhouse in the same way as many other children were – cart-loads at a time. My mother did not know where he was for two years. He was taken off in the dead of night without her knowledge, and the parish officers would never tell her where he was.

It was the mother of Joseph Russell who first found out where the children were, and told my mother. We set off together, my mother and I, we walked the whole way from Bristol to Cressbrook Mill in Derbyshire. We were many days on the road.

Mrs. Newton fondled over my mother when we arrived. My mother had brought her a present of little glass ornaments. She got these ornaments from some of the workmen, thinking they would be a very nice present to carry to the mistress at Cressbrook, for her kindness to my brother.

My brother told me that Mrs. Newton's fondling was all a blind; but I was so young and foolish, and so glad to see him again; that I did not heed what he said, and could not be persuaded to leave him. They would not let me stay unless I would take the shilling binding money. I took the shilling and I was very proud of it.

They took me into the counting house and showed me a piece of paper with a red sealed horse on which they told me to touch, and then to make a cross, which I did. This meant I had to stay at Cressbrook Mill till I was twenty one.

Sarah Ashton, interviewed in *The Ashton Chronicle*, 23 June 1849

2 Now read Source 2, which is an article from a newspaper. As you read, think about the following questions:

- What is this article about?
- What are you learning about the writer's viewpoint?
- What methods is the writer using to communicate their viewpoint to the reader?

Source 2

Britain's child soldiers

Denying those under the age of 18 the right to leave the army is outdated, immoral and in breach of UN guidelines

At 16 you are not old enough to vote, buy a pint in a pub or ride a motorbike. Yet you can join the armed forces, and commit yourself for four years beyond your 18th birthday. On becoming legally adult you can then be sent to the frontline in Afghanistan. A 16-year-old soldier can train with live ammunition, yet when he goes back to barracks in the evening he isn't old enough to rent an X-rated DVD of Apocalypse Now, a film dealing with the horrors of war – because it is too violent.

Notions of childhood change. During the siege of Mafeking in 1900, Robert Baden Powell recruited 12-year-old boys to deliver messages under fire. They wore khaki and their leader was the 13-year-old Warner Goodyear. But today Britain is the only European country to recruit into the regular army at 16. Perversely those young recruits are required to serve two years longer than those recruited at 18. Far from

being a curious legal relic, this rule was re-introduced by the Labour government in 2008. After a six-month 'cooling-off' period there is no right to leave. While 'unhappy minors' may leave at the discretion of their commanding officer, the fact that there is no 'discharge as of right' leaves them uniquely open to bullying and that bullying is more serious if it happens because they cannot leave.

The situation of 16-year-old soldiers is sometimes compared to that of apprentices. Yet in what other 21st century apprenticeship can a breach of discipline lead to a court martial and time spent in military prison? In what other apprenticeship do you face such dangers? How many apprentice carpenters, brick layers or plumbers are found dead whether shot in the head or hanging from a beam? Yet that is what happened to four young recruits training at Deepcut barracks. A carpenter's skills are a guarantee of security in an economic downturn. There are more limited openings for trained marksmen. An infantryman returning from Helmand province has no guarantee of a job. David Cameron's call for a 'national change' in attitude towards mental health problems among former soldiers is highly welcome, but could his proposed 24-hour helpline be extended to soldiers who are currently serving or training in barracks?

While the UK no longer has conscription, those joining the army at 16 often come from the poorest and least educated backgrounds. For youngsters without other jobs to go to, a career in the army may be hard to resist. What other choices do they have? It is true that 16- and 17-year-olds are no longer deployed to conflict zones but decisions made as a child have irrevocable consequences as an adult. At the moment a young person making a decision at 16, with his parents' consent, has no right at the age of 18 to review that decision with an informed conscience.

Michael Bartlet, *The Guardian*, 11 March 2011

Your task

Both sources are about attitudes towards children.

Compare the writers' different viewpoints of childhood.

Checklist for success

A successful response should:

- demonstrate your understanding of both sources
- use quotations from the sources to support your answer
- compare the writers' viewpoints by looking at the similarities and the differences
- compare the methods used by the writers to communicate their viewpoints to the reader.

Reflecting on your progress

3 Read the following response to this task. As you read, think about what the student has done well and what advice they might need in order to make more progress.

Response 1

The writers have different viewpoints in these two texts as one is biographical so it is from the child's point of view and the other one is an article about child soldiers from the writer's point of view. The first text gives lots of information about the girl's experience. She tells the reader that she had a hard life when she was little because her father died; 'my father died when I was eight years old'. She tells the reader about her brother being sent away and that she had to go on a long journey with her mother.

clear awareness of the main difference in perspective

uses relevant supporting evidence

relevant further comment

The second text is more emotional than the first text because the writer has strong opinions about the child soldiers. The writer of this text addresses the reader directly and uses strong facts to make the point that they think the age of being a young soldier is wrong: 'be sent to the front line in Afghanistan'.

relevant comparison of the tone between the two texts

clear difference identified

relevant supporting evidence from second text, but it could be better integrated

The main difference between these texts is that the perspective is different. The girl in the first text doesn't seem to be so aware that her experiences seem very hard for such a young child, whereas the writer of the second text presents lots of arguments to support their view that the age of soldiers is far too young.

clear explanation of the difference in viewpoint of the two texts

Comments on Response 1

This response attempts to compare, although there are only two comments actually comparing the two texts. The first sentence shows that the student has identified a key difference in viewpoint between the two texts. There are some relevant supporting quotations from both texts. The final sentence summarises the key difference between the texts again.

4 How could this sample response be improved? Using the middle rung of the Check your progress ladder at the end of this chapter, think about what advice you might give to this student in order to improve their work.

5 Now read Response 2. As you read, think about what the student has done that is an improvement on Response 1, and what advice this student might need in order to make even more progress.

Response 2

These two texts are both about the unfair treatment of young people, although they have been presented with very different viewpoints: one is from the point of view of a young child and one is presumably written by an adult. — clear understanding of the difference in viewpoint

The child in the first text doesn't seem to have a strong view about her experience at first. She gives lots of facts about her life without any emotive language or opinion, so it seems very impersonal. — effective comment on the effect of the perspective

However, the details about her 'father dying' and her brother going off with a 'cartload' of children suggest that her experience is very unhappy as they imply a sense of loneliness and being abandoned. — perceptive inference into the effect of quotation

Her brother going 'the same way as many other children' makes this seem very usual, as if children are being used like cattle. — another clear inference

The second text also describes the way young soldiers are treated, saying they are 'trained with live ammunition', 'sent to the front line in Afghanistan' and 'cannot 'leave', as if they also are powerless to control their environment. — strong connection between the two texts, supported with quotation

Both these texts are about the powerlessness of children and how they should have more rights. However, the second is much more emotive, partly because it is written by an adult rather than the child themselves. It is clear that the writer of Source 2 has very strong opinions about this issue: he argues 'decisions made as a child have irrevocable consequences as an adult'. In contrast, the writer of Source 1 tells us that she 'had to stay at Cressbrook Mill till I was twenty one' without offering any opinion on how this felt or whether her treatment was fair.

clear comparison and explanation of key difference, though this could be explored further

evidence to support differences between two texts

Comments on Response 2

This is a much better response as the student has identified the key difference between the texts and compares them throughout, rather than dealing with the texts separately. The evidence is used well as the student is inferring meaning from the quotations, thinking about what they suggest as well as what they literally tell the reader.

Responding to an English Literature task

1 Read the following poem, 'The Hero'. As you read, think about the following questions:

- What is this poem about?
- What ideas and feelings do you think the writer is communicating?
- What do you notice about the ways the poet has communicated these ideas and feelings to the reader?

The Hero

'Jack fell as he'd have wished,' the Mother said,
And folded up the letter that she'd read.
'The Colonel writes so nicely.' Something broke
In the tired voice that quavered to a choke.
She half looked up. 'We mothers are so proud
Of our dead soldiers.' Then her face was bowed.

Quietly the Brother Officer went out.
He'd told the poor old dear some gallant lies
That she would nourish all her days, no doubt.
For while he coughed and mumbled, her weak eyes
Had shone with gentle triumph, brimmed with joy,
Because he'd been so brave, her glorious boy.

He thought how 'Jack', cold-footed, useless swine,
Had panicked down the trench that night the mine
Went up at Wicked Corner; how he'd tried
To get sent home, and how, at last, he died,
Blown to small bits. And no one seemed to care
Except that lonely woman with white hair.

Siegfried Sassoon

2 Now read the following poem, 'Arms and the Boy'. As you read, remember to think about the following questions:

- What is this poem about?
- What ideas and feelings do you think the writer is communicating?
- What do you notice about the ways the poet has communicated these ideas and feelings to the reader?

Arms and the Boy

Let the boy try along this bayonet-blade
How cold steel is, and keen with hunger of blood;
Blue with all malice, like a madman's flash;
And thinly drawn with famishing for flesh.

Lend him to stroke these blind, blunt bullet-heads
Which long to nuzzle in the hearts of lads.
Or give him cartridges of fine zinc teeth,
Sharp with the sharpness of grief and death.

For his teeth seem for laughing round an apple.
There lurk no claws behind his fingers supple;
And God will grow no talons at his heels,
Nor antlers through the thickness of his curls.

Wilfred Owen

Your task

Compare the ways the poets present attitudes towards young soldiers in 'The Hero' and 'Arms and the Boy'.

Checklist for success

A successful response should:

- compare the poems, looking at the links and connections between them

- demonstrate your understanding of ideas and feelings in both poems

- include some well-selected evidence to support your comparison

- analyse the effects of particular words, literary techniques and structural features, linked to the ideas and feelings in both poems.

Reflecting on your progress

3 Read the following section of a response to this task. As you read, think about what the student has done well and what advice they might need in order to make more progress.

Response 1

Both of these poems are about war. The poem is about a   — simple connection between the poems

mother who has heard that her son has died in the war.

The poem is sad because the mother thinks her son was   — simple awareness of content

brave but the soldier who comes to tell her says that he

was a coward. The mother is described as if she is weak

and old: 'tired old voice that quavered to a choke'. This

makes her seem weak and also that she is upset because — comment on effect of word choices

'choke' sounds like she is trying not to cry. The second

poem is also about soldiers in the war. This poem is all   — link between the two poems

about the dangers of war. The poet uses words like: 'blood' — comment on effect of word choices

and 'flesh' and 'bullet' to show that war is dangerous.

Both poems talk about lives being wasted in war and   — structured comment on the similarity between the two poems

how it is tragic. Both use the word 'boy' to describe the

soldiers. This suggests that the soldiers are young and   — use of evidence to support connection between the poems

the poets both suggest that war wastes lives.

Comments on Response 1

This response deals quite well with the surface level of the poems. Rather than comparing, it deals with both poems separately and then brings them together to make a clear link towards the end. The student makes a straightforward link between the content of the poems and uses clear supporting evidence, although more ideas about what both poems are concerned with would be useful.

4 How could this sample response be improved? Using the middle rung of the Check your progress ladder at the end of this chapter, think about what advice you might give to this student in order to improve their work.

5 Now read Response 2. As you read, think about what the student has done that is an improvement on Response 1, and what advice this student might need in order to make even more progress.

Response 2

Both poems are concerned with the effects of war. Both suggest that innocent lives are lost, although one focuses on one particular boy, 'Jack', and the other refers to a nameless 'boy', which suggests that it is all innocent boys that the poet is concerned with.

> clear connection between the poems

> clear comparison between how ideas are presented

The title of Sassoon's poem is ironic, as the boy is clearly not a 'hero' to the soldier. He is described as being 'cold-footed' and a 'useless swine' although it is clear that the poet doesn't see the boy this way. The reader infers that the boy was desperately suffering from the horrors of war: 'panicked' and 'tried to get sent home'.

> embedded evidence used to support ideas

The title of Owen's poem is also significant because it links together 'arms' or weapons, with the idea of 'boy' – a word that is also used by Sassoon to describe the soldier in his poem. Owen describes how boys are too innocent and vulnerable to be given weapons and sent off to war, and personifies the weapons as 'hunger', 'malice' and 'famishing' in order to make them seem very threatening. Owen, like Sassoon, shows the reader that the boy is precious: he describes him as 'laughing', 'the thickness of his curls' and having 'supple' fingers, as if he is full of life which should not be wasted. Sassoon presents a similar idea of the boy being precious, but this time uses the figure of the mother to show how much he will be missed and how proud she is of her 'precious boy'.

> developing comparison of use of title in both poems

> clear understanding of the main idea in the poem

> correct use of technical term

> developed comparison of the ways ideas are presented

Comments on Response 2

This is a clear comparative response. The student is dealing with both poems at the same time, explaining clearly what they are both about and how both poets have presented their ideas. Evidence is used well to support the explanation of ideas, and there is a correct identification of a specific technique with some examples.

Check your progress

- I can comment in detail on the connections between texts.
- I can present a comparison between the viewpoints expressed in two texts.
- I can select and use details from both texts to present a detailed comparison of viewpoint.
- I can analyse the similarities and differences between the ways a similar idea or topic is presented in two texts.

- I can clearly explain the connections between texts.
- I can make clear comparisons of viewpoint based on inferences from the texts.
- I can use evidence from both texts to present my comparisons between different viewpoints.
- I can make clear comparisons between the ways writers use language and structure to express their viewpoints.

- I can identify the connections between texts.
- I can identify different viewpoints and explain what the similarities or differences are.
- I can select some appropriate evidence from both texts to support my points about similarities and differences.
- I can identify similarities and differences between how ideas have been presented in two texts.

Chapter 8

Writing creatively

In this chapter, you will learn about how writers craft vivid and creative texts, using skills of description and narration, and apply what you have learned to your own writing. You will learn how to evoke convincing settings, create memorable characters, structure descriptions and stories in interesting ways and how to come up with original ideas quickly and effectively.

In this chapter, you will learn

- how to describe setting and atmosphere
- how to describe people and events
- how to structure description
- how to build ideas for a descriptive task
- how to structure narratives effectively
- how to use characterisation and voice effectively
- how to generate ideas for your narrative response
- how to apply your skills to an English Language task.

	English Language GCSE	**English Language GCSE**
Which AOs are covered?	AO5 Communicate clearly, effectively and imaginatively, selecting and adapting tone, style and register for different forms, purposes and audiences Organise information and ideas, using structural and grammatical features to support coherence and cohesion of texts	AO6 Candidates must use a range of vocabulary and sentence structures for clarity, purpose and effect, with accurate spelling and punctuation
How will this be tested?	Questions will require you to apply what you have learned about the overall organisation of texts so that they are both clear and engaging. They will also require you to write for one of two purposes – to describe or to narrate, so you will need to show your ability to adapt and craft language appropriately.	Questions will require you to think of original yet accurate ways of expressing yourself in sentences. You will be expected to demonstrate a wide but appropriate vocabulary. You will need to show that you can spell those vocabulary choices accurately and punctuate those sentences effectively and accurately.

Describe setting and atmosphere

Learning objectives
You will learn how to
- use a range of techniques to make your descriptions of places vivid and memorable
- convey atmosphere through the language you use.

Assessment objectives
- English Language AO5, AO6

How can you describe settings and atmosphere in a memorable way?

Getting you thinking

Look at this photo.

1 Write a paragraph describing what you see in this picture. What sort of feeling or atmosphere is created by it? Think about the different elements to the photo – what is in the foreground and background, for example?

Explore the skills

You need to be precise when you describe settings or locations, but you also need to convey the 'feeling' or mood.

Read the following description of the same parsonage from the photo, written in 1857.

The house is of grey stone **1**, two stories high, heavily roofed with flags, in order to resist the winds that might strip off a lighter covering. It appears to have been built about a hundred years ago **2**, and to consist of four rooms on each story; the two windows on the right **3** (as the visitor stands, with his back to the church, ready to enter in at the front door) belonging to Mr. Brontë's study, the two on the left to the family sitting-room. Everything about the place tells of the most dainty order, the most exquisite cleanliness. **4** The door-steps are spotless; the small old-fashioned window-panes glitter like looking-glass. **5**
Inside and outside of that house cleanliness goes up into its essence, purity. **6**

Elizabeth Gaskell, from *The Life of Charlotte Brontë*

1 noun phrase conveys colour and texture of building

2 **adverbial** of time

3 **prepositional phrases**

4 further noun phrases

5 simile develops the overall description

6 final summary sentence

2 What precise 'factual' information does the writer provide in the paragraph?

3 What impression or 'feel' is given? What words or phrases tell us this?

4 How is the overall tone in this description different from the paragraph you wrote earlier?

Read the following alternative description of the parsonage based on the photo.

The parsonage is a gloomy/bright/lively place to grow up in. The echoey/polished/plush corridors seem never-ending, and the watchful/comfy/looming trees in the graveyard cast long/short/thin shadows on the earth, and the gravestones are covered/ smothered/layered with moss and leaves.

Key terms

adverbial: a phrase which tells us something more about a verb or a sentence

prepositional phrase: phrases which help us understand the relationship between things or ideas: for example, when they occurred or where they are positioned

5 Look at the highlighted words above.

a Select and note down the adjectives or verbs which convey a less pleasant or more threatening tone.

b Write a sentence explaining the effect of using that word. For example:

'gloomy: means dark and dull, and suggests a damp, shadowy place.'

6 Continue the description in a similar gloomy style. For example, write one or two sentences describing a fireplace, a particular gravestone, or something else of your own choice. You could find a picture to help you come up with ideas.

Develop the skills

Building description around a noun is a very effective way of getting your reader to 'see' what is in your head. For example:

Below me, I can see the narrow, stony path which winds and twists across the snowy moors

- adjectives
- main 'thing' being described
- verbs also describing the path
- further detail about where the path is

7 Can you build a similar description around the nouns highlighted below?

By the path is a .... flower, which sways and .... in the icy earth. The ....clouds race above me in the wintry sky. Ahead is a .... cottage, which is battered and ....by the fierce gales.

Another key aspect of descriptive writing is **imagery**. This is particularly effective when you want to create original or vivid word pictures in your reader's mind.

8 For example, in the parsonage extract in Activity 1, what simile does Gaskell use to describe one key feature of the building? What is the effect it creates?

Now read this extract from a book by an English writer describing the Cisa pass near Parma in Italy.

9 Where does Jones use imagery here? For example, think about the way he uses verbs to describe the road, or how he describes the villages. Copy and complete the following table.

> It's a spectacular road that lifts you above the fog of the plain: supported on concrete stilts it struts over valleys, and its long tunnels puncture the mountains. A few hundred metres below the asphalt, picturesque mountain villages huddle around their bell-towers, appearing from above like random piles of matchboxes. Now, in October, the mountain colours are crisp and autumnal: white wood-smoke gusting between dark green pines.
>
> Tobias Jones, from *The Dark Heart of Italy*

Imagery	Example	Effect
metaphors	'struts over valleys'	He **personifies** the road, making it sound as if it is walking in giant steps, almost boastfully.
simile		

10 Complete these descriptions using your own similes and metaphors. Use **personification** where appropriate.

> The shimmering river glistens like a ....
> as it winds and curves across the desert. Here and
> there, palm-trees are dotted across the landscape
> like ....
>
> The dunes are like all-knowing gods: they
> .... us as we pass, showing little
> emotion on their .... faces.

Key term

personification: when an object or location is described as if it had human characteristics, for example, 'as the storm gathered, the thunder *grumbled* above us, and the rain *tiptoed* across the window pane…'

11 Jones also draws on a range of sensory perceptions to create the scene. For example, the 'crisp' mountain colours tell us that he can see things sharply and clearly. What other senses does he draw on?

Apply the skills

12 Complete the following task.

Look at this photo, and then write 1–2 paragraphs describing the setting and the atmosphere.

Checklist for success

- Describe things precisely, for example, using numbers, size or scale.
- Consider age, condition.
- Refer to the weather, if appropriate.
- Use powerful and original imagery to create word pictures.
- Consider sound, smell, texture, taste and sight.

Check your progress:

▲▲▲ I can describe settings using a wide range of vocabulary, and thoughtfully selected language features, such as imagery.

▲▲ I can describe settings using appropriate vocabulary and language features, including imagery in places.

▲ I can describe settings precisely and choose some vocabulary for effect.

Describe people and events

Learning objectives
You will learn how to
- use a range of techniques to make your descriptions of people vivid and memorable
- convey experiences and events in a convincing way.

Assessment objectives
- English Language AO5, AO6

How can you describe people and events in a memorable way?

Getting you thinking

When you want to create a convincing portrayal of someone, it is important to consider a range of different aspects. For example, it is better to **show** how they look, speak and behave rather than **tell** the reader what someone is like.

Look at this image of Bill Sikes, a famous villain from Charles Dickens's *Oliver Twist*.

Key term

show, not tell: rather than say what someone or something is like, for example, 'nasty', show them being nasty or their 'nasty' appearance.

1 Basing your ideas on the picture, make notes on Sikes's appearance, how you think he might behave, and how he might speak.

Explore the skills

Here is Dickens's own description of Sikes:

> He had [...] a beard of three days' growth: and two scowling eyes; one of which displayed various parti-coloured symptoms of having been recently damaged by a blow.
> 'Come in, d'ye hear?' growled this engaging ruffian.
> A white shaggy dog, with his face scratched and torn in twenty different places, skulked into the room.
>
> Charles Dickens, from *Oliver Twist*

- facial feature implies he can't be bothered to shave
- 'scowling' means angrily or in a bad temper
- the description of the bruised eye suggests he has been in a fight
- verb 'growled' tells us his tone of voice
- 'engaging' means 'pleasant' or 'welcoming' – presumably meant sarcastically

2 What is the overall impression given of Sikes?

3 Why do you think Dickens adds the detail about Sikes's dog?

4 Choosing one of the aspects *not* mentioned in Dickens's description, for example, the stick in the picture, write another sentence about Sikes.

For example:

- use a verb to describe how Sikes is moving or gesturing
- use one or more adjectives to describe the item or feature concerned.

Develop the skills

Read the following description of the writer Lorna Sage's grandmother.

> Asthma lent a breathy vehemence to her curses and when she laughed she'd fall into wheezing fits that required a sniff of smelling-salts. She had a repertoire of mysterious catchphrases that always sent her off. If anyone asked her the time, she'd retort, 'just struck an elephant!' and cackle triumphantly. Then, 'Dew, Dew' she'd mutter as she got her breath back – or that's what it sounded like – meaning 'Deary me', or 'Well, well', shaking her head. That 'ew' sound was ubiquitous with her. She pronounced 'you' as 'ew', puckering up her small mouth as if to savour the nice or nasty taste you represented.
>
> She had lost her teeth and could make a most ghoulish face by arranging the false set, gums and all, outside her lips, in a voracious grin. [...]

> She was soft and slightly powdery to the touch, as though she'd been dusted all over with icing sugar like a sponge cake. She shared her Edwardian generation's genteel contempt for sunburn and freckles, and thanks to her nocturnal habits her skin was eerily pale.
>
> Lorna Sage, from *Bad Blood*

5 What do we learn about how Lorna Sage's grandmother looks, acts and speaks from this extract?

6 The writer uses several of the five senses to create this portrait: which ones, and where?

7 The writer says that the grandmother squeezed her lips together when she spoke as if deciding whether someone tasted 'nice' or 'nasty'. What fairy tale or story does this remind you of?

8 What simile does the writer use to describe the feel of her grandmother's skin? Why is this an appropriate comparison when describing a grandmother?

9 Write your own descriptive paragraph about an older person, but make it about someone who appears warm and comforting, and not witch-like!

In this further extract from *Bad Blood*, Lorna Sage describes learning to swim with her friend Gail.

Learning to swim was the first important thing we did together. Gail was good at gym and athletics, but like me she'd been put off swimming by high school excursions to Whitchurch public baths – small, steamy, stinking of chlorine, with cracked tiles and deafening echoes, the gym mistress counting to three then pushing you in. Now, in the summer holidays, she and I went down to the mere like other Hanmer kids (who didn't much speak to us since we'd passed the eleven plus), changed on the bank among the goose and duck droppings, and fooled around in warm water that smelled of rain until we found we could float and then swim – although in a style that horrified the gym mistress when we went back to school. Even now, if I say to myself 'dog-paddle' I can see Gail's head sticking up out of the soupy mere water in her rubber bathing hat, her eyes hard as pebbles with determination, her eyelashes glued together with the wet, while she paddled furiously and hardly moved at all. I kept pace and did the same, we both learned to dog-paddle and soon it was easy to swim whole lengths, even in the horrible baths.

topic sentence introduces the experience

sums up the look, feel and smell of the baths

tells us about a specific person and her behaviour

Lorna Sage manages to bring together descriptions of people *and* places to evoke the experience.

10 What do we learn about the public baths and the mere? What attitude does Lorna Sage have to them?

11 What do we learn about: the gym mistress; the other children in the village; Gail? What impression does Lorna Sage want us to have?

12 What descriptive phrase perfectly links the final sentence to the beginning?

Switching between descriptions of people and places in this way will make past events or experiences all the more realistic and vivid for your readers.

Apply the skills

13 Choose one of these three experiences or events:

- learning to ride a bike or a pony
- helping a relative or family friend out with a job
- going on public transport on your own for the first time.

Jot down quickly a few notes about:

- 1–2 people involved (could be a friend, or someone in authority)
- the scene, setting or place, for example, your street, a house, a train station
- your feelings about the experience or people involved.

Now complete the following task.

> Write a description of the experience in no more than 175 words.

Checklist for success

- Create a convincing portrayal of the people involved through showing the reader details about appearance, behaviour and speech.
- Create a realistic picture of the experience itself through details about the setting and what happened and your response/feelings about it.

Check your progress:

▲▲▲ I can write about people and experiences in convincing ways by carefully selecting from a wide range of vocabulary and using similes or metaphors where appropriate.

▲▲ I can use well-chosen vocabulary to portray an experience and the people involved.

▲ I can write about people and experiences with some reference to how people look, speak and behave.

Structure a description

Learning objective
You will learn how to
• use a range of techniques to structure your descriptions in ways that keep readers interested and engaged.

Assessment objectives
• English Language AO5, AO6

How can you structure your descriptions to keep readers interested?

Getting you thinking

Imagine you write a description of walking by the sea or a lake and being caught in a storm.

1 What particular things would you describe or comment on? List 3–4 ideas, for example:

• aspects of the weather

2 What order would you describe them in? Is there a 'right' or logical order? Or could you describe them in any sequence?

Explore the skills

Structuring a description is all about *what* you choose to focus on, *the way you look at it* and the *order in which you reveal the details*.

Read this extract from a short story called 'Rain'.

> Still the grumbling clouds hold back, occasionally letting go a thunderclap or a flash of lightning like a stinging slap across someone's cheek, a sharp insult that cuts through the skin. There is no release, just a regathering of explosive anger, like a mad woman screaming down a carpeted hallway.
>
> The sweat gathers on the back of her neck, under her thick black hair, steaming her face, each wiry hair sticking to her fingers when she tries to brush it off.
>
> On the subway, she has the bad luck of getting into an un-air conditioned car and the air is more suffocating than ever, the heat holding the smells of the bodies around her: sweat, deodorant, stale cigarette smoke, old hamburgers.

Someone stands up as she gets in and she squeezes in between an old Chinese man, curled like a shrimp over the shopping bag he clutches in his tiny hands, and a hugely fat woman, her body overflowing into the seat beside her. No one ever rushes at rush hour.

Ameena Meer, from 'Rain'

3 How does Ameena Meer structure her writing? *What* does she focus on in each separate paragraph?

4 Imagine Ameena leaves at the next station. *Plan* (don't write!) three further paragraphs about her experience of travelling in the city in the rain. Decide on a *focus* for each paragraph and *why it has been chosen*.

The first has been done for you…

- Paragraph 5: The stairs on the way out of the station up to the pavement… (why? Because she is pressed against the grimy wall)
- Paragraph 6:
- Paragraph 7:

5 Another key feature of Ameena Meer's writing is **how** she describes each aspect in her description. For example, she 'zooms in' (rather like using a camera) on one very specific detail in paragraph 2.

   a What is it?

   b How does this help us understand how she is feeling?

6 Plan your own 'zoom in' detail (or two) for paragraphs 5, 6 and 7. The first has been done for you.

Paragraph 5: stairs on way out of station
Zoom-in detail: a tatty poster of a model, peeling off the wall

7 Finally, consider the **order** of your paragraphs. A typical sequence would follow Ameena's journey in time, but there are alternatives. How has this student 'played around with time'?

Paragraph 5: leaving the station via the stairs

Paragraph 6: at her apartment that night, looking out at the city

Paragraph 7: remembering a beggar in the street at the top of the stairs

Develop the skills

The order of your sentences in each paragraph is equally important. For example, here is a student's first paragraph about the storm:

At first, there is little sign of the storm. There is blue sky and a few fluffy smudges in the distance, but soon these approach the still lake, getting darker all the time. Suddenly, the tiny patch of blue sky has gone.

— short topic sentence introduces the scene

— second sentence explains more or adds detail

— final sentence emphasises the change

8 Decide:

- your **focus** for the next paragraph
- a **detail** to zoom in on.

9 Now, write your own three-sentence paragraph based on your plan.

- Start with a topic sentence.
- Add a second with a zoom-in detail.
- Finish with a third that sums up, or emphasises a key idea or aspect.

In descriptive writing, you can also:

- use repetition of key sentences or paragraphs to create an almost poetic patterning, or echoes of ideas
- vary your sentence and paragraph style to introduce a new mood or cut from one thing to another.

For example:

> I am sitting on a narrow ledge by the side of the lake. The warm sun makes my skin glow, and the water sparkles and glitters. I am alone, but feel peaceful.
>
> The face of the mountain is calm and smiles down on me.
>
> At first, there is little sign of the storm. There is blue sky and a few fluffy smudges in the distance, but soon these approach the still lake, getting darker all the time. Suddenly, the tiny patch of blue sky has gone.
>
> In a few minutes, rain is spattering my face, and the surface of the sea is a million pinpricks on a black dress. A small boat which was bobbing gently now rocks violently from side to side, the rusted letters of its name blurred and almost invisible. The water swells, and then rises like a dormant beast, waking from its slumber to threaten the path on which I stand.
>
> Now, when I glimpse the mountain it is not smiling.

10 How does the writer use different paragraph lengths to **focus on different aspects**?

11 What **patterns** or **repetitions** can you see?

12 How is the **order of what is happening** made clear? (Think about linking words and phrases.)

Apply the skills

Now, read this task and complete the activities that follow it.

> Write a blog entry describing your experience of an extreme weather event, for example, heatwave, flood, snowstorm, fog.

13 Plan four to five paragraphs, deciding what you would include in each.

14 Draft the paragraphs, thinking carefully about how the structure can alter the effect.

Checklist for success

- Use topic sentences in paragraphs to introduce or create a focus.
- Deal with a different aspect or focus in each paragraph of your description.
- Consider varying the sequence of your paragraphs or of your sentences *in* paragraphs to create particular effects.
- Use a variety of sentence and paragraph lengths to maintain your reader's interest.

Check your progress:

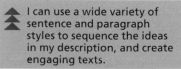
I can use a wide variety of sentence and paragraph styles to sequence the ideas in my description, and create engaging texts.

I can use topic sentences and paragraphs which deal with separate parts of my description, and vary my structure.

I can write a description which is split into different paragraphs, each with a new focus.

Build ideas for a descriptive task

Learning objective
You will learn how to
• generate ideas for a descriptive writing task.

Assessment objectives
• English Language AO5, AO6

How can you quickly come up with ideas for your descriptive task?

Getting you thinking

Read this task.

> A travel website is running a competition asking people to write about an exciting outdoor experience they have had. Write a description suggested by this picture.

A person responding to the task has begun to make notes based on the photo.

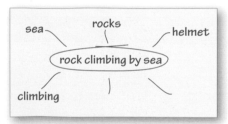

1. This is a good start, but can you add any further words that come to mind based on:

   • what else you can see in the photo
   • the climber's feelings or the mood of the picture
   • anything you *can't* see but could perhaps be seen by the climber in the picture?

2. **a** Try out one or more of these other ways of generating ideas:

   • a list of words
   • words dotted all over the page with lines between them to show links
   • a table with headings (sights/sounds/textures/smells/tastes).

   b Which works best for you?

3. Once you have your list or other diagram, select the most vivid or interesting ideas, or cut the least interesting ones.

Explore the skills

When you generate initial words or phrases, develop them by adding precise detail. For example, you could add sensory detail: '*bright, sparkling* surface of the water'.

4   Can you add further 'sense' adjectives to these nouns?

> '........................... rock face' (feel, texture)
>
> '.......................rope' (colour, appearance, size)
>
> '.......................sea air' (taste, smell?)
>
> '...................seagulls' (sound?)

Develop the skills

5   If you plan very quickly, you can even organise your initial ideas into paragraphs. Can you add two further 'areas' to this student's plan?

> Paragraph 1: Looking down at the sea
>
> Paragraph 2: The feel of the rocks
>
> Paragraph 3: Looking up at the sky above
>
> Paragraph 4:
>
> Paragraph 5:

Apply the skills

6   Now look at this writing task.

> Your local railway station is running a competition about people's memories of train journeys. Write a description suggested by this picture.

Generate ideas for this task using the methods you have found out about.

Checklist for success

* Select your preferred method for generating ideas.
* Generate ideas quickly and efficiently, selecting the ones which have most potential.
* Add vivid details and divide into paragraphs.

Check your progress:

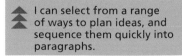

▲▲ I can select from a range of ways to plan ideas, and sequence them quickly into paragraphs.

▲ I can use different methods to generate ideas, and can add details to them.

▲ I can come up with some ideas using a spider diagram before I start writing.

Structure narratives effectively

Learning objective
You will learn how to
- use a range of techniques to structure your narratives in ways that keep readers interested and engaged.

Assessment objectives
- English Language AO5, AO6

How can you structure your stories to keep readers interested?

Getting you thinking

Read these openings to stories.

1. Which of these openings would make you want to read on? Why?

2. What differences do you notice between them?

'They murdered him.'

> Robert Cormier, from *The Chocolate War*

'During the whole of a dull, dark, and soundless day in the autumn of the year, when the clouds hung oppressively low in the heavens, I had been passing alone, on horseback, through a singularly dreary tract of country; and at length found myself, as the shades of the evening drew on, within view of the melancholy House of Usher.'

> Edgar Allan Poe, from *The Fall of the House of Usher*

'The morning had dawned clear and cold with a crispness that hinted at the end of summer. They set forth at daybreak to see a man beheaded, twenty in all, and Bran rode among them, nervous with excitement. This was the first time he had been deemed old enough to go with his lord father and his brothers to see the king's justice done. It was the ninth year of summer, and the seventh of Bran's life.'

> George R.R. Martin, from *A Song of Ice and Fire*

'You must go back with me to the autumn of 1827.'

> Anne Brontë, from *The Tenant of Wildfell Hall*

Explore the skills

Writers often use openings of stories to establish particular things such as:

- the mood/atmosphere or time
- the setting or location
- a particular character or relationship
- a key event or action
- direct contact with the reader.

Or they raise questions about them: for example, who has been murdered?

3 **a** Which of the story openings establish these aspects or ask questions?

b Do any combine these approaches?

Imagine you have been asked to write a short story called 'The Visit'.

Read this opening line which establishes location and mood.

> The long corridor had a worn, dark red carpet with cigarette burns dotted along it...

4 Jot down some ideas for what the story might be about (who is its **protagonist**, what is happening, or will happen).

Now note down some descriptive details, for example:

- the wall: *smoke-stained, yellowing, torn wallpaper*
- objects such as paintings, candles, lamps
- smells, textures.

Key term

protagonist: the central character in a novel, play or film

5 Now choose one or two of these details to write a second 'location and mood' sentence.

6 **a** How would you need to change or adapt your opening if you wanted to make 'direct contact' with the reader?

b Write an alternative sentence addressing the reader directly ('You don't believe me?' or 'I need to tell you...').

Develop the skills

Often writers **withhold** (or keep back) information from a reader leaving them guessing: Who? What? When? Where?

7 Which of the four openings at the start of this section withholds information most effectively?

Here are two attempts by students at writing the opening to a story called 'The Visit'.

Student A

> I arrived at number 1 Park Avenue clutching the letter from my great uncle telling me to meet him at his house.

Student B

> *The letter in my hand, I arrived at the house. He had told me to meet him there.*

8　**a** Which of these holds information back?

　　b How?

9　Now you try: copy and adapt the opening to the story below so that the names are changed to pronouns, and you don't reveal it is a watch until the final sentence.

Original version	Your version
As I entered the huge lounge, I could see my uncle Frederick standing at the window. Frederick turned and spoke to me: 'I have some news for you, Stephen. I have decided to give you this gold watch that belonged to your father.' He handed me the watch, and I looked at it in my hand. It was a beautiful piece, with pearl numbers and hands made of inlaid gold.	As I entered the huge lounge, I could see him standing at the window.

The structure of a short story includes the elements you learned about in Chapter 2.

For example, here is a different story:

- **Introduction:** Boy on school trip goes to a museum.
- **Complication:** Gets lost and finds himself in the Egyptian room.
- **Rising action/development:** A 'mummy' seems to move, gets up and walks towards him.
- **Climax:** He searches desperately for a way out, and faints as the mummy approaches.
- **Resolution:** He awakes to find himself sitting on the coach with his class. He learns that no such room exists as it was destroyed by fire some years back.

10　However, the events of the story can be revealed in different ways. For example:

- Do you have to begin with the boy arriving at the museum? Where else could the story start?
- How or where could you use **flashback?**

Key term

flashback: a point in a story when a character remembers or goes back over previous events

The way you order and structure the events of your story, and your paragraphs, are vital in engaging your reader and keeping them interested. Read these four opening paragraphs from the same story about the mummy.

11 At what stage of the original plan does this version begin?

12 Where does the writer mention the school visit, if at all?

13 What is the effect of the single word paragraph 'Idiot.'?

14 Add a fifth paragraph that goes back in time and tells us a bit more about:

- where Dai is and how he came to be in the Egyptian room
- who he is, what he's like.

You could start…

> His school had arrived at the museum at 2pm. Dai hadn't wanted to go…he hated history, so…

> The thing moved. Although the glass case was dusty, and the inscription on the label was too worn to read, Dai was certain of it. Yes…there it was again! The tight rolls of bandaging seemed to slip or shift. But, it couldn't have, could it?
>
> Dai was furious with himself for getting lost. If only he'd stuck with their teacher, he'd have been ok.
>
> Idiot.
>
> He looked at the glass case again, as if in a trance. It was sitting up! The pale stiff dead thing was slowly raising its body from the case.

Apply the skills

15 Complete the following task.

Plan your own story based on the title 'The Visit' and write the first 2–3 paragraphs of it.

Think about how you can engage the reader.

Checklist for success

- Make sure your story has an interesting 'complication'.
- Consider using devices such as flashback or starting **in medias res**.
- Use a range of paragraph lengths and styles to keep your reader interested.

Key term

in medias res: 'in the middle of things' – you begin your story right in the heart of the action, without an 'introduction'

Check your progress:

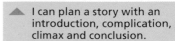 I can adapt and alter my plan so that it engages the reader's interest straight away, and maintains it throughout through clever use of paragraph styles and focuses.

 I can plan a story and choose different ways of opening it to get the reader interested.

I can plan a story with an introduction, complication, climax and conclusion.

Create convincing characterisation and voice

Learning objectives
You will learn how to
- improve characterisation in a variety of ways
- develop a distinctive voice.

Assessment objectives
- English Language AO5, AO6

How can you make your characters or narrators interesting?

Getting you thinking

1 Read this extract from the novel *Small Island*. In it, the narrator, called Hortense, has just arrived in England from Jamaica.

I did not see what now came through the door, it came through so fast. It could have been a large dog the way it leaped and bounded towards me. It was only when I heard, 'Hortense,' uttered from its mouth that I realised it was my husband. 'Hortense. You here! You here at last, Hortense!'

I folded my arms, sat on my trunk and averted my eye. He stopped in front of me. His arms still open wide ready for me to run into. 'Don't Hortense me, Gilbert Joseph.'

His arms slowly rested to his sides as he said, 'You no pleased to see me, Hortense?'

I quoted precisely from the letter. 'I will be at the dockside to meet you. You will see me there jumping and waving and calling your name with longing in my tone.'

'How you find this place, Hortense?' was all the man said.

'Without your help, Gilbert Joseph, that's how I find this place. With no help from you. Where were you? Why you no come to meet me? Why you no waving and calling my name with longing in your tone?'

Andrea Levy, from *Small Island*

2 What do we find out about what's happened from this conversation?

3 What impression are we given of Hortense and Gilbert?

Explore the skills

Characterisation is the way in which writers build a convincing portrayal of a person. This can be done in many ways (see 8.2), but **dialogue** is key. This can show us what a person is like.

For example:

- use of **dialect** in the short exclamation: 'You here!'

- explanations: 'Without your help, Gilbert Joseph, that's how I find this place'

- questions: 'Where were you? Why you no come to see me?'

- and through the descriptive detail around dialogue.

<aside>
Key term

dialect: specific vocabulary or grammar form linked to a particular culture or country. 'You here!' rather than 'Are you here?'
</aside>

> I folded my arms, sat on my trunk and averted my eye. He stopped in front of me. His arms still open wide ready for me to run into. 'Don't Hortense me, Gilbert Joseph.'

shows us the narrator's actions and implies her mood

shows us Gilbert's actions and response

simple line of speech conveys exactly how Hortense feels

The way Hortense speaks gives us a strong sense of her character: proud, disappointed... and rather sarcastic!

4 Continue the dialogue after the end of the extract.

- Add one line of Gilbert's spoken response to the accusation (perhaps his reason for not being at the dockside).

- Add one further line of speech from Hortense.

- Include at least one action or gesture on Gilbert's part (does he sit on the step? Go to help Hortense stand up?).

5 Now check and edit your work. Make sure you set out dialogue correctly using speech marks, and use other punctuation accurately.

Develop the skills

Character can also be revealed through what someone observes, not just their speech.

Read this short extract from 'The Ice Palace' by F. Scott Fitzgerald. Sally Carrol, from the southern states of America, is staying with her fiancé's parents in the North.

> It was a large room with a Madonna over the fireplace and rows upon rows of books in covers of light gold and dark gold and shiny red.

> All the chairs had little lace squares where one's head should rest, the couch was just comfortable, the books looked as if they had been read – some – and Sally Carrol had an instantaneous vision of the battered old library at home, with her father's huge medical books, and the oil-paintings of her three great-uncles, and the old couch that had been mended up for forty-five years and was still luxurious to dream in. This room struck her as being neither attractive nor particularly otherwise. It was simply a room with a lot of fairly expensive things in it that all looked about fifteen years old.
>
> F. Scott Fitzgerald, from 'The Ice Palace'

Fitzgerald uses Sally's own observations and opinions to tell us about her as a person.

6 In what way are the objects in her fiancé's house different from her own? Think about:

- the books
- the couch.

7 What do these observations suggest or imply about her views of her fiancé's house (and perhaps him too)?

8 **Voice** can also be conveyed, even when a character isn't speaking. Can you hear Sally's voice in the final two sentences? What tone or manner are they expressed in?

9 What overall sense do you get of Sally from this passage?

Characterisation can also be conveyed by the style and type of sentences. Read these two extracts by students responding to a similar task.

Student A

You think I was pleased to get here? Let me tell you the truth. The city was a disappointment. I had expected bright lights, cafés open till midnight, limousines carrying film-stars. No. I got a gloomy street with rubbish in the gutters. All the houses were dark.

— direct question to reader, and short sharp answer

— clear statement of fact

— negative adjectives

Student B

She pressed her face against the train's window as the sparkling streets with their necklaces of light curved and swirled towards her and the stars glittered above the cathedral rising majestically from the beating heart of the city.

— use of third person

— imagery suggests precious vision

— verb continues same idea

— city is personified

10 How do the different sentence styles match the mood of the characters in each case?

11 What do the language choices tell us about the way the characters feel? Which text tells us directly; which implies it?

> ### Apply the skills

12 Complete the following task.

Write two opening paragraphs from a story in which your main character arrives in a city from the countryside.

Checklist for success

- Use dialogue to convey how your character feels.
- Use description within the dialogue to add detail to what they do or how they react to others.
- Describe how they observe their surroundings or what happens to them.
- Use sentence style to match their mood or observations and establish their voice.
- Decide whether to use first- or third-person narration to match the effect you wish to create.

Check your progress:

I can use dialogue convincingly to convey character and also adapt sentence style to suggest voice and viewpoint.

I can use dialogue and description to tell the reader what is happening and convey character.

I can use direct speech to tell the reader something about my character.

Generate ideas for your narrative response

Learning objective
You will learn how to
- plan and generate ideas for a story quickly and efficiently.

Assessment objectives
- English Language AO5, AO6

How can you come up with good ideas for a short story or short story opening in a short space of time?

Getting you thinking

1 Look at this story task.

> Write the opening to a story about a place that has been used for junk or rubbish.

    a In no more than five minutes, write down 2–3 ideas for a story based on this subject.

    b How easy was this to do? What would have helped you (apart from more time!)?

Explore the skills

If you have little time to plan a story, it is important you have a basic structure to work to, even if you only jot down a few key details.

Think about **who, what, when** and **why.** (The 'where' has been decided for you, although you could be more specific or creative: the 'where' could be a box, trunk, even someone's head!)

Here is one student's set of notes:

However, one thing is missing: this really needs some sort of **development**. Where is the story going?

2 Can you come up with at least one idea for what might happen to her when she is at the scrap yard?

    Think about:
- someone she might meet
- an event or happening

    OR

- a combination of both of these.

3 Share your ideas and evaluate which of the ideas you hear or learn about have the most potential.

Where?	Scrap-metal yard (all sorts, not just cars)
Who?	Taylor, a girl of 15
What (is she doing)?	Bunking off school
When?	Early morning
Why?	Can't face her exam – hasn't revised properly

Develop the skills

Of course, in your planning, it is great if you can think 'outside the box': in other words, come up with original ideas or unusual scenarios.

The same student has made some further quick notes. Here they are:

4 What unusual or original ideas did the student come up with?

> Taylor is in a wheelchair and has wheeled herself to the scrap yard. It's an old abandoned one, full of old medical equipment and a place she goes whenever she feels low.

5 If you have another character, think about how they will interact in an interesting way with your main character. For example:

- young main character meeting someone old, or vice versa
- main character meeting ghost of him or herself
- person meeting someone they hate or love
- someone in trouble meeting an authority figure (teacher or police officer)
- family member meeting another family member.

Which of these would you select if you were attempting the task?

What story is suggested by your choice?

Apply the skills

6 Read this task, and then plan your response in 4–5 minutes maximum.

> Write the opening part of a story that takes place in an abandoned building or setting.

Check your progress:

 I can generate a range of interesting, well-developed ideas and turn these into a plan with the key ingredients of a story.

 I can generate some good ideas and create a structured plan from them.

I can generate ideas and write a basic plan from them.

Checklist for success

- Plan quickly by making notes about **who** (protagonist), **what** (is happening), **when** (time of day, season and so on) and **why** (plus a bit more detail about the **where**).
- Note down additional details, such as other characters, and anything that will make your text original or different.

Apply your skills to an English Language task

Learning objectives
You will learn to
- apply the key skills from this chapter to an unseen English Language task
- reflect on your progress through looking at different responses to the task.

Assessment objectives
- English Language AO1, AO2

Responding to English Language tasks

1 Read the following task.

> You are going to enter a creative writing competition. In the competition, you have to write a description suggested by the photo.

Think about:

- What can you see in the picture? Where do you think it is?

- How could you create a vivid and detailed description for the reader?

Checklist for success

A successful response should include:
- vivid details of natural and man-made things in the picture

- a sense of the mood or atmosphere suggested by the image

- a sense of voice and perspective.

Reflecting on your progress

2 Read the following response to this task. As you read, think about what the student has done well and what advice they might need in order to make more progress.

Response 1

As I look in front of me I can see this big pile of cars which go on forever. They look like a mountain of cars which no one could ever climb. There must be literally hundreds of them.

effective simile describing what can be seen

I ask myself as I look at them, how did they get here?

question gives some variety to the narration

I can see one car which has this blue and grey colour. It looks like one of those American big limo type cars which you see teenagers in in rom-coms. It is empty now of course and it is leaning over as if it is going to fall any minute! But because it is all rusty it would probably break up into a million pieces anyway.

new paragraph moves onto one car in particular

I clamber up onto the heap of rubbish and try to open the handle. It feels grimy and greasy in my hand, so I change my mind and just peer in the window. The seats have lost their stuffing and there are bird droppings everywhere. The windows are all dusty and the dashboard is cracked, probably when the car was dumped, I guess.

reference to the sense of touch makes description more realistic

specific vocabulary term, relevant to cars

discourse marker signifies narrator's change of direction

Then I move round to the front of the car and inspect it. The front wheel on the driver's side is completely gone. Maybe it was stolen by someone who was rebuilding their own car? I know I should go from this deserted spot as it is dangerous but something like a magnet makes me stay.

It is sad to think about all these silent, old cars. Once they were loved by their owners but now they are just abandoned like toys. The way they are piled on top of each other is upsetting. If they were people they would be in pain, I think.

attempt to personify the cars to create a more original idea

However, my final thought as I leave this creepy place is that this would make a great film-set. There could be lots of actors and lights, and then the place would come alive again. This would be better than if it is a deserted old place with no one about.

last paragraph takes reader into new area

Comments on Response 1

This response focuses on the task set and has stuck to description rather than slipping into narrative. There are some attempts at detailed description in the features of some of the cars, but in places the vocabulary is repetitive and there is limited use of imagery. The student begins to suggest a mood and voice towards the end, when they start to personify the cars, but the idea is left undeveloped. The idea about the film-set is undeveloped and the description rather trails off.

3 How could this sample response be improved? Using the middle rung of the Check your progress ladder at the end of this chapter, think about what advice you might give to this student in order to improve their work.

4 Now read Response 2. As you read, think about what the student has done that is an improvement on Response 1, and what advice this student might need in order to make even more progress.

Response 2

The sharp blue sky contrasts with the dull tones of the cars that greet me as I enter the scrap-yard. As far as the eye can see there are vehicles piled up and it is amazing I haven't seen this place before. It is hidden behind high trees as if the owners are embarrassed.

Perched at the top of the mound, I can see a huge blue van or wagon tipped up with its boot high off the ground. It looks like a huge animal bending over! However, unlike any animal it is completely silent. In fact, in this car graveyard all you can hear is the wind whistling through the trees and the open car doors. It is kind of weird and makes me uneasy.

Closer to where I'm standing an old Chevvy is on its side. It still has that cool look that reminds me of 50s movies with Drive-Ins and American teens sitting on the bonnet drinking Coke with straws. The silver metal side parts glint in the sun, reminding me that this was once a car of style and importance. What is its history I wonder?

vivid opening noun phrases set scene

alternative opening phrase gives variety to description

interesting simile which is partially developed

paragraph allows reader to 'zoom in' on one specific detail on the car

From time to time, the sun bounces off metal and blinds me, making me feel almost seasick as I tread carefully between the uneven rows of trash. I go further into the depths of the yard and find myself lost in a shadowy part which is cold and icy. I don't remember how I got here and it's like I'm deep inside some horrible fairy tale. The cars are monsters and I can't escape.

imagery cleverly develops the 'fairy-tale' idea

Then the sun changes its angle and I can see a way out. I breathe a sigh of relief.

short paragraph effectively signals writer's sudden escape

By the gate I look back at the heaps of twisted metal and crumpled doors. It seems bizarre that objects that once made so much noise are now silent and still. I think of all their drivers, perhaps they too are in their own graveyards or perhaps they are in their beds dreaming of their lost loved belongings. I imagine them coming back here to visit the cars and see them for one last time.

prepositional phrase effectively helps reader see narrator's perspective

imaginative link takes us outside the world of the picture to a new idea

Comments on Response 2

The student has communicated their vision of the scrap yard convincingly, with a number of vivid details, developed from wider description of the setting. There is wide-ranging vocabulary and the whole description is structured successfully, using a variety of paragraphs to convey the changing mood and experience of the narrator, although there is some 'telling' when 'showing' would reveal more: for example, it would be better to show how the narrator feels 'uneasy' through his or her actions rather than simply telling the reader. The ideas are linked carefully, and the writer moves fluently from one area to another.

Check your progress

- I can generate a range of interesting, well-developed ideas and turn these into a structured plan quickly and effectively.
- I can describe settings and people using carefully selected vocabulary and a range of language features, such as imagery.
- I can use a wide variety of sentence and paragraph styles to sequence ideas and create texts that interest the reader.
- I can adapt my structure so that it engages the reader's interest straight away, and maintains it throughout through clever use of paragraph styles and focuses.
- I can use dialogue convincingly to convey character and also adapt sentence style to suggest voice and viewpoint.

- I can use different methods to generate ideas and create a structured plan from them.
- I can describe settings or people using appropriate vocabulary and imagery in places.
- I can use topic sentences and paragraphs effectively, and vary my overall structure.
- I can organise a story and choose different ways of opening it to get the reader interested.
- I can use dialogue and description to tell the reader what is happening and convey character.

- I can generate ideas for stories or descriptions and write a basic plan from them.
- I can describe settings and people precisely and choose some vocabulary for effect.
- I can write a description which is split into different paragraphs each with a new focus.
- I can organise a story with an introduction, complication, climax and conclusion.
- I can use direct speech to tell the reader something about my character.

Chapter 9
Point of view writing

What's it all about?

In this chapter, you will encounter a range of different text types and draw out particular skills which you then put to use, such as using topic sentences, varying length of sentences for impact, selecting punctuation both to make your meaning clear and to assist your argument, and choosing positive or negative vocabulary to affect the reader's response.

In this chapter, you will learn how to

- understand what point of view writing is

- match tone and register to task and audience

- match features to text types and conventions

- select appropriate vocabulary to make an impact

- vary sentences and verbs for effect

- use punctuation for effect and impact

- shape whole texts cohesively

- shape sentences into paragraphs effectively

- apply your skills to an English Language task.

	English Language GCSE	English Language GCSE
Which AOs are covered?	AO5 Communicate clearly, effectively and imaginatively, selecting and adapting tone, style and register for different forms, purposes and audiences Organise information and ideas, using structural and grammatical features to support coherence and cohesion of texts	AO6 Candidates must use a range of vocabulary and sentence structures for clarity, purpose and effect, with accurate spelling and punctuation
How will this be tested?	Questions will require you to apply what you have learned about the organisation of texts so that they are clear, persuasive and engaging. They will also require you to write in a variety of forms, but always with the intention of expressing your view or attitude to a particular issue.	Questions will require you to think of original, yet accurate ways of expressing yourself in sentences. You will be expected to demonstrate a wide, but appropriate vocabulary.

What is point of view writing?

Learning objectives
You will learn how to
- express your point of view
- select particular techniques writers use to express their viewpoints.

Assessment objective
- English Language AO5

What does it mean when you have to write from a particular point of view?

Getting you thinking

When we talk about someone's 'point of view' we usually mean their attitude towards a subject or issue, or their opinion on it.

Here are three points of view on different topics:

Student A

> I remember my first day at school as pretty awful. I didn't know anyone as we had recently moved to the area, and my parents hadn't had time to get me a proper uniform, so the first thing I had to do was borrow something from the school office. I felt very lonely and isolated.

Student B

> Breakfast clubs? What a great idea. Clearly there are lots of children who don't have time for a proper breakfast or whose parents don't provide one for them. Ok, so you have to get into school early, but they are sociable and set you up for the day.

Student C

> I think the role of a paramedic must be very rewarding, but I'm not sure it's something I could do. People who do that job should be paid twice as much as they are. To have to deal with trauma, family tragedy, but also feel you have helped people in distress would be such an honour, but you have to be a special type of individual, and I'm not sure I'm that person.

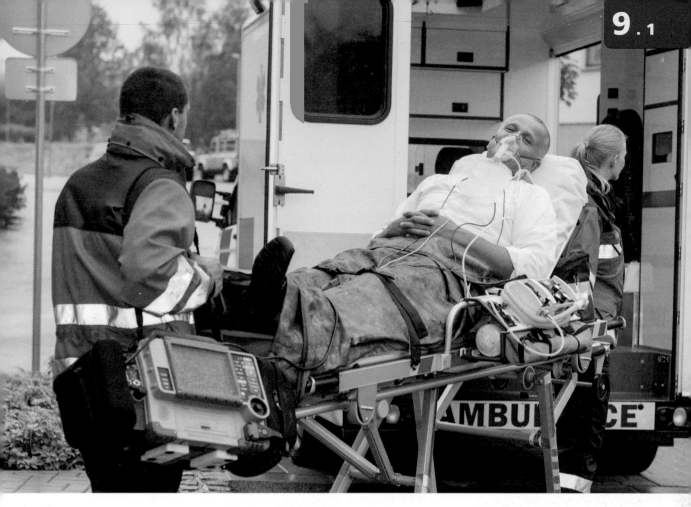

1 Each of the student's views' deals with something different: an issue or idea, an experience or event, or a person or role.

- Which one is which?
- What point of view is expressed in each case?
- How do you know?

2 What is your own opinion on each of these topics?

Explore the skills

It is clear we can have opinions on all sorts of things. But, how is that opinion expressed? Now read these different comments on the same topic.

> I dislike the way these faceless, corporate coffee chains invade our high streets like alien armies. They will damage local businesses, make us lose our identity, and just get bigger and bigger. I say 'No way!'
>
> Speech by town councillor

> Do you like a tasty cappuccino with oodles of froth or are you a Mocha guy or girl? Do you like your beans de-caff or with soya milk? Well, it doesn't matter – because you can have them all. In many towns there are now ten or more coffee shops and bars… with more opening all the time. For some this is coffee heaven; for others, coffee hell.
>
> *Feature article, broadsheet magazine*

Logged **in** ✕

Monday, 17 October

I love the smell, the rich warming aroma, the tantalising notion that I have stepped into a coffee bar in Bolivia, a fiesta of flavours ahead of me.

Blog by student

3 What is the common topic that these three texts share?

4 What are the different points of view expressed?

5 How does each writer use language (such as choice of vocabulary) and evidence (supporting facts or information) to make their points?

Develop the skills

Point of view is about **perspective** (the way we see things, or the 'angle' we take). This often means a **positive** or **negative** view of something, but we can also have a more balanced or **neutral** view, too.

6 Look again at the three examples above. Which would you say is 'positive' about coffee shops? Which 'negative'? Which 'neutral'?

7 Positive or negative points of view can be conveyed through using a number of devices. Copy and complete this table, adding your own examples from the three snippets above.

Key terms

positive: seeing the good side of things

negative: seeing the bad side of things

neutral: having a balanced view, or not taking sides

Technique	Negative	Positive	Balanced
adjective choice	'*faceless*, corporate coffee chains'		
verb choice		'I *love* the smell of…'	
imagery (similes and metaphors)	'invade our high streets *like alien armies*'		
types of sentence		statement: 'I love the smell…'	

Apply the skills

8 Read this opening to an article about coffee bars by one student.

Decide:

- what the **viewpoint** is (positive, negative or neutral)
- what **techniques** are being used (vocabulary, verbs, imagery).

I was walking to school yesterday through the town centre, half-asleep after staying up late to watch that vital episode of *Game of Thrones*, when a thought struck me: I need a coffee! So, I rubbed my eyes and looked around. That's when it struck me: our high street had ten (I'm not kidding) coffee shops or bars. Ten! It's like we're on a coffee planet.

I mean, how many coffee bars does a town need? What is this sudden obsession? Are we mad, or what? Surely one or two would do? Now, I like a coffee as much as the next sleepy student, but I also like bookshops, sports shops, and cinemas. Are there any of these in our town? No, not one. Not a sausage. Well, there are sausages – you can get them in sandwiches at (you've guessed it) the coffee bar.

9 Now complete this task.

Either write your own paragraph on the same topic. You could either continue in the same style and with the same opinion

OR

you could write from another point of view, perhaps adopting a different style.

Checklist for success

- Select sentences which match your opinion and strength of feeling.
- Select vocabulary (especially adjectives and verbs) which are positive, negative or neutral according to your view.

Check your progress:

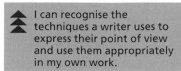 I can recognise the techniques a writer uses to express their point of view and use them appropriately in my own work.

I can recognise the techniques a writer uses to express their point of view and apply some of them in my own work.

I can recognise the basic point of view of a writer.

Match tone and register to task and audience

Learning objective
You will learn how to
- select the right tone and register when you express a point of view.

Assessment objective
- English Language AO5, AO6

Why does it matter what tone or register you use?

Getting you thinking

Tone is the feeling or mood created by the writer's language choices, for example: mocking, sad, informal or formal.

Register generally refers to the vocabulary and sometimes grammar structures or patterns you use in specific contexts or for particular audiences.

For example:

- you might use 'dad' or 'pa' when speaking *to* your father, but 'father' when speaking *about* him to someone else

- you might use specialist terms about a hobby to other enthusiasts, but simpler vocabulary to people who are not so knowledgeable.

Read this short report on a youth television channel about a rock festival.

1. How would you describe the tone of the writer here? (Is he happy? Relaxed? Shocked? Or…?)

2. What is wrong with his register? Think about the audience and the context.

3. Pick out any words or sentences you would change, and suggest some alternatives.

> **Reporter:** I am afraid to say I find the behaviour here extremely immature. For a start, youthful gentlemen and ladies are gyrating about in some sort of place called a 'mosh-pit'. And as for their attire – most of their garments are covered in soil. It is a most unedifying spectacle!

Explore the skills

Using the wrong tone and register may put off your audience. Read this further extract from a report on Glastonbury.

> Going to festivals can be a pretty wild **1** experience, but I'd **2** recommend it to anyone. Sure, **3** you might get covered in mud, but that's half the fun. Embrace it! **4** You'll have a fab **5** time.

1 **informal adjective**, using 'pretty' rather than the more formal 'rather'

2 **abbreviation** for 'I would' adds to the chatty style

3 **tag** links this to spoken dialogue

4 **short direct sentence** with exclamation mark

5 **shortened form** of 'fabulous'

The tone here is lively, engaging and informal, matching the youth audience.

4 Now read this further formal account in the left-hand column of the table below. Go through the text and identify any of the words, phrases or punctuation you could change using the devices from the annotation list to make it have a more informal tone.

5 Once you have done this, complete the whole account.

Formal tone	Informal tone
Here is a further observation with regard to the sanitary arrangements. These leave something to be desired as you are required to line up for an extended period of time. Once you reach the cubicle, you will be astounded by the inferior facilities. It is preferable to bring your own personal toiletries.	As for the toilets, here's the deal: you've got to...

Develop the skills

Look at these two tasks:

- Write a letter to the headteacher of your school asking them for time off to go to a rock festival.

- Email a friend to persuade them to go with you to a rock festival.

6 What register would you use for each? Why?

7 What key points would you include to persuade them?

Apply the skills

8 Read the following task.

Write the first two paragraphs of the letter and the email in the task above. Make sure they have contrasting tones.

Checklist for success

- Consider if and where abbreviations or shortened forms are appropriate.
- Judge what vocabulary would set the right tone.
- Decide if tags or other 'chatty' usages are suitable.
- Think about the role of punctuation and its effect.

Check your progress:

I can adapt my tone and register according to the task and audience.

I can write in a formal way for particular audiences, and an informal way for others.

I can understand the difference between formal and informal language.

Match features to text types and conventions

Learning objective
You will learn how to
- select suitable features which match particular forms and conventions.

Assessment objectives
- English Language AO5, AO6

What features will make your point of view more convincing?

Getting you thinking

There are a number of **conventions** that guide the way you write texts. For example, it is normal for business letters to have a polite, formal tone.

This then guides the particular **features** you use, for example, as we saw in 8.2, shortened or full forms of words or names ('Dear Mrs Cook' rather than 'Oi, Cookie!').

1 Each of the following texts has particular conventions, so the language features shown are likely to be different in each case. Can you match the text in each case to the language examples?

a Letter to your local MP arguing logically for improved transport for young people between the ages of 11 and 16.

b Blog to your personal 'followers' expressing your feelings about bad fashion/clothing decisions.

c Speech to your classmates urging them to take personal responsibility about their use of water.

Openings
Well, what can I say about today?

Dear Sir/Madam,

I'd like to talk to you about something I feel strongly about…

Middle sections
Another key reason I feel we need to change our behaviour is…

On the one hand, it is true that… …yet, on the other, it is clear…

Now, let's check out something else (hey, don't be afraid, it's only a photo!)…

Endings
Yours faithfully

Thank you for listening, and I hope what I have said gives you food for thought.

Marie x

Explore the skills

Blogs and opinion pieces

The conventions of **blogs** and **opinion pieces/articles** are that they tend to be personal, often reflect on recent or ongoing issues or events, and establish a familiar tone with their reader. Read the following short extract from children's writer Helena Pielichaty in which she discusses a talk she gave at a writers' conference.

> I think the session went down OK – it's always difficult to tell with an adult audience as they're usually polite even if they've been bored rigid. Nevertheless, I did that thing I always do after an event and I over-analysed my performance and convinced myself I was atrocious. *I should have said this* and *why did I say that?* It's nuts, really – it's not as if you can change anything.
>
> Helena Pielichaty, 31 March 2014
> http://www.helena-pielichaty.com/blog/

2 What language devices or features does Helena use which fit with the conventions of blogs? Find examples of the following:

- the narrative form used (first or third person)
- the formal or informal language
- words or phrases that suggest she is sharing her thoughts with the reader
- use of humorous or exaggerated observations.

Speeches

The **conventions of speeches** are that they will also be personal, but are often used to call for change or to persuade the audience to do or believe something. This may lead to the use of more rhetorical devices and emotive or powerful language to create an impact.

For example, in this speech from 1852, former slave Frederick Douglass addressed citizens of his hometown, Rochester, USA, about the injustice of slavery.

> Whether we turn to the declarations of the past, or to the professions of the present, the conduct of the nation seems equally hideous and revolting. America is false to the past, false to the present, and solemnly binds herself to be false to the future. Standing with God and the crushed and bleeding slave on this occasion, I will, in the name of humanity, which is outraged, in the name of liberty, which is fettered, in the name of the Constitution and the Bible, which are disregarded and trampled upon, dare to call in question and to denounce, with all the emphasis I can command, everything that serves to perpetuate slavery – the great sin and shame of America!
>
> Frederick Douglass, 'What to the slave is the fourth of July?', 5 July 1852

3 Identify:

- references to the audience (and the speaker himself)
- examples of emotive imagery or vocabulary
- repetition or patterns used for rhetorical effect and impact
- a clear statement of the purpose of the speech – what needs to change
- any other features you would expect to see in persuasive speeches of this nature.

Letters

Letters will be personal, but the conventions of formal and informal letters mean that the language and features will change accordingly. In this formal example, a young woman sends a letter to an employer after he has offered her a job.

Dear Mr Malone,

Thank you for inviting me to the interview for the role of trainee mechanic at your garage. However, I will be declining the offer of a job as I felt the environment was completely unsuitable for a woman.

Firstly, there is the lack of basic washing or toilet facilities. Added to that is the lack of respect which I was shown when being shown around the workshop which I found extremely demeaning. Finally, the salary you propose is 20% less than you are paying to your other (male) trainees, something which is particularly unacceptable.

I will, of course, be willing to reconsider my decision if these issues are addressed, but I cannot join your company until they are.

Yours,

Lorna McCloud

4 Can you identify:

- where and how the letter sets out or introduces the issue at hand
- the formal features of language used, such as choice of vocabulary
- the logical and explanatory language used to get her point across
- the 'call to action' which she suggests to the employer?

Develop the skills

Imagine you have been given the following task.

> Write a blog in which you explain your point of view on this statement:
>
> 'Some jobs are better suited to men than women; it's no good pretending that women can do them equally as well as men.'

Here is one student's attempt at beginning the blog.

> It is clear that in the world today, there are a number of jobs that women simply *cannot*, nor *should not* do. This is not a matter of equality, nor is it a matter of male pride or domination. No, it is a matter of *common sense*.
>
> The undeniable evidence is this: in general, women are physically weaker than men. Thus occupations which require muscular strength, such as building work, policing and so on, are simply unsuitable for the female sex.

5 What is wrong with this as a **blog**? What form or type of text is it closer to?

6 What **features** would you need to change or adapt to make it fit the type of text (blog)?

Apply the skills

7 Read the following task.

> Write the blog expressing your own opinion on the topic.

Checklist for success

- Consider the **conventions** of blogs (what readers expect them to be like in terms of structure and style).
- Use the **features** of blogs you have learned or read about in this lesson and elsewhere to draft your text.

Check your progress:

- I can adapt the content of my writing according to the conventions and features of the particular text type.
- I can use some different features according to the conventions of the type of text.
- I can understand that certain texts have different conventions and features.

Select appropriate vocabulary to make an impact

Learning objectives
You will learn how to
- select powerful and interesting vocabulary for discursive or persuasive writing
- switch between telling and showing readers how you feel.

Assessment objectives
- English Language AO5, AO6

How can your choice of words influence the reader?

Getting you thinking

Your choice of specific words and phrases – your **vocabulary** – is a vital tool you can use to influence your reader or make them think.

In 'Rewriting the rules on logos', Naomi Mdudu explores the changes fashion brands are making.

Rewriting the rules on logos

Logos fell out of favour with the onset of the **recession**. Labels known for their distinctive branding, such as Gucci, Louis Vuitton and Burberry, went to great pains to tone it down. It all looked a bit crass and a reminder of the excessive culture of **consumption** that helped get us in trouble in the first place. Understatement became the statement.

But designers are now approaching logos and branding in a different way. What we are seeing are fun and witty slogans and branding instantly attributable to a label but not in the brash way of the 2000s.

Naomi Mdudu, *Metro*, 20 March 2014

1. What do we learn about the popularity of logos and branding:
   - in the recession
   - from 2000 onwards?

   Which particular words or phrases tell you this?

2. How does Naomi Mdudu feel about the new approaches? What words or phrases tell you this?

Glossary

logos: identifiable words, phrases and/or images linked to a brand

recession: period of financial problems and unemployment

consumption: buying or using up

Explore the skills

It is important to select words or phrases that convey your feelings on a particular issue. Read this short discussion between two students on logos and branding. What are their different viewpoints?

Student 1

> I am totally appalled by the influence of branding. I mean, what's the point? Clothes are to be worn...they do a job. They need to be functional, smart (for work) and comfortable. Branding is an unnecessary complication. As long as you don't look a mess, who cares who made them?

Student 2

> Brands make a bold statement about who you are. Seeing someone else wearing a brand you like creates an instant, electric connection. They can be incredibly powerful in helping you find like-minded people. Who wants to be an outsider?

3 Can you find examples of the following:

- **adverbs** used to strengthen an adjective
- **adjectives** and **nouns** or **noun phrases** describing clothing or the effect clothes create?

Copy and complete the second and third columns of the table.

Vocabulary type	Example(s)	Effect
adverbs used to strengthen an adjective or verb	'totally appalled by...'	How powerfully anti-branding they are. 'Totally' leaves no room for argument.
adjectives	'functional'	
nouns or noun phrases	(who wants to be an) 'outsider'	

Key terms

adverbs: words that change or simplify the meaning of a verb, and usually answer how or when an action was done, for example, 'angrily', 'later'

adjectives: words that tells us more about a noun, for example, 'the *pretty* hat'

noun phrases: a noun phrase acts as a noun containing additional words to add more information or modify its effect ('witty (*adj.*) slogans (*noun*)')

Sometimes writers' feelings can be conveyed in more subtle ways. For example, Student 2 uses the word 'outsider'. This suggests something negative without saying it directly.

Here are some alternative nouns or phrases they might have used:

individual	reject	trail-blazer	visionary
leader	weirdo	outcast	loner

4 Which of these are positive and which negative? Are there any you would call 'neutral' (could be positive or negative). Place them on a line with the most positive to the right.

Negative ——————|————————|————————|————————|——— Positive

5 Now choose the most suitable one for each of the following sentences, and copy and complete them.

I felt like an utter .... when I turned up at the party wearing my dad's old T-shirt.

Nobody was wearing bow-ties to night-clubs when I started the trend. Now, I'm considered as a ....

When it comes to groups of friends, I generally prefer my own company, so I guess you could call me a ....

Develop the skills

Vocabulary can reveal your feelings in different ways.

For example, by:

- *telling* the reader directly what your feelings are ('totally appalled by')
- *showing* what you feel through vivid description.

In this extract from *No Logo*, Naomi Klein does both these things as she describes a visit to an industrial zone in the Philippines that makes clothing for well-known brands.

Inside, it's obvious that the row of factories, each with its own gate and guard, has been carefully planned to squeeze the maximum amount of production out of this swath of land. Windowless workshops made of cheap plastic and aluminium siding are crammed in next to each other, only feet apart. Racks of time cards bake in the sun, making sure the maximum amount of work is extracted from each worker, the maximum number of working hours extracted from each day. The streets in the zone are eerily empty, and open doors – the ventilation system for most factories – reveal lines of young women hunched in silence over clamoring machines.

Naomi Klein, from *No Logo*

6 Identify:

- a verb which tells us how hard 'they' have tried to get as much work as they can from the zone
- a verb phrase which tells us how close the workshops are to each other
- a verb that makes work sound like something being taken out by a syringe.

7 What is the effect of the following noun or adverb phrases in the extract:

- 'windowless workshops made of cheap plastic'
- 'streets…eerily empty'
- 'young women hunched in silence over clamoring machines'?

8 Now write a further paragraph which describes a particular woman working in the factory. Convey your attitude to her working conditions (positive, negative or somewhere in between) through the vocabulary you use.

Apply the skills

9 Complete the following task.

Imagine you have been asked to write a blog post giving your own opinions about branding in general, and logos specifically.

In your blog post, include a description of a large fashion brand's store, including what it looks like and the behaviour and appearance of the customers and staff.

Checklist for success

You will need to:

- *tell* the reader directly how you feel through your choice of positive or negative vocabulary
- *show* the reader through some descriptions of people, places or experiences
- *select* vocabulary that is positive or negative
- *consider* your use of nouns or noun phrases, adverbs and verbs.

Check your progress:

I can make a range of detailed vocabulary choices which both tell the reader directly, or show more subtly, what my feelings are on a particular issue.

I can select vocabulary carefully with awareness of how positive or negative my word choices are.

I can make my viewpoint clear in my writing by using simple adjectives or verbs to make my feelings clear.

Key techniques: varying sentences and verbs for effect

Learning objective
You will learn how to
- vary your verbs and sentences to convey your viewpoint to influence the reader.

Assessment objective
- English Language AO5, AO6

How can you use different types of sentence and verbs to influence the reader?

Getting you thinking

Read this article by Pam Allyn about reading aloud.

READ ALOUD. CHANGE THE WORLD.

Many years ago, my mother read to me from the book, *Blueberries for Sal* by Robert McCloskey. I remember as if it were yesterday, hearing her voice at my side on a cold wintry night sharing those words: 'Kerplink, kerplank, kerplunk...' as little Sal's blueberries thunked into her pail. My mother's words changed my world.

Long before I could read on my own, she shared with me the strength and beauty of McCloskey's language – a profound story of a little girl and her mother out in nature, co-existing with a mother bear and her own baby. The power of story, of language and of my mother, all came together. And happened many times after that, over and over. The 'read aloud' made me a reader. All these years later, I was reading aloud a picture book to a small child in a classroom. His life, so far, had not been easy. His childhood was troubled by poverty and loneliness. In that moment, in the joy of the read aloud, he had an idea that started something big.

March 5 is World Read Aloud Day, a grassroots movement that my organization, LitWorld (http://litworld.org), created four years ago to honor this young boy's wish for everyone to be able to have a read aloud every day. His eager, glowing smile has reverberated with me every day since then. What he said was this: 'Mrs. Allyn, let's make sure everyone knows how good this feels. Let's have a holiday for the read aloud.'

Since the day he shared that good idea with us, World Read Aloud Day has become a worldwide event reaching over one million people in more than 65 countries around the world.

Pam Allyn, *Huffington Post,* 3 March 2014

---

1 How does Pam Allyn feel about her experiences of being read to as a child?

2 How does this relate to her reason for writing the article?

3 Which sentences and **verb** (or verbs) stand out in the first paragraph?

> **Key terms**
>
> **verb:** the force behind a sentence; it can describe movements or actions or states, and tell us when something happened
>
> **simple sentences:** these tend to be quite short, punchy and terse; they contain a subject and a verb

Explore the skills

Pam Allyn uses a range of sentence types and verbs for different reasons:

- short **simple sentences** ('My mother's words changed my world.') for a clear statement about her perspectives on the topic
- longer sentences to *explain* how her world was changed ('Long before I could read on my own…and her own baby.')
- variety of verbs on the same topic ('*read* to me', '*hearing* her voice', '*sharing* those words') to describe the impact of that experience
- more concrete verbs to describe specific effects on her and the world ('thunked', 'reverberated').

4 Read this student's sentence about the importance of music to him.

I was eleven when I first picked up a guitar and strummed that clumsy first chord but it was a moment I will never forget.

Rewrite it as two short sentences which have more emotional impact.

5 Now read this further extract from the same student.

Music opened up a new world to me. It did this in the way it opened me to artists and musicians I'd never heard of.

Rewrite these two sentences as one long single explanatory sentence. You could also try to find a synonym for the repeated verb 'opened'.

6 The same student also wanted to include how his parents reacted when he first performed:

It also changed the way my parents saw me. I remember their reaction when I played at a school concert when they revealed they had no idea I was so good.

Rewrite the second sentence so that it includes the actual words they said with speech marks.

Develop the skills

Compound sentences can be used to signal a shift in an argument, or a link between ideas. Read these later sentences from the same 'Read aloud' article:

> Children who grow up as readers become engaged citizens of the global world, and every child deserves that right to read.

Two equally weighted points (the first half of the sentence about children 'engaging' with the world; the second about their right to reading) are joined by 'and'.

7 Below are some sentences on the topic of music.

Create compound sentences by joining each of the two separate sentences together with one of the following conjunctions:

'and', 'so', 'yet', 'but', 'for', 'or', 'nor'.

- Yes, learning an instrument is a challenge. There are countless books and videos to help you.
- You may never be very proficient. It won't be wasted time.
- The tunes you learn will always be there. In the future, you can dig them out for generations to come.

Key term

Compound sentences: sentences made up of equal clauses or sections, usually joined by conjunctions such as *and*, *so*, *yet*, *but*, *for*, *or* and *nor*

Another way in which you can vary verbs in order to affect your reader's response is by using **modal verbs**.

> Playing an instrument <u>will occupy you</u> when you're on your own, and <u>it could open</u> social doors. Just think of the friends <u>you might make</u> if you form a band, or join an orchestra. What's more, playing music is cool. It <u>could be</u> the thing that turns you from Billy No Mates to Mr. Desirable.

> ### Key term
>
> **modal verbs:** verbs such as *could, should, might, will, must, would* slightly alter the meaning of the verbs they are attached to

8 Here, the student uses modal forms to express different levels of certainty. Plot these on a line from 'very certain' to 'uncertain'.

9 Write this paragraph out twice.

> Finally, if you want fame and fortune, playing a musical instrument............... be your passport to wealth. You............find that the simple tune you made up with your mates becomes a worldwide hit.

a In the first version, add modals to the gaps to make the point of view very clear and certain.

b In the second version, add modals to make your point of view more cautious.

Apply the skills

10 Now complete the task.

Write the opening paragraph to an article in which you write about either the benefits of private reading, or the benefits of sport.

Checklist for success

- Use simple, short sentences and verbs to state a point of view clearly.
- Use longer sentences (such as compounds) to explain your view.
- Use well-chosen verbs to create emotional impact or authority.
- Use modal verbs to express levels of certainty.

Check your progress:

▲▲▲ I can switch between short and long sentences, including minor ones, and various verb forms, including modals, to express my views.

▲▲ I can use different types of sentence and verbs to explain my viewpoint.

▲ I can write simple and long sentences which explain my viewpoint.

Key techniques: using punctuation for effect and impact

Learning objective
You will learn how to
- use different forms of punctuation to explain your ideas or support your point of view.

Assessment objectives
- English Language AO5, A06

How can punctuation help you to get your message across?

Getting you thinking

Read this short extract on the issue of safer cycling.

1 What different types of punctuation have been used in this extract?

2 What tone of voice does this create?

> *Cycling? Who needs it? It should be considered an extreme sport! As I ride my bike to school I see dangers everywhere (and miss lots of others). It'd be safer swimming with sharks – honest!*

Explore the skills

Punctuation contributes to the tone of your text, and therefore, affects the point of view which is conveyed to the reader.

For example:

Logical, clear, rational argument	Chatty, more informal persuasion
Colon: to introduce an explanation or example: 'Cycling is clearly very dangerous: wayward lorries, potholes and even cats and dogs all threaten your journey.'	Brackets, or dashes, for comic asides: '(and miss lots of others) – honest!'
Semicolon: to balance or contrast two related statements. Each statement must be a complete sentence that would make sense on its own: 'Cycling is increasingly popular; complaints from cyclists are increasingly bitter.'	Exclamation marks for outbursts or comic effect: 'It should be considered an extreme sport!'
	Apostrophes for shortened, chatty forms: 'It'd' rather than 'It would'

3 Rewrite these sentences to make them sound more logical. For each one, choose either a colon or a semicolon, to link two ideas. You will need to remove some punctuation, too, and possibly add a word (such as 'and').

a Lorry drivers are the worst! They can't hear you! Their mirrors are too high! They can't see you at left-hand junctions!

b Yet roads can never be completely free of danger. You take a risk whenever you get into a car, or ride a bike.

c The only real solution is to educate drivers of all road vehicles. The alternative is more accidents, more anger.

Develop the skills

Read this opening to a campaign editorial from *The Times*.

Since Mary's accident, more than 100 cyclists have died on Britain's roads. The youngest was eight years old; the oldest was 80. So far in 2012, eleven have died in London, three in Edinburgh, and two on the same stretch of the A1 outside Nottingham. Those who survived injury in 2011 — of whom Mary was one — number a startling 19,108, with more than 3,000 seriously injured.

The Times, 5 November 2012

5 How does the writer of the editorial use these punctuation marks?

Punctuation	Example	Effect?
comma	2nd sentence to list three statistics	Rhetorical pattern of three adds support to argument.
semicolon		
dashes		

6 Add a semicolon and a pair of dashes to the paragraph below to make the explanation logical and clear. You may have to change some of the sentences.

Lorry drivers have a different perspective. City cyclists are reckless. Country cyclists lack awareness. They change direction suddenly often without signalling so drivers have little chance of avoiding them.

Apply the skills

7 Complete the task below.

Write two paragraphs about the perils of being a pedestrian on country roads. In the first, make your tone emotive and (if appropriate) comical; in the second, be logical and reasonable.

Check your progress:

▲▲▲ I can use a range of punctuation marks such as colons, semicolons, dashes and brackets to make my point of view clear.

▲▲ I can make use of exclamation marks appropriately.

▲ I can use exclamation marks to make a point strongly.

Shape whole texts cohesively

How can you organise your writing as a whole to make your point of view persuasive and clear?

Getting you thinking

Read this task.

> In recent years, 'Gap Years' – a period when young people travel abroad before they go to college, or start a job – have become increasingly fashionable.
>
> Write an article for your school/college website in which you give your point of view about gap years, and whether they are a good idea.

A student has jotted down their plan for the article, as follows:

Approach 1

Paragraph 1: Introduction
<u>For</u>
Paragraph 2: Need a break from studying and work
Paragraph 3: Broadens your mind – meet new people, friends
Paragraph 4: Use Gap Year to help others by volunteering
<u>Against</u>
Paragraph 5: Costs a lot of money – not fair to rely on parents
Paragraph 6: Doesn't really broaden your mind – it's just a holiday really
Paragraph 7: Can be dangerous, and you could get lonely
Paragraph 8: Conclusion

1 In what other ways could they have organised their answer?

Explore the skills

There are several ways of organising your ideas when you wish to persuade your reader. You can also structure your ideas as follows:

Approach 2

> Paragraph 1: Introduction
> Paragraph 2: For – need a break from work, etc.
> Paragraph 3: Against – costs a lot of money, etc.
> Paragraph 4: For...etc.
> Paragraph 5: Against...etc.

2 How is this different from Approach 1 in the 'Getting you thinking' section?

3 Now look at this third approach:

Approach 3

> Although gap years can be incredibly expensive and most students will need financial support from parents or to undertake fundraising, it will be money well spent. After all, everyone needs a break from work to refresh their minds and bodies, and after being at school since the age of five it is money well spent if your travels help you consider your next step in life.

a What is the point of view of the writer? How do you know?

b Where are the 'for' and 'against' arguments here?

c How is this different from Approach 2?

There are different ways of introducing a counterargument.

You can include it in the first clause of your sentence, using words or phrases such as:

'While', 'Although', and 'Even though'.

These words and phrases are known as **discourse markers** as they mark a shift in the tone, idea or topic of your piece of writing.

Or you can introduce it with phrases such as:

- 'Some people believe that...', and follow this with a **new sentence** beginning with, 'However', or 'On the other hand', avoid using 'and so on' in this context.

4 Copy and complete the examples below using one of these approaches.

Select from the **discourse markers** in the box.

> While   Although   Some people believe that
> Some argue that   However   On the other hand
> Nevertheless   Yet   Even though

a ....travelling abroad for a long time could make you feel lonely, and there are many dangers you could face..

b ....a year out just makes you restless. ...., it could be said that you come back realising what is good about your home life, friends and family.

c ....travelling alone takes courage, some might say that it is less stressful when you only have yourself to look after.

Develop the skills

The style and length of your paragraphs can also create an impact on your reader. For example, read these final two paragraphs from one student's essay.

> I know that everyone says that a year out is a precious experience and the memories will last forever, but, as far as I am concerned, the thing that will last the most is the debt! Volunteering overseas is incredibly expensive. I don't come from a rich family and university is going to cost me a lot anyway.
>
> The truth is, the biggest 'gap' will be in my wallet.

5 What is the writer's point of view?

6 What is different about the two paragraphs?

7 Why do you think the writer chose to end the essay in this way?

It is important to stick to a separate idea or point in each paragraph, but the information you select is key.

The average gap year will cost between £3000–£4000 – meaning that 22% of parents contribute to their child's travel, spending approximately £763 to help them, often more. The cost of the year can be even higher if the student does organised trips, or wants specialist experiences such as whale-watching or doing the Inca trail, things that can cost upwards of £500 alone.

However, such costs can create unforgettable memories, and enable students to do things they will never have a chance to do once they are in a job or married. Just imagine sitting in some dull office job, staring out at the rain and traffic, and wishing you had done something exciting while you could!

Information from Lattitudes website:
http://www.lattitude.org.uk/2013/03/gap-year-by-numbers/

8 What has the writer included in the first paragraph to support their argument?

9 How is the style and focus of the second paragraph different?

Apply the skills

10 You have been asked to give a talk at your school on your views about whether it is a good idea to take a break when you leave school before you choose a career or go on to further study. Complete the following task.

Plan your speech, deciding on approaches 1, 2 or 3.

Write the first three paragraphs of your speech, using the approach you have chosen.

Checklist for success

* List your for/against points.
* Decide what sequence or order you wish to present your ideas in.
* Use a variety of paragraph styles to get your message across.
* Add different types of content to each paragraph.

Check your progress:

⬆⬆ I can plan an essay, considering all three possible approaches, and then vary my paragraph style and content to create an impact on the reader.

⬆ I can plan an essay, and write the first three paragraphs so that the arguments for and against are clear to the reader.

▲ I can plan an essay which has two halves – the first dealing with the pros, the second dealing with the cons.

Shape sentences into paragraphs effectively

Learning objectives
You will learn how to
- order sentences to explain or stress particular points or ideas
- link sentences together so your ideas are clear and logical.

Assessment objective
- English Language AO6

How can you arrange your sentences to make your viewpoint clear and have an impact on your readers?

Getting you thinking

Read the opening to an article below by Hadley Freeman.

Why black models are rarely in fashion

I unashamedly love fashion, but there is much for — which the fashion industry deserves to be criticised: the obsession with skinniness, the **fetishisation** of youth, the misogynistic promotion of fashion items that are, quite frankly, torturous (6in heels, I'm looking at you). But the grotesque element in fashion that I personally find the most **egregious** is its blatant racism. Black models never, with single-digit exceptions in a decade, appear on the cover of major fashion magazines, because, as the black model Jourdan Dunn told the Guardian last year, 'people in the industry say if you have a black face on the cover of a magazine it won't sell.'

— topic sentence

— specific focus on key issue

— supporting example

Then there are the fashion shows. Until this season it was by no means uncommon to go to a show and see only white models on the runway. Jezebel.com has charted the presence of models of colour at New York fashion week and there is no doubt there has been an improvement: at the shows this time six years ago, 87% of the models were white, 4.9% were black, 5.4% were Asian and 2.7% were Latina. This month the stats were, respectively, 78.69%, 7.67%, 9.75% and 2.12%. The shows in London have also shown an increased effort at acknowledging diversity, with special credit going to Burberry, Topshop and Tom Ford. Whereas several shows last season were all white, as the Sunday Times pointed out last weekend, this time none of them were.

The Guardian, 18 February 2014

Glossary

fetishisation: an excessive obsession

misogynistic: women-hating

egregious: outstandingly bad

1 What is Hadley Freeman's main point of view in this article?

2 Where, in the first paragraph, do we find this out?

3 How does the second paragraph:

  a provide further evidence of her main viewpoint

  b subtly alter it?

Explore the skills

The order of the **first paragraph** is key to both understanding Hadley Freeman's point of view, and to the impact she wants to make.

- The first sentence **sets the context** by explaining the writer's love of fashion and her understanding of some of the obvious things wrong with it.

- The second sentence, however, focuses in on the single **more serious, and perhaps surprising point she wants to make**.

- The third sentence hammers this home with a very **specific example to support the previous point**.

4 Why couldn't the order of these three sentences be changed? (For example, why couldn't the second sentence come first?)

5 Re-order these three sentences on a similar issue into a new paragraph so that it works in the same way.

> This is especially true of the 'skinny' look; if young women didn't want it, why do they continue to buy into it? They are only reflecting what society seems to want in terms of body style. It is wrong to blame fashion magazines for promoting a particular look.

6 Now go back to Hadley Freeman's article and read the **second paragraph** and answer these questions:

  a How is the first sentence of the second paragraph different in style from the first sentence of the opening paragraph?

  b How does it link back to the first paragraph?

7 What is the structure of the second paragraph?

  a What is the job of the first two sentences?

  b What do sentences three, four, five and six add?

Develop the skills

Hadley Freeman links her sentences (and paragraphs) together to explain her point of view in a fluent way. Read this further extract:

> But **2** let's look at these **1** stats with standards that are slightly higher than a grasshopper's knee. For a start, **2** for American designers to choose more than three-quarters of their models from the Caucasian demographic is, to say the least, hardly reflective of the country. Some of those formerly all-white London shows, such as Paul Smith, cast a grand total of one black model and a whopping two Asian models. Insert slow applause. Moreover, **2** these **1** changes have only come about with heavy effort from the Council of Fashion Designers of America in the US and the British Fashion Council in the UK, which sends out letters every single season to designers specifically asking them to reflect London's diversity.

8 Look at the highlighted words and phrases.

  a How does the use of the **determiner** 'these' **1** link back to the previous sentences or paragraphs?

  b How do the linking words or phrases, 'But', 'For a start', and 'Moreover' **2** help to guide us through her argument?

Key term

determiner: a word or phrase which indicates the distance between ideas or things in a text. For example, 'those books' (far away); 'these books' (close to hand)

9 Look at this table.

pronouns/determiners (useful for referring back to previously mentioned items)	this, these, that, those, such
	I, we, he, she, they, you, him, her, them, us
words/phrases which explain contrasts	yet, but, however, on the other hand, in contrast
words/phrases which add to or stress a point	moreover, furthermore, also, in addition
words/phrases which give reasons or describe an effect	for example, as, in this way, thus, therefore, because
words/phrases that indicate sequence or time order	recently, later, firstly, secondly, finally, then, next, before that, now

Select appropriate words or phrases and copy and complete the following passage, using them to fill the spaces.

.... treatment of black models is unacceptable. ...., it is probably illegal, as the same rights that apply in other professions should apply here. ...., how can you change things? If the industry is so misguided, then forceful action must be taken. .... customers must boycott fashion brands. .... would then see a change, perhaps.

Apply the skills

10 Complete this task.

'The fashion industry is responsible for lots of society's problems.'

Write the first two paragraphs of a blog article in which you explain your viewpoint on this issue.

Think about:

- how people of different colours and races are represented and treated
- how the use of skinny models affects us
- the use of young models.

Checklist for success

- Engage the reader with detailed, relevant ideas.
- Write clear paragraphs linked in a logical manner.
- Use a range of connecting words and phrases to signal and develop your point of view.

Check your progress:

▲▲ I can write paragraphs which use a range of sentence sequences and linking words and phrases to get my point of view across to the reader.

▲ I can write paragraphs which focus on one main idea and explain my points clearly and fluently.

▲ I can write paragraphs which begin with simple topic sentences explaining my views.

Apply your skills to an English Language task

Learning objectives
You will learn to
- apply the key skills from this chapter to an unseen English Language task
- reflect on your progress through looking at different responses to the task.

Assessment objectives
- English Language AO5, AO6

Responding to English Language tasks

1 Look at this practice task and think about how you would approach it.

'Keeping up with the latest fashions is a waste of time and of money; you do not need to be wealthy or have lots of free time to look cool.'

Write an article for a broadsheet newspaper in which you explain your point of view.

Think about:

- what your viewpoint on this subject is
- how you can argue your key points effectively and convincingly.

Checklist for success

A successful response should include:

- a clear sense of your point of view and your reasons for it
- a convincing argument, supported by well-developed ideas
- style and tone matched to the task and audience
- a structure that is persuasive and logical.

Reflecting on your progress

2 Read the following response to this task. As you read, think about what the student has done well and what advice they might need in order to make more progress.

Response 1

I think this is true because I don't have loads of money but I think I'm quite trendy and wear quite cool things.

viewpoint expressed in first sentence

This is because I am dead careful about what I buy and — *informal vocabulary*
this means that I don't just follow what my mates do and
just buy anything that celebs wear.

I think that you can shop around and find great deals if
you're clever. Like last weekend there were these big sales
on but I ignored the obvious things right near the front
of the shop and went and looked at the back. There are — *paragraph clearly deals with one area*
always these rails with odd sale items on which you can
get if you know where to look. My friends think I'm mad but
who is the mad one when they've paid loads and I've paid
nothing?

Another thing is that you can go to charity shops and you — *linking phrase, if slightly chatty in tone*
can find great bargains there. Ok, loads of the stuff was
left by older people but there is the odd gem if you look
hard enough. I found this Gap dress that was like three
pounds! I wore it to the school prom and no one knew — *example supports point*
where I'd got it. I just said it was in this sale and all my
mates believed me.

The other thing is boot sales or jumble sales. My mum and
dad love them and have their own stall so they're always
dragging me along at the crack of dawn. The bad side is
that I have to get up so early but on the good side we get
to the field before most ordinary people. It means I can
have a sneak look at what's on offer. Last month I bought
an iPhone charger, which costs lots on the web if you want — *example is not really relevant to topic*
a proper one. I also saw these posters which were going
cheap which were great for my art project.

So it is basically completely not the case that you need — *topic sentence attempts to sum up argument*
to be rich to be fashionable. There is no way I would call my
family rich, my dad is a taxi-driver and my mum is a lunchtime dinner lady at my brother's school. You do need time
to hunt stuff out, I give you that, but it's actually quite — *rhetorical question used to connect with reader*
fun and I just think when I see my mates spending loads,
who's the idiot now?

Anyway, I would definitely recommend charity shops,
jumble sales and things like that if you want a bargain.
You just need to know where to look I think. — *final short sentence restates point of view*

Comments on Response 1

The point of view expressed is reasonably clear, but ideas are somewhat jumbled and there is no real progression in the argument. The tone is also sometimes inappropriate with too much informality, especially in vocabulary choices. There is some attempt to use rhetorical devices, and to draw on anecdotal evidence for effect, but the language is not as fluent as it could be.

3 How could this sample response be improved? Using the middle rung of the Check your progress ladder at the end of this chapter, think about what advice you might give to this student in order to improve their work.

4 Now read Response 2. As you read, think about what the student has done that is an improvement on Response 1, and what advice this student might need in order to make even more progress.

Response 2

Last weekend I was in town, shopping and I noticed something. There were no more second-hand shops in our town. Now, they are all called 'Vintage Fashions'! This is a bit of a con really. It's the same old items, but now with fancy labels and a price tag to match. I stared through the window and thought, 'You're not fooling me!' and set off for the big shops in the arcade. — anecdote draws reader in

I suppose you could argue that even with the bigger prices that vintage shops charge, they are still cheaper than going to the H and M's or Primark's, and there are always the charity shops. But hunting around does take a lot of time, and one thing I have noticed is that you sometimes end up buying items because they're cheap, not because they are the right ones. Then you feel a fool when you never wear them and have to go and buy new? VM anyway! — quite a sophisticated point, but could be expressed a little more clearly

(effective short sentence to end paragraph)

It really is a minefield if you are a fashion shopper nowadays. — clear topic sentence
On the one hand, you have articles saying how it is wrong that clothing is made so cheaply in sweat shops, yet on the other hand we all like a bargain. I suppose if you are rich you don't have that problem. Being rich takes away those sorts of questions, doesn't it? — rhetorical question using question tag

Anyway, back to my shopping trip last weekend. I was looking — cohesive use of 'back to' signals return to first point for a blue shirt for the school prom. I'm not the world's best shopper – I tend to go straight in, ask for what I want, maybe try it on, then get out as fast as I can. But I thought I'd take my time this time. But oh what a time it took! In the charity shops I was knocked over by a little old lady half my height. She was after a pair of slippers and she thought I was after them too. It was like war! Anyway, after half an hour of battle I escaped. But with no shirt.

useful comic analogy on 'war'

The truth is, the one I really wanted was in this designer men's shop on our high street called, 'Trend One'. But it was £60. Yes, you heard me – sixty! Well, I had thirty so I thought maybe they would do a deal. But no way. The door was shut in my face before you could say 'excuse me...'.

direct short statement

It definitely is a waste of time trying to be cool. I missed half the England game while I was looking for that shirt. I ended up spending all afternoon traipsing round the shopping centre. As I said, I ignored the vintage shops as they were just a con, and the charity shops were like modern warfare. The big department stores were so massive I just gave them a miss.

topic sentence signals more on issue of 'time'

I know what I have got to do. I will need to plead with my mum and dad to lend me the extra so I can go back to 'Trend One' for the shirt I like. Maybe you don't need to be wealthy to keep up with the fashions but it would sure help!

effective short final paragraph but mostly about money

Comments on Response 2

The general tone and approach is well judged, and the points are generally clear and well made, with supporting evidence as required. The use of humour to create impact is also well judged. There is effective use of a variety of sentences, including rhetorical ones, and punctuation is chosen for its effect. The ideas are well linked for the most part, although the point of view is not immediately apparent; paragraph 3 might have been better as the first one, although starting with an anecdote does draw the reader in. Vocabulary is reasonably wide, although occasionally some more vivid details would have added to the accounts of the shopping trips.

Check your progress

- I can recognise the techniques a writer uses to express a point of view and use them appropriately in my own work.
- I can adapt my tone and register according to the formality of the task and audience.
- I can make vocabulary choices which tell the reader directly, or show more subtly, what my feelings are on a particular issue.
- I can use a range of punctuation marks, including colons, dashes and brackets, to strengthen my point of view.
- I can select from a variety of ways to plan a point-of-view essay, and vary my approach to create an impact on the reader.
- I can write paragraphs which use a range of sentence sequences, linking words and phrases to get my point of view across.

- I can recognise the techniques a writer uses to express a point of view and apply some of them in my own work.
- I can write in a formal way for particular audiences, and an informal way for others.
- I can select positive or negative vocabulary carefully to help express my point of view.
- I can use punctuation such as exclamation marks appropriately.
- I can plan and write a point-of-view essay in which the arguments for and against are clear to the reader.
- I can write paragraphs which focus on one main idea and explain my points clearly and fluently.

- I can recognise the basic point of view of a writer and express my own opinions.
- I can understand the difference between formal and informal language.
- I can make my viewpoint clear in my writing by using simple adjectives or verbs.
- I can use punctuation marks to make a point strongly.
- I can plan a simple essay of two parts: one for a particular point of view, the other against it.
- I can write paragraphs which begin with simple topic sentences explaining my views.

Glossary of key terms

adjective: a word that describe nouns – a *tennis* ball, a *pink* teddy

adverbial: a word or phrase used to modify a verb, adjective or adverb to tell you how, when, where something is happening. Adverbials modify meaning to give the reader more information. For example:
The boy ran *clumsily* across the road.
The boy ran *gracefully* across the road.
Resolutely, the boy ran across the road.
Without looking, the boy ran across the road.

adverb: a word that changes the meaning of a verb, and usually answers how or when an action was done: for example, *angrily*, *later*

allegory: a story which can be interpreted to have a hidden meaning, usually moral or political

auxiliary: the verbs *to have* and *to be* can be used to assist other words to make verb phrases and communicate actions, states of being and time much more specifically: for example, I *have* finished, she *was* swimming

chronological: told in the order that it happens

cohesion: what glues a united, whole text together

colloquial: informal language

colon: a colon is a punctuation mark which goes before a list, description or explanation. It must always be preceded by a complete sentence

command: a sentence that tells us to do something by putting the verb first to emphasise the action

complex sentence: when an extra idea is added to a simple sentence or man clause: for example, Although it was raining, we decided to walk.

compound sentence: when two ideas (which could be simple sentences) are joined together: for example, The bus arrived and I jumped on board. They are joined with conjunctions such as *for, and, nor, but, or, yet, so*

connotations: ideas or feelings invoked by a word because of its associations

coordinating conjunction: joining words such as *and, nor, but, or, yet, so*, used in compound sentences

couplet: a pair of lines that rhyme

dashes: punctuation marks used to add an aside or interjection

determiner: a word that goes in front of a noun such as *a*, *an* and *the*

dialect: the form of English used in a particular place

effect: what readers think, feel, or picture in their minds' eyes as they read

emotive language: a deliberate choice of words to elicit an emotional response from the reader and enable the reader to infer the writer's viewpoint

exclamation: a sentence that expresses an emotion such as shock, anger, joy, surprise

explicit meaning: the basic information on the surface – the true or literal; what is stated directly

figure of speech: a word or phrase that means something additional, or different, to its literal meaning

first-person narrator: using *I*

flashbacks: past events inserted into a narrative

form: a set of agreed conventions, or rules, that give an identifiable shape to a piece of literary writing; these rules might relate to structure and organisation, layout, content or language

genre: a particular type or category of writing with its own purpose, features and conventions

hyperbole: exaggeration used for emphasis or effect

iambic pentameter: line of poetry with ten syllables, five stressed and five unstressed, creating five 'di dums' or heartbeats (iambs)

imagery: language used to create a picture (image) in the mind of the reader, often a comparison (simile or metaphor)

implicit: below the surface, implied rather than stated directly

infer: to work out meanings from clues given in the text; to 'read between the lines'

inference: the explanation of what you have been able to read between the lines

in media res: 'in the middle of things' – you begin your story right in the heart of the action, without an 'introduction'

interpretation: your overall response to a text made up of all the clues and evidence you have gathered

literal: surface, basic, obvious meaning

main clause: a simple sentence with a subject and a verb

minor sentence: a sentence that doesn't contain a main clause: for example, *'Run!'* or *'My one shot.'*

modal verbs: verbs such as *could, should, might, will, must, would,* which modify or alter the meaning of the verbs they are attached to

narrator: the speaker in a text; usually (although not always) the central character of the story

negative: seeing the bad side of things

neutral: having a balanced view, or not taking sides

noun phrase: a noun phrase is a phrase (a group of connected words) with a *noun* as its main word; a *noun phrase* can normally be used in place of a *noun* within a sentence

noun: a labelling or naming word – *teddy, ball, cup*

omniscient narrator: a narrator who writes in the third person, is 'outside' the story, not part of it, and is 'all knowing', having access to the thoughts and feelings of the characters as well as the plot of the whole story

pathetic fallacy: when the writer describes the conditions of the natural world to add to the atmosphere of the story

personification: when an object or location is described as if it had human characteristics, for example, 'as the storm gathered, the thunder *grumbled* above us, and the rain *tiptoed* across the window pane…'

perspective: point of view

prefix: added to the beginning of words in order to turn them into other words

prepositional phrase: a phrase which helps us understand the relationship between things or ideas, for example, when they occurred or where they are positioned

pronoun: a word such as *I, he, she, we, they* or *it* which replaces a noun in a sentence

protagonist: the central character in a novel, play or film

purpose: the reason a text is written

rhetorical question: a question addressed directly to an audience in order to make a point

rhetorical technique: a language technique used to persuade a reader to consider an idea from a different point of view

scanning: reading to pick out particular information such as the cost of an item or the closing date for an application

semantic field: a collection of words that have a similar meaning or create a similar idea in the mind of the reader

simple sentence: this will contain one idea; it will have one verb or verb phrase as the sentence will only have one action, event, or state within it, for example: The baby was very tired.

skimming: reading for gist; a speed read without reading every word

Standard English: the most widely used form of English, which is not specific to a particular place or region

statement: a sentence that declares something and presents it as a fact or opinion

structural features: these can include listing; use of short / long sentences; questions and answers; punctuation; order and sequence of ideas; the function of the start and end

structure: the way in which a writer chooses to organise a text; this may include the order of ideas or topics; paragraphing; sentence structure; narrative perspective (first person or third person); chronology (sequencing of events) ; pace; patterns within the writing such as repetition, contrasts

subordinate clauses: clauses attached to the main clause to add extra information; they don't make sense alone

suffix: a word ending added to the end of words to turn them into other words

tone: the mood, voice or feeling created by the writer's language choices: for example, humorous or sarcastic

verb: a verb is the force behind a sentence; it can describe movement, action or state, and tell us when something happened

viewpoint: an attitude, opinion or point of view

Acknowledgements

The publishers gratefully acknowledge the permissions granted to reproduce copyright material in this book. Every effort has been made to contact the holders of copyright material, but if any have been inadvertently overlooked, the Publisher will be pleased to make the necessary arrangements at the first opportunity.

'How Not to Be a Woodlouse' from How to Be a Dragonfly by Patricia Debney (Smith|Doorstop Books, 2005). WaterAid Leaflet by permission of WaterAid. Extract from The Generation Game by Sophie Duffy published by Legend Press reprinted by permission of Legend Press Ltd. Space Poem Three – Off Course from Selected Poems by Edwin Morgan 1985 reprinted by permission of Carcanet Press Limited. Extract from Junk by Melvin Burgess reprinted by permission of Andersen Press Ltd, a division of Random House PLC. Extracts from A Kestrel for a Knave by Barry Hines reprinted by permission of Penguin Books UK and The Agency (London) Ltd © Barry Hines 1968. Extract from The Princess and the Pea by Lauren Child, Penguin 2006, reprinted by permission of David Higham. Extract from the Curious Incident of the Dog in the Night-time (play) by Mark Haddon adapted by Simon Stephens reprinted by permission of Bloomsbury Publishing Plc. Extract from The Year of the Flood by Margaret Atwood reprinted by permission of Curtis Brown Group Ltd, London; Bloomsbury Publishing Plc; McClelland & Stewart, a division of Random House of Canada Limited, a Penguin Random House Company; and by permission of Nan A Talese, an imprint of the Knopf Doubleday Publishing Group, a division of Random House LLC. on behalf of O.W. Toad copyright © O.W. Toad 2009. The following extracts from The Guardian reprinted by permission of Guardian News and Media Limited. Teenage stowaway survives flight over Pacific in jet wheel well by Jonathan Hayes from The Guardian 21 April 2014. Children's Behaviour at School Deteriorating by Jeevan Vasagar from The Guardian 18 April 2011. Extract from River Town by Peter Hessler © Peter Hessler 2001 reprinted by permission of Headline Publishing Group and William Clark Associates. Extracts from The Curious Incident of the Dog in the Night by Mark Haddon copyright Mark Haddon 2003 reprinted by permission of Aitken Alexander Associates. Extract from the Curious Incident of the Dog in the Night-time (play) by Mark Hadden adapted by Simon Stephens reprinted by permission of Bloomsbury Publishing Plc. Extract from Our Day Out by Willy Russell reprinted by permission of Negus-Fancey Agents Ltd. NSPCC Leaflet reprinted by permission of National Society for the Prevention of Cruelty to Children (NSPCC). Extracts from A Kestrel for a Knave by Barry Hines reprinted by permission of Penguin Books UK and The Agency (London) Ltd © Barry Hines 1968. 'Cold' from The Bees by Carol Ann Duffy copyright © Carol Ann Duffy. Reproduced by permission of the author c/o Rogers, Coleridge & White Ltd. 'Havisham' by Carol Ann Duffy copyright © Carol Ann Duffy. Reproduced by permission of the author c/o Rogers, Coleridge & White Ltd. Swedish man Peter Skylberg survives frozen car months eating handfuls snow by Allan Hall from Mail Online 22/2/2012 reprinted by permission of Solo Syndication. Extracts from 'Your Shoes' from during Mother's Absence by Michelle Roberts © Michelle Roberts reprinted by permission of Little, Brown and Aitken Alexander Associates. 'The Veldt' from The Illustrated Man by Ray Bradbury reprinted by permission of Abner Stein. The following extracts from The Guardian reprinted by permission of Guardian news and Media Limited: Teaching in prisons is where I can make a real difference by The Secret Teacher; Sleeping rough for charity hides the real homelessness crisis by Alastair Sloan. Extract from Would you take your child on holiday during term time by Joanna Moorhead from The Guardian 29 January 2014. Extract from Britain's child Soldiers by Michael Bartlet from The Guardian 11 March 2011. Extract from Hole in the Wall Project and The Power of Self-Organized Learning by Sugata Mitra Edutopia April 13 2014 reprinted by permission of the author. Extract from Small Island by Andrea Levy © Andrea Levy 2004 reprinted by permission of Headline Publishing Group. Arms and the Boy from Wilfred Owen: The Complete Poems and Fragments" by Wilfred Owen ed. Jon Stallworthy (Chatto & Windus, 1983). Extracts from An Inspector Calls and other plays by J B Priestley reprinted by permission of United Agents on behalf of the Estate of J B Priestley. Extract from Animal Farm by George Orwell (copyright © George Orwell, 1945) reprinted by permission of Bill Hamilton as the Literary Executor of the Estate of the Late Sonia Brownell, and also used by permission of Houghton Mifflin Harcourt Publishing Company. All Rights Reserved. Extracts from If Nobody Speaks of Remarkable things by Jon McGregor 2003 reprinted by permission of Bloomsbury Publishing Plc. 'A Case of Murder' by Vernon Scannell reprinted by permission of the Estate of Vernon Scannell and Jane Scannell. Extract from Would you take your child on holiday during term time by Joanna Moorhead from The Guardian 29 January 2014. Extract from Britain's child Soldiers by Michael Bartlet from The Guardian 11 March 2011. Extract from The Rights and Responsibilities of a Children's writer by Helena Pielichaty reprinted by permission of Ms Helena Pielichaty. Extract from Rewriting the rules on logos by Naomi Mdudu reprinted by permission of Solo Syndication. Extract from http://www.huffingtonpost.com/pam-allyn/read-aloud-change-the-wor_b_4892116.html reprinted by permission of Pam Allyn. Extracts from Why black models are rarely in fashion by Hadley Freeman from The Guardian 18 February 2014 reprinted by permission of Guardian News Media. Extract from 'Second Gear: The response to our Cities Fit for Cycling' is heartening but it has not gone far enough the times November 5th 2012 reprinted by permission of News Syndication. Rain by Ameena Meer reprinted by permission of Ms Ameena Meer. Extract from http://www.lattitude.org.uk/2013/03/gap-year-by-numbers reprinted by permission of Lattitude Global Volunteering.

The publishers would like to thank the following for permission to use reproduce pictures in these pages:

Cover images © amiloslava/Shutterstock, Marzolino/Shutterstock

p8: © Joris Van Ostaeyen/Alamy; p11: Hulton Archive/Getty Images; p13, top: Nicram Sabod/Shutterstock.com, bottom: Scorpp/Shutterstock.com; p14: Hank Morgan/Science Photo Library; p17: © Redsnapper/Alamy; p20: Georgios Kollidas/Shutterstock.com; p23: © Stephen Dorey/Alamy; p24: Walker Art Library/Alamy; p27: © Moviestore Collection Ltd/Alamy; p29: Underwood Archives/Getty Images; p30: Dennis van de Water/Shutterstock.com; p32: Paul Stringer/Shutterstock.com; p37: Bruno Morandi/Getty Images; p42: Iberfoto/SuperStock; p44, top: Oli Scarff/Getty Images, bottom: © Yakoniva/Alamy; p45: The Granger Collection/TopFoto; p47: Ulrich Baumgarten/Getty Images; p53: © Mim Friday/Alamy; p54: © Col Pics/Everett/Rex Features; p55: © John Hayward/Alamy; p56: DeAgostini/Getty Images; p59: Illustration from 'The Tale of Peter Rabbit.' © Frederick Warne and Co, 1902, 2002; p61: © Vincenzo Dragani/Alamy; p63: © The Protected Art Archive/Alamy; p68: Richard Boll/Getty Images; p70: ATGImages/Shutterstock.com; p72: © Augusto Colombo, Italy/Alamy; p77: Erik Astrom/Scanpix/TT News Agency/Press Association Images; p79: © Frances Roberts/Alamy; p80: Peter Walker (Heritage) Ltd/The Kobal Collection; p83: Leifur/Getty Images; p84: Laborant/Shutterstock.com; p85: © Gary Roebuck/Alamy; p89: © AF Archive/Alamy; p91: © AF Archive/Alamy; p93: © Moviestore Collection Ltd/Alamy; p94-95: © Wayne Hutchinson/Alamy; p97: © Mark Harvey/Alamy; p98: © Sergio Azenha/Alamy; p100: Popperfoto/Getty Images; p105: Paul Bradbury/Getty Images; p106: Museum of London/Heritage Images/Getty Images; p109: © Serge Vero/Alamy; p117: Mary Evans/Peter Higginbotham Collection; p118-119: Mary Evans/Grenville Collins Postcard Collection; p120: Craig Shepheard/Demotix/Press Association Images; p122: © Adrian Sherratt/Alamy; p124: Maria Isaeva/Shutterstock.com; p125: © Mary Evans Picture Library/Alamy; p128: Robert Workman/ArenaPAL; p130: Giorgio Fochesato/Getty Images; p132-133: © John Worrall/Alamy; p134: Birmingham Museums and Art Gallery/Bridgeman Images; p136, top: © Amoret Tanner/Alamy, bottom left: © Carrie/Alamy, bottom centre: British Library Board/TopFoto, bottom right: The Granger Collection/TopFoto, p138: © Travelib/Alamy; p140-141: © David J. Green/Alamy; p143: © ImageBroker/Alamy; p155, top: © AF Archive/Alamy, bottom: Fine Art Images/Heritage Images/Getty Images; p157: © United Archives GmbH/Alamy; p158: © The Art Archive/Alamy; p161: © Classic Image/Alamy; p162: © Stefano Paterna/Alamy; p163: The Print Collector/Getty Images; p166: DeAgostini/Getty Images; p168: © Theatrepix/Alamy; p170: © Mary Evans Picture Library/Alamy; p171: Yale Center for British Art, Paul Mellon Collection, USA/Bridgeman Images; p174: © ImageBroker/Alamy; p177: Philippe Le Tellier/Paris Match/Getty Images; p184: 4contrast_dot_com/Shutterstock.com; p187: Suzanne Tucker/Shutterstock.com; p188: The Print Collector/Getty Images; p189: The Bridgeman Art Library/Private Collection/Getty Images; p193: LiliGraphie/Shutterstock.com; p195: Planet News Archive/SSPL/Getty Images; p197: Hepp/Getty Images; p198: © Nadezhda Bolotina/Alamy; p201: © Age Fotostock Spain, S.L./Alamy; p204: Michael Steele/Getty Images; p206: © Aflo Co. Ltd./Alamy; p208: © Photos 12/Alamy; p214: © Photos 12/Alamy; p220: altanaka/Shutterstock.com; p223: IanC66/Shutterstock.com; p224, top: MaraZe/Shutterstock.com, bottom: Sergey and katerina/Shutterstock.com; p225: Courtesy Hole-in-the-Wall Education Project, New Delhi, India; p226: Hulton Archive/Getty Images; p229: Universal History Archive/Getty Images; p230: © The Art Archive/Alamy; p232: TopFoto; p234, top far left: PaulPaladin/Shutterstock.com, top centre left: pchais/Shutterstock.com, top centre: Eric Isselee/Shutterstock.com, top centre right: ppl/Shutterstock.com, top far right: autsawin uttisin/Shutterstock.com, centre far left: Michal Dzierzynski/Shutterstock.com, centre left: indigolotos/Shutterstock.com, centre: Kuttelvaserova Stuchelova/Shutterstock.com, centre right: stocksolutions/Shutterstock.com, centre far right: Mark William Richardson//Shutterstock.com, bottom: kilukilu/Shutterstock.com; p235: Ulrich Baumgarten/Getty Images; p237: © Travel Pictures/Alamy; p238: © Everett Collection Historical/Alamy; p240: Carl Court/AFP/Getty Images; p243: © Geoffrey Welsh/Alamy; p244: Popperfoto/Getty Images; p250: © Ball Miwako/Alamy; p253: © Alan Novelli/Alamy; p254: © Authentic-Originals/Alamy; p257: © Andrey Armyagov/Shutterstock.com; p258: ToskanaINC/Shutterstock.com; p259: © David Grossman/Alamy; p262: Gail Johnson/Shutterstock.com; p263: Paul Kennedy/Getty Images; p264: © AF Archive/Alamy; p266: starryvoyage/Shutterstock.com; p268: Still from "Small Island" © Television Ruby (Small Island) Ltd. Used with kind permission of Ruby Films Limited; p270: © Keith Taylor/Alamy; p274: Hans Engbers/Shutterstock.com; p277: Hans Engbers/Shutterstock.com; p281: CandyBox Images/Shutterstock.com; p283: Chaloemphan/Shutterstock.com; p285: © Roger Cracknell 01/classic/Alamy; p286: Mark Noak/Shutterstock.com; p288: Fotosearch/Getty Images; p293: © SCPhotos/Alamy; p294: © Bob Ebbesen/Alamy; p296: Henrik Sorensen/Getty Images; p298: © Julian Marshall/Alamy; p300: R. Tyler Gross/Getty Images; p303: Steve Hoarsley/Shutterstock.com; p305: Mark Mainz/Getty Images.

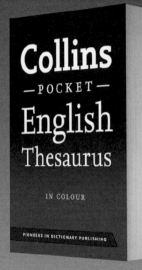

Notes

Notes